VETO BARGAINING

PRESIDENTS AND THE POLITICS OF
NEGATIVE POWER

The late twentieth century gave rise to the most concentrated period of divided party government in American history. With one party controlling the presidency and the opposing party controlling Congress, the veto became a critical tool of presidential power. This book analyzes the politics of the presidential veto. Combining sophisticated game theory with unprecedented data, it shows how presidents use vetoes and threats of vetoes to wrest policy concessions from a hostile Congress. Case studies of the most important vetoes in recent history add texture to the analysis. The first book-length attempt to bring rational choice theory to bear on the presidency, *Veto Bargaining* is a major contribution to our understanding of American politics in an age of divided party government.

Charles M. Cameron is Associate Professor of Political Science at Columbia University.

T0381781

Series Editors
Randall Calvert, *University of Rochester, New York*
Thráinn Eggertsson, *Max Planck Institute, Germany, and University of Iceland*

Founding Editors
James E. Alt, *Harvard University*
Douglass C. North, *Washington University of St. Louis*

Series list continues on page after Index

VETO BARGAINING

PRESIDENTS AND THE
POLITICS OF NEGATIVE POWER

CHARLES M. CAMERON
Columbia University

CAMBRIDGE
UNIVERSITY PRESS

PUBLISHED BY THE PRESS SYNDICATE OF THE UNIVERSITY OF CAMBRIDGE
The Pitt Building, Trumpington Street, Cambridge, United Kingdom

CAMBRIDGE UNIVERSITY PRESS
The Edinburgh Building, Cambridge CB2 2RU, UK   http://www.cup.cam.ac.uk
40 West 20th Street, New York, NY 10011–4211, USA   http://www.cup.org
10 Stamford Road, Oakleigh, Melbourne 3166, Australia
Ruiz de Alarcón 13, 28014 Madrid, Spain

© Charles M. Cameron   2000

First published 2000

Typeface Sabon 10/12 pt.   *System* DeskTopPro/ux®[BV]

A catalog record for this book is available from the British Library.

Library of Congress Cataloging in Publication data
Cameron, Charles M. (Charles Metz), 1954–
Veto bargaining : presidents and the politics of negative power / Charles M. Cameron.
p.   cm. – (Political economy of institutions and decisions)
Includes bibliographical references and index.
ISBN 0–521–62391–X (hb). – ISBN 0–521–62550–5 (pb)
1. Veto – United States.   2. Presidents – United States.
3. Executive power – United States.   4. United States – Politics and
government – 1945–1989.   5. United States – Politics and
government – 1989–   I. Title.   II. Series.
JK586.C23   1999
352.23'0973—dc21   99–12886
                                                                                      CIP
ISBN 0 521 62391 X   hardback
ISBN 0 521 62550 5   paperback

Transferred to digital printing 2004

To LLJ

Contents

Tables and Figures

TABLES

Tables and Figures

Preface

The Founders erected the new American state upon two pillars: federalism and the separation of powers. The Civil War and the Roosevelt revolution knocked the first aside – not entirely, but largely so. The breathtaking expansion of the executive apparatus during the twentieth century shook but failed to topple the second pillar. The separation-of-powers system remains the foundation of that amazingly complex and ever changing construction, the American federal government.

In a system of "separated institutions sharing powers," bargaining between the executive, legislative, and judicial branches becomes the modus operandi of governance. Of course, building legislative coalitions and managing bureaucratic hierarchies are also key features of American government, as they are in parliamentary governments. But in no system but the American is bargaining across the distinct branches of the government so formal and so important.

This book is about one type of interbranch bargaining, veto bargaining between president and Congress. When the policy preferences of the president and Congress differ dramatically, as they often do during periods of divided government, veto bargaining is instrumental in shaping important legislation. The process works through anticipation, through threats, and through vetoes, including vetoes of repassed legislation. This book examines all these mechanisms. Because we are living in the most concentrated period of divided government in our nation's history, a theory of veto bargaining is essential for understanding the recent operation of American government. It is also necessary for understanding American political history.

The book contributes to what Barry Weingast, perhaps somewhat grandly, calls "the new theory of the presidency," by which he means an institutionalist conception of that office grounded squarely on rational choice theory. This study is the first sustained, book-length effort to bring formal rational choice theory to the study of the presidency. It is also one of the more ambitious efforts to test formal, rational choice models of political institutions against real data.

No one who reads this book would wish it longer. Nonetheless, if time and space were without limit I would include other important topics. The president's ability to convert votes during override battles is an important part of veto politics that I do not discuss. Fortunately, Keith Krehbiel has undertaken a fascinating analysis of this phenomenon, one that is sure to stimulate additional work (1998: chaps. 6–7). In parts of the book, I allude to Groseclose and McCarty's intriguing idea of a "blame-game veto," that is, veto bait offered by Congress in order to hurt the president at the polls (1996). Their highly original and provocative analysis naturally suggests an empirical study of the impact of vetoes on public opinion. This is a promising direction for research. There is much more to say about vetoes and appropriations politics, building on the excellent work of Kiewiet and McCubbins (1988). The line item veto retains a fascination for many, and political analysts have constructed several interesting models (Schap 1986, inter alia). However, the Supreme Court probably killed the political prospects of the line item veto when it struck down the powers given the president by the 104th Congress. I doubt whether the line item veto will ever play a large role in veto politics at the federal level but if it does, this topic will surely be revisited by others.

To say that I incurred heavy debts writing this book is an almost laughable understatement. Fortunately, unlike Dr. Johnson, I have *not* "protracted my work till most of those, whom I wished to please, have sunk into the grave, and success and miscarriage are empty sounds." It just felt that way. At long last I can enjoy the pleasant duty of thanking colleagues, students, friends, and family for their patience and assistance.

Two acknowledgments take precedence. My friend and sometime-colleague, game theorist Susan Elmes, patiently suffered my presence in three graduate classes, answered endless questions, and performed the intellectual heavy lifting in a collaborative paper on the theory of sequential veto bargaining. I am sure she must often have longed for an apter pupil, but I never wished for a better teacher. The contribution of Harry J. Paarsch will be less obvious to a reader but not to me. During many difficult months when I struggled futilely with the measures of legislative significance, Harry offered not only his cheerful comradeship but the benefit of his remarkable insights as an econometrician. His suggestions ultimately provided the key to unlocking the data, without which this book would not be possible.

It has been my good fortune and great pleasure to work with remarkable graduate students – keen, able, hardworking, careful, and candid.

Two stand out: William Howell and Charles Riemann, who helped at every turn. In addition, John Lapinski was instrumental with the material on veto threats, and Yuen Kwok was indispensable in conceptualizing, collecting, and analyzing the data on concessions. Nina Fischman was present at the creation and made the first illuminating assay of early data on sequential veto bargaining.

One of the great book doctors in political science, Barry Weingast, lavished some of his exuberant creativity on an early version of the manuscript. Not only did he understand what I was trying to do, he saw what I *could* do, and helped me see it. Robert Y. Shapiro patiently read many versions of the manuscript and associated papers and invariably offered sound, and timely, advice. He provides a model of collegiality. My longtime friend Doug Arnold helped me at a difficult time in ways that perhaps only the two of us can appreciate. The comparativist Sunita Parikh, an extraordinary colleague and wonderful friend, worked indefatigably to broaden the intellectual horizons of a mere Americanist (but it didn't always work). The business strategist Warren Boeker patiently suffered through many descriptions of event histories of vetoes, a subject he could hardly be less interested in, and offered useful suggestions about how to think about such data. Richard Neustadt's graceful comments at a conference at Columbia meant much to the recipient. Readers from Cambridge and Princeton University Presses offered excellent suggestions as did seminar participants at Stanford and Harvard and various political science meetings. Jennifer Gandhi, Brad Joseph, Patrice Johnson, Jason Lynch, Rebecca Miller, Anita Ramen, and Eric Reinhardt provided excellent research assistance. Meike Klingauf performed marvels on the illustrations. In assisting with innumerable excruciating details at the end, Rose Razaghian supplied not only help but mercy. My wonderful secretary Aida Llabaly kept the remainder of my academic responsibilities on track despite my best efforts otherwise, and made the office a lively and enjoyable place – a sentiment shared by *all* her "favorite" professors.

The Hoover Institution's timely provision of a National Fellowship allowed me to concentrate my energies on the book during 1995–96. Without the Fellowship I would not have benefited from the indispensable help of Howell, Paarsch, or Weingast. Only the generous support of the National Science Foundation (grant SES-9223396) allowed the collection of the extensive new data used in the book.

Many friends bore with good humor my indentured servitude to old newspapers, fat green books, and the computer. Thank you Peter, Mary Lou, Paula, Greg, Walter, Stephanie, Seth, Julie, Jane, Warren, Warren, Colette, Barry, Ann, Jim, the Coles (especially Maggie), Ted, Carol,

Preface

David, Frank, Joanne, Frank Jr., and Nick (see, there really was a book). The family thanks Sylvia Yanagisako and John Sullivan and the other folks who made our tour of Palo Alto houses so enjoyable.

Words cannot possibly express my gratitude to my wife for her support, not only for this project but every other one; nor my thankfulness to Eliza and Ian for their many interruptions, delightful distractions, and welcome intrusions.

1

Divided Government and Interbranch Bargaining

American political scientists have rediscovered what the foremost historian of the Founding Era calls "the major justification for all the constitutional reforms the Republicans proposed" in 1789, the principle "expanded and exalted by the Americans to the foremost position in their constitutionalism," in fact "the dominant principle of the American political system" (Wood 1969:449, 604). That principle is the separation of powers.

The impetus for the rediscovery is no mystery: the continuing reality of split party control of Congress and the presidency, "divided government." In the half century since the end of World War II, from 1945 to 1994, the Republican and Democratic parties simultaneously controlled different parts of the American federal government in twenty-eight years, 56% of the time. By the late 1980s the pattern had become the norm, and political scientists could no longer dismiss divided government as anomalous. The resulting intellectual shock was neatly captured by the title of James Sundquist's influential 1988 article: "Needed: A Political Theory for the New Era of Coalition Government in the United States."

How could political scientists need a theory of divided government in 1988, when the American federal government had shown such a persistent tendency toward split party control – 40% of the time in the century and a half since the full emergence of the party system in the 1830s? The answer lies in the theory of American government forged around the turn of the century by the founders of modern political science in the United States. For key members of this generation, the separation of powers was not the genius of the American system; it was the problem with the system. In their view, separation of powers led to gridlock, incoherent policy, and corruption. Typical was Woodrow Wilson's heartfelt cry, "no government can be successfully conducted upon so mechanical a theory [as that of checks and balances] . . . you cannot compound a successful government out of antagonisms" (1908:54, 60).

1

Studying such a system on its own terms was beside the point. It needed to be fixed or junked, replaced with a Westminster parliamentary system.

The intellectual foundations for Wilson's view had been supplied by another of the great figures of early political science, the now neglected Henry Jones Ford. In his tour de force, *The Rise and Growth of American Politics*, published in 1898, Ford documented the self-interest that led the Founders to devise an impossibly fragmented government. Then he exposed the flaws of the resulting system, its incoherence and corruption. Finally, he proposed an extraconstitutional solution to the botched work of the Founders: strong, disciplined political parties. A strong party led by the president and controlling both houses of Congress could join together what the Founders had set asunder. Unified party government under strong presidential leadership was the formula for compounding successful government from the system's misguided antagonisms.

Ford's remarkable analysis – resoundingly vindicated for later generations by Franklin Roosevelt's first term – is easily traced through the 1940s and 1950s in V. O. Key's *Politics, Parties, and Pressure Groups*, E. E. Schattschneider's *Party Government*, and the American Political Science Association's 1950 recommendations on "responsible party government." There were dissenting voices, especially that of the great public law scholar Edward S. Corwin. But by the late 1950s Corwin was "substantively and methodologically at odds" with the bulk of a profession that had accepted the Ford-Wilson credo (Bessette and Tulis 1981). The main currents of thought about American political institutions in the 1960s and 1970s – represented by (among others) Robert Dahl's blistering attack on the political theory of James Madison, James Sundquist's elaborate tracing of party realignments, Samuel Huntington's assault on an antiquated Congress, and Richard Neustadt's analysis of presidential power – continued along the lines first mapped by Ford (Dahl 1956; Sundquist 1973; Huntington 1965; Neustadt 1960). In sum, the reason why political scientists in the late 1980s needed a theory of divided government was that most of the theory they knew attacked the system of separated powers rather than analyzed it.

No longer. A burst of creative new work is changing our understanding of this most fundamental of American political institutions. In a pathbreaking book, David Mayhew has argued that surges and slumps in the enactment of significant legislation do not correspond in any simple way with unified and divided government (Mayhew 1991). Mainstream presidential scholars, notably Mark Peterson, Charles Jones, and Jon Bond and Richard Fleisher, have removed the president from the center of the political universe (Peterson 1990; Jones 1994; Bond and Fleisher 1990). This "tandem institutions" view treats the presidency as a coordinate body in a constellation of institutions sharing power. On

the electoral side, Morris Fiorina, along with Alberto Alesina and Howard Rosenthal, argues that divided government is no accident (Fiorina
1996; Alesina and Rosenthal 1995). Instead, voters (or at least some of
them) may deliberately choose divided government in an attempt to
counterbalance one overly extreme party with another.

Of particular importance for this book is the work of what are sometimes called the new, analytical, or rational choice institutionalists. During the 1980s, this group of scholars revolutionized how political scientists think about Congress.[1] Then, during the late 1980s and early 1990s,
they turned their attention to how other branches interact with Congress. Examples include Calvert, Moran, and Weingast's study of executive, legislature, and agency interactions (1989); McCubbins, Noll, and
Weingast's analysis of congressional control of the bureaucracy (1987);
Eskridge's investigation of battles between Congress and court over statutory interpretation (1991); Ferejohn and Shipan's model of Congress,
presidents, courts, and agencies sequentially acting to create bureaucratic
policy (1990); and Krehbiel's theory of gridlock (1996, 1998). To this
group might be added Moe's study of the evolution of the office of the
presidency (Moe and Wilson 1994, inter alia).

Much separates the distinct strands of this new work, but a theme
knitting them together is *interbranch bargaining*. The separation-of-
powers system was explicitly predicated on the notion of internal balance and dynamic tension among the three branches. What passes for
governance in the American system is often the product of pulling and
hauling, haggling and bargaining among the three branches. Though this
cliché can be found in any textbook on American government, it is only
with the recent work on divided government that political scientists have
placed interbranch bargaining at the center of theories of American
politics.

In this book I study a particular kind of interbranch bargaining, one
in which the president looms large: veto bargaining. I study which bills
get vetoed, what happens to bills after they are vetoed, how presidents
use vetoes and veto threats to wrest policy concessions from Congress,
and their success and failure in doing so. I also study the depressing
effect of the veto power on Congress's legislative productivity. In other
words, I study the president and the politics of "negative power" – the
consequences of an institutionalized ability to say no. The research I
report is often the first systematic empirical evidence on these matters.
Moreover, the *way* I approach the research is also distinctive. As an
analytical institutionalist, I use "rational choice theory" to study the
presidency. In fact, this is the first book-length study of the presidency

---

[1] An outstanding review can be found in Krehbiel 1991, chaps. 2 and 3.

to adopt an explicit, formal, and sustained rational choice perspective. But unlike many works in the rational choice tradition, this one neither begins nor ends with theory. It opens with systematic evidence and empirical puzzles; it uses theory to think through the data and solve the puzzles; then it returns to the data afresh and uses the theory to find additional insights. The investigation takes us deep into the operation of the Founders' system of separated powers, a system we must live with, for better or for worse.

VETOES IN THE SEPARATION-OF-POWERS SYSTEM

The range of veto politics runs from the critical to the mundane, and sometimes from the sublime to the ridiculous. Two cases illustrate this remarkable diversity.

A Tale of Two Vetoes

Case 1: Carter Kills a "Special Interest Bill." In 1977 Representative Keith Sebelius (R-Kansas) had what he thought was a good idea, one concerning rabbit meat. Under the 1946 Agricultural Marketing Act, the federal government inspects "minor species" meat like that of rabbits. The program is voluntary and paid for by the meat processors themselves, who have an obvious interest in building public confidence in offbeat products. At least in the case of rabbit meat, the bulk of the costs have always fallen on a few large producers in what is a very small industry – only about $10 million in 1977. In fact, rabbit meat has never caught on with American consumers. Moreover, domestic producers face steep competition from imported rabbit meat. Thus Representative Sebelius's bright idea: make the inspection program mandatory for large processors and financed by tax dollars, and require imported rabbit meat to be processed under U.S. government standards. This would have the twin effect of lowering the price of domestic rabbit meat and effectively excluding most foreign producers. Sebelius's gift to the rabbit producers passed Congress in late October 1977 – only to run into a brutal check from the executive. President Jimmy Carter vetoed the bill, declaring it special-interest legislation (*CQ Almanac* 1977:444–45, 64-E).

The tale of this veto seems quite straightforward. Sebelius had good reason to believe the executive branch was not kindly disposed to his bill, since the Agriculture Department had opposed it. But he hoped the president would not weigh in on such a minor matter. Too late to change the bill's content, he found he was wrong. The results were fatal for the bill.

4

Case 2: Clinton "Ends Welfare as We Know It." The stunning victory of the Republicans in the 1994 midterm elections propelled welfare reform to the top of the legislative agenda in the 104th Congress.[2] Also critical for the Republicans was their plan to balance the budget. These priorities impelled welfare reform down two legislative tracks, the first leading toward a freestanding reform bill (H.R. 4), the second toward the budget reconciliation bill (H.R. 2491). The latter was the vehicle for balancing the budget. Huge savings in federal programs would be needed if a balanced budget was to be combined with simultaneous tax cuts, also a Republican goal.

The House moved rapidly down the first track. In March 1995 it passed an exceedingly tough welfare reform bill, H.R. 4, by a relatively narrow and extremely partisan vote, 234–199 (only 9 Democrats voted in favor of the Republican plan). As the Republicans' Contract with America had promised, the reform proposal turned most federal welfare programs into block grants to be administered by the states and imposed time limits on welfare benefits. The proposal thus ended a sixty-year guarantee of federal benefits for the poor. It also made deep budget cuts. According to the Congressional Budget Office, the cuts amounted to $102 billion over seven years, over 10% of federal expenditures on social services exclusive of Medicaid. Yet the narrowness of the bill's support meant it was vulnerable to a veto, if the president had the stomach to oppose the Republicans. In fact, he issued a veto threat directed at the House bill. But he denounced only the plan's severe cuts in child welfare services. Tellingly, he made no objection to the block grants or time limits on benefits.

In the Senate, the minority-party Democrats could filibuster a bill with narrow support. Majority Leader Robert Dole needed to fashion a bill that retained the core of the House reforms but nonetheless mustered 60 or more votes in the Senate, to invoke cloture. Dole deftly positioned the Senate bill to achieve the needed support, plus some. He retained the block grant approach and ended the federal guarantee of welfare but softened some of the harsher parts of the House plan and substantially reduced the budget cuts, to about $66 billion over seven years, some $36 billion less than the House bill. The Senate passed Dole's bill in September 1995 by a vote of 87–12: 52 Repub-

---

[2] This account draws on various issues of *Congressional Quarterly (CQ) Weekly Report* (1995: March 25:872–75, September 23:2908–11, October 28:3290–91, November 4:3381, November 11:3459–60, November 18:3541–45, November 25: 3613–16, December 2:3662, December 9:3745, December 23:3889–91; and 1996: January 6:37–38, January 13:95, 103, February 3:304–5, February 17:394–5, March 2:558–60, April 20:1023–29, May 25:1465–7, June 8:1597–99, June 15:1684–86, June 22:1761–2, June 29:1877–8, July 13:1969–70, July 20:2048–51, July 27:2115–19, August 3:2190–6, 2216–18, 2232).

licans and 35 Democrats voted for the bill; only 11 Democrats and 1 Republican voted against it. President Clinton pointedly did not threaten the bill, which may have been veto-proof in any case. The bill then went to conference.

Unfortunately for the Republicans, the Senate bill simply did not make cuts deep enough to achieve all the Republicans' goals. Accordingly, the Republicans turned to the second track, the Budget Reconciliation Bill. Because such bills cannot be filibustered, the Republicans could attach proposals that were too controversial to pass the Senate in a freestanding bill, so long as the proposals were related to deficit reduction (the so-called Byrd Rule could be used to remove other policy changes). Without the hindrance of a filibuster, the Republicans could ram the bill through the Senate using only their partisan base. The Republican conferees on H.R. 4 had worked out an agreement that essentially split the difference between the House and Senate versions of the bill. The Republican leaders simply grafted the conferees' recommendations onto the Reconciliation Bill. After doing so, the Reconciliation Bill cut about $81 billion dollars from welfare over a seven-year period. The Byrd Rule knocked out some of the policy changes that House members desired, but many others remained.

The Reconciliation Bill passed the House and Senate in bitterly partisan votes, much as the Democrats had passed a tax increase in the 103rd Congress. The Senate vote on the conference report on the final reconciliation bill was 52–47. Not a single Democrat voted for the bill, and only one Republican voted against it. In the House, the equivalent vote was 237–189; only five Democrats and one Republican crossed party lines.

The president vetoed the Reconciliation Bill the first week in December 1995. His veto message highlighted his opposition to cuts in Medicare and Medicaid, not welfare. The welfare provisions in the bill were cited as objectionable principally because of their excessive cuts. To highlight his willingness to balance the budget, the president released his own plan the day after the veto. It included $46 billion in welfare cuts but less stringent limits than those in the Reconciliation Bill.

Despite the veto, the Republicans did not give up. The conferees brought out H.R. 4, making some changes from the original agreement fashioned before the veto of the Reconciliation Bill. The actual conference report carried a slightly lower savings tag than even the original Senate bill – about $64 billion over seven years[3] – but tougher provisions, more along the lines of the House bill. For example, Medicaid eligibility was tightened and payments to mothers of children born out

---

[3] Early estimates put the savings at about $58 billion; the CBO put the savings at $64.1 billion (*CQ Weekly Report*, February 17, 1996:395).

of wedlock were curtailed. Thus, the conference report bore a strong resemblance to the Reconciliation Bill, except it's cuts were less deep. The House adopted the conference report December 21 by a vote of 245–178. The Senate followed suit a day later, with an overwhelmingly partisan vote of 52–47. Only one Democratic senator, Max Baucus of Montana, voted for the bill. Since overriding a veto was clearly hopeless even in the House, the bill's only chance of enactment was presidential acceptance. On January 9, 1996, Clinton vetoed H.R. 4 – but two weeks later in his State of the Union Address urged Congress to send him a bipartisan bill, promising he would "sign it immediately."

Still the Republicans persisted. As their legislative vehicle, the Republicans used H.R. 3734, designating the new welfare reform bill as a reconciliation bill to head off filibusters in the Senate. The bill saved about $61 billion but maintained many provisions the administration objected to. H.R. 3734 passed the House 256–170 in mid-July, a margin far short of the approximately 290 votes needed to beat a veto. The Senate passed its version of the bill a few days later, 74–25. The Senate version softened some of the more draconian features of the House bill. For example, opponents used the Byrd Rule to remove the so-called family cap, which would have prohibited federal welfare funds for children born to welfare recipients. Medicaid eligibility requirements remained unchanged; the food stamp program escaped conversion to a block grant; states remained free to use funds from the social services block grant to support children whose parents had exceeded the time limits on benefits. The Senate bill's savings were estimated at about $55 billion.

In conference, the Republicans included the Democrats in deliberations for the first time. The conference report largely followed the lines of the Senate bill, softening some of the more extreme provisions in the House bill. When the report emerged from conference, House members used procedural measures to delay consideration of the conference report until the president announced his intentions. On July 31, after a meeting with his top advisors, the president indicated his willingness to sign the bill. The House immediately passed it 328–101, with the Democrats splitting 98–98. The bill breezed through the Senate 78–21, with the Democrats splitting 25–21. President Bill Clinton signed H.R. 3734 shortly thereafter. A landmark bill was law.

These cases illustrate the range of veto politics. Are these politics worth understanding?

Veto Bargaining

Are Vetoes Worth Studying?

Time and again, vetoes have bounded onto center stage in the drama of American politics. In the hands of President Andrew Jackson "the veto developed a terrible power. His twelve vetoes descended upon Congress like the blows of an iron flail" (Ford 1898:180). Tyler used the veto to put at defiance a Congress controlled by his own party, provoking an impeachment vote (Spitzer 1988:39–53; Watson 1993:16; Jackson 1967: 56–74). Buchanan's veto of the Homestead Bill so alienated northern workingmen and farmers that it materially aided the election of Abraham Lincoln in 1860 (Ford 1919; Jackson 1967). Johnson's obstinate vetoes of Reconstruction legislation sparked a genuine constitutional crisis. His impeachment remains one of the most dramatic moments in the history of the presidency. Grover Cleveland, in one of the more spectacular examples of presidential "knight-errantry" used the veto to wage a personal war against corruption in veterans' pensions (Ford 1919: chap. 6, esp. 116ff.). His vetoes killed literally hundreds of private bills and became an important issue in the following presidential campaign. Harding's, Coolidge's, and Hoover's vetoes of veterans' "bonus" legislation assured a continuing buildup of tension during the 1920s and early 1930s, a tension that exploded into riots during the so-called Bonus Expeditionary Force of 1932. Franklin Roosevelt used the veto as an opportunity for grand political theater, on one occasion vetoing a bonus bill before a joint assembly of Congress broadcast over radio to the nation. Vetoes flew fast and furious during Truman's confrontation with a Republican Congress he branded "the worst ever." President Bush's veto of the Family Leave Act handed the Democrats a campaign issue for the 1992 presidential election. The stunning capture of Congress by the Republicans in 1994 seemed to signal a knockout of the Clinton presidency. But the supine president staggered back onto his feet and used a lightning burst of vetoes to pound the overconfident Congress into shocked immobility – at least for a time.

These episodes illustrate memorable vetoes. But the existence of memorable vetoes tells us nothing about the systematic importance of the veto as an institution. This is a critical issue. Political scientists do not collect historical curios simply for their own sake; that is antiquarianism, not social science (Finley 1985). Our interest is understanding the main currents of the separation-of-powers system. From this perspective, the presidential veto is worth studying only if it *frequently* affects the content of *significant* legislation.

Casual observation suggests this is a hard case to make. Consider the extreme rarity of vetoes. Between 1945 and 1992, Congress presented presidents with over 17,000 public general bills (i.e., bills other than private bills, so these bills have some policy import). From this flood of bills, presidents vetoed only 434. In other words, presidents in the postwar period vetoed only 25 public general bills per 1,000 passed, while 975 per 1,000 escaped unscathed.[4] Several presidents – Kennedy and Johnson are recent examples – vetoed only a handful of bills; some nineteenth-century presidents – John Adams and Thomas Jefferson, for instance – vetoed none at all. From the perspective of simple counts, the presidential veto appears little more than a statistical fluke.

Because vetoes are rare events, can we conclude that they resemble the strike of a lightning bolt: a dramatic and memorable event, calamitous for the unfortunate target, but hardly an important factor in everyday life? *No.* Understanding why requires thinking systematically about the structural incentives embedded in the American separation of powers system.

A BARGAINING PERSPECTIVE ON THE VETO

How can a weapon that is hardly ever used shape the content of important legislation under frequently occurring circumstances? A bargaining perspective on the veto suggests a five-step answer:

1. The institutional design specified by *the Constitution almost guarantees periods when the president and Congress differ over major policy objectives.* Those periods have become a signature of contemporary American politics. We live in an age of divided government.
2. When president and Congress disagree, *the president has a strong incentive to use the veto* if Congress presses its objectives too vigorously.
3. Accordingly, *Congress will anticipate vetoes and modify the content of legislation to head them off.* The veto power will have shaped the content of legislation without actually being used. Veto threats play an important role in this process.
4. However, congressional concessions will sometimes be insufficient to satisfy the president. When that happens, *the president may use actual vetoes not only to block legislation but to shape it.* The president may veto a bill in order to extract policy concessions in a repassed version of the vetoed bill. Congress may alter and repass the bill, groping for a version the president will accept or that can beat his veto. Because this bargaining unfolds through a series of back-and-forth actions, it constitutes *sequential veto bargaining* (SVB).

---

[4] More precisely, 17,198 public laws were enacted. Presidents vetoed 434 bills, but 44 of these vetoes were overridden. So the rate of vetoes per bill presented to the president was $434/(17,198 + 434 - 44) = .025$.

5. *The true significance of veto bargaining is masked by the passage of large numbers of unimportant bills* about which the president cares little. Among the many fewer important bills in play at any given moment, the probability of vetoes is quite high and the incidence of sequential veto bargaining substantial, at least during periods of divided government.

In sum, divided government and the politics of the veto go hand in hand. Veto bargaining is an essential part of a theory of divided government. Each step in this argument deserves a closer look.

Policy Differences between President and Congress

A good place to begin is Figure 1.1, which displays some fundamental data on the macropolitics of American political institutions. The figure shows the occurrence of divided party government from the 24th to 104th Congress, 1835 to 1996. Of course, divided government is only a rough indicator of policy differences between president and Congress, which can emerge even under unified party government. President Carter's battle with Congress over water projects supplies an example. However, policy differences are frequent and profound during divided government, even in its less conflictual periods, such as the early Eisenhower Congresses. So the data in Figure 1.1 supply an approximate lower bound on the recurrent tendency for policy divisions to emerge between president and Congress.

In the Figure 1.1, the hash marks or "rug" at 0.0 indicates each Congress in which unified government prevailed. The hash marks at 1.0 show each Congress in which divided party government occurred. The undulating line is the fit from a nonparametric, locally weighted regression model of the data.[5] Much the same effect would result from a running average of the 0–1 values but the local regression has superior statistical properties and is just as easy to interpret. Given the scoring of the data, the line indicates the estimated probability that government will be divided at each point in time. For example, the model estimates the probability of divided government at the time of the Congress of 1871–72 as 50%.

[5] The data are taken from the *Congressional Quarterly* 1985:182–83 and table 1–18 in Ornstein, Mann, and Malbin 1997. On locally weighted regression, see inter alia Cleveland 1993, Hastie 1993, and Beck and Jackman 1998. The model shown was fit as a general additive model in the statistical language S-plus, employing the loess function lo (span = .4, degree = 2, family = binomial). The regression diagnostics discussed in Cleveland, Grosse, and Shyu 1993, as well as an analysis of deviance using approximate chi-square tests, suggested no obvious lack of fit, nor are the broad patterns particularly sensitive to changes in the span or use of robust methods (Tukey's bisquare).

10

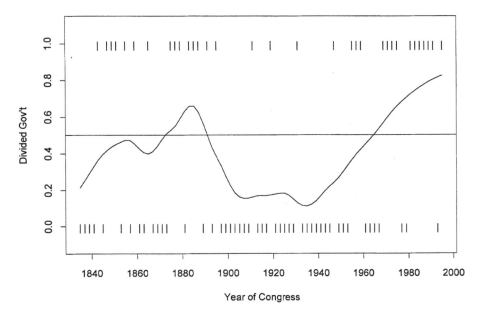

Figure 1.1. Divided Government, 1835–1996

The data display a striking periodicity. First, there was a period stretching from the late 1840s to the election of 1896 in which the probability of divided government fluctuated around 50%. (The dip just after 1860 results from the South's expulsion from Congress during and immediately after the Civil War.) This period was characterized by vigorous policy differences between the parties, first over slavery and civil rights, and later, as a rural agrarian nation struggled to transform itself into an urban, industrialized one, over labor laws, tariffs, and monetary policy.

The first period of mixed unified and divided government came to a crashing end with the realigning election of 1896. This remarkable event ushered in a half century of unified government, its most prolonged period during the 160 years shown in Figure 1.1. Of course, the Republican Party held the government during the first part of this period, while the Democratic Party dominated politics in the second half, following the New Deal realignment of 1932–36. Partisan and policy change was thus abundant during this period. What was rare was divided party government, whose probability the model estimates at less than 20%. In fact divided government occurred only three or perhaps four times, depending on how one dates the end of the era. The three clear-cut cases

11

are Taft and the Democratic House in 1911–12, Wilson and the Republican 66th Congress in 1919–20, and Hoover and the Democratic House in 1931–32. The remaining case is Truman and the Republican 80th Congress in 1947–48.

The regression model indicates that the great era of unified government drew to a close in the mid-1950s. A convenient watershed is the sudden appearance of a Republican president and Democratic Congress in 1955, the first such apparition since Rutherford Hayes found himself facing the 46th Congress in 1879. The model suggests that the probability of divided government continued to increase steadily throughout this new era. By the early 1960s it passed the 50% mark. At present, the probability of divided government is about 80%. Thus, we are living in the greatest period of divided government in more than a century and a half. It needs no regression model to see that we live in the most concentrated such period since the 1880s and 1890s. One can see this simply by looking at the distribution of hash marks at 1.0.

Figure 1.1 suggests an obvious explanation for political scientists' failure to develop a theory of divided government: historical accident. The beginning of the great period of unified government coincided almost perfectly with the emergence of professionalized universities and the new discipline of political science (Ross 1991). The early pioneers saw the unsavory party politics of the 1880s, lived through the amazing election of 1896, experienced Wilson and Theodore Roosevelt, and some two decades of unified government. Their students lived through the equally amazing New Deal realignment, the stupendous Franklin Roosevelt, and two more decades of unified government. How could the political science they created *not* afford a central place to unified government, strong presidents, and (after the second shock) realigning elections?[6] However, if professional political science had emerged fifty years earlier or fifty years later, its central concepts for understanding American government would have looked very different.

A fine-grained explanation for the patterns in Figure 1.1 continues to elude political scientists. In broad terms, however, the source of the system's potential for divided government is quite clear: it is an inevitable by-product of the Founders' design. It is quite literally built into the system.

In puzzling out why the American constitutional order almost guarantees periods of disagreement between the president and Congress, it is helpful to consider the logic of the system from the perspective of "principal-agent theory." Principal-agent theory is a powerful set of tools for analyzing delegation, hierarchy, fiduciary relationships, contracts, and

---

[6] V. O. Key's seminal article on "critical elections" appeared in 1955.

the like. Employing this perspective, it is useful to distinguish between two broad classes of governmental designs, the *unitary-agent design* and the *multiple-agent design.*

The unitary-agent design envisions the delegation of power from the people (the principal) to a single team of governors (the agent). The people grant the team a temporary franchise to govern, during which it has a relatively free hand with policy. Periodically, though, the franchise is declared open. Other teams may then compete for the franchise through an election. The prospect of competition creates powerful incentives for the incumbent team to supply the people with good government.[7] Parliamentary democracies provide the clearest example of this simple and readily understandable design. Perhaps partly because this design is so easy to understand, it is widely employed.

The multiple-agent design is more complex and used less often. Here, the people delegate power not to a single team that temporarily controls the entire government but to several standing entities with somewhat overlapping jurisdictions over policy making. Each entity specializes in an activity but has a monopoly over none. The entities then engage in structured competition among themselves. In addition, the people periodically provide feedback to some or all of the entities separately, via elections. The structured competition among the distinct entities, in conjunction with feedback directed at them individually, is intended to create incentives for good governance.

The most famous example of the multiple-agent design is, of course, the American system of government. Why did the founders favor the multiple-agent design over the unitary-agent one? The unitary-model has a danger that is easily illustrated in an extremely simple model of governmental performance, shown in Figure 1.2. In this simple Markov model, the political system may be in either of two states: the "virtuous" state V or the "tyrannical" state T. There are a series of discrete periods, 1, 2, 3, and so on. Regardless of which state the system is in at time t it must make a transition to a subsequent state at time $t + 1$. Possible transitions are shown by the arrows. Each transition arrow may occur with a particular probability, the likelihood of making the transition to V or T given the present state (either V or T).

In the unitary design, competitive elections are supposed to keep the government in the virtuous, nontyrannical state in each period. Consequently, given such a constitutional design, if the system is in state V at time t it is very likely to remain there at time $t + 1$. For the sake of concreteness, assume this probability is .98. Unfortunately, there remains

---

[7] Palmer 1995 provides a lengthier elaboration of this general perspective, focusing on Westminster parliamentary systems.

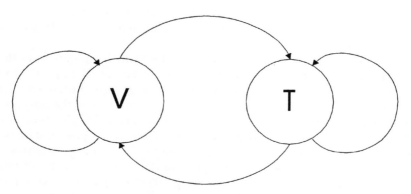

Figure 1.2. Two-State Markov Model of Governmental Performance

a small chance the other transition could take place. This could happen because a team that had previously performed well becomes corrupted by power and delivers a self-coup, the well-known *autogolpe* of Latin American politics. Or a newly entering team might turn out to be very bad, unexpectedly. Or, the people in a momentary fit of passion might select a team that calmer reflection would suggest is bad. All these are unlikely events – in our tinker-toy polity, they happen on average only one election in fifty. But they *can* happen. If they do, the system flips into the tyrannical state. One of the great tragedies of human history is the difficulty of escaping from tyranny, since tyrants so ruthlessly maintain their power. The difficulty of escape is reflected in the transition probability out of *T*. Again for the sake of concreteness, assume the transition probability out of *T* to be one-tenth that out of *V*. This is a small probability but not absolutely zero. As the collapse of the Soviet Union reminds us, transitions from tyranny are possible.

Given the transition probabilities shown in Figure 1.2, how much time will the system tend to spend in the virtuous and tyrannical states? To put it another way, what are the long-run probabilities of being in *V* and *T*? The answer is easy to calculate once we set up the problem in the form of Figure 1.2. Simple algebra (provided in the appendix to this chapter) shows the probability of being in *T* is 95%! The probability of being in *V* is only 5%. This example illustrates quite vividly how even small chances of disaster become calamitous over the long haul, the *Challenger* principle of politics.

The multiple-agent design is intended to be very resistant to the slide into tyranny. To see its logic, return to the two-state model of government performance. Continue to suppose there is a 2% chance that a bad agent comes to power in any given period. In the multiple-agent design, however, a single bad agent cannot create a despotism by itself because the other agents can block its moves. Suppose there are three agents each with the power to block the others' slide into tyranny. Then the system's one-period probability of a transition from virtue to tyranny falls from .02 to $.02^3 = .000008$ – from 1 chance in 50 to 1 chance in 125,000! The same type of calculation carried out earlier shows that the long-run probability of being in the virtuous state is now 99.6%. The corresponding chance of being in a despotism is less than one-half of 1%. The example is contrived but the logic of the multiple-agent model is clear.

The historical experience of parliamentary democracies suggests the Founding Fathers may have exaggerated the vulnerability of the unitary-agent model to tyrannous breakdown, though systematic studies of the evidence are rare. On the other hand, simple statistics are likely to be deceptive since we will tend to see the unitary design only in places where it is likely to succeed. Countries in which the unitary-agency model is fragile are not likely to select it as their constitutional design, an example of what statisticians call "selection bias." Regardless of the real probabilities, though, there is abundant evidence of the Founders' fear of tyranny. The corrupting influence of power was an obsessive concern of Whig political science. *Federalist 10*, for example, discusses the vulnerability of republics to temporary madness propagated by demagogues (Hamilton, Madison, and Jay 1787). The American constitutional design reflects this fear of tyrannous breakdown.

How does the logic of the multiple-agent design play out in the American system? The key is the way the Founders constructed the electoral foundations of each branch to frustrate seizure of the whole government by any unified agent. First, the Founders staggered the length of terms across the presidency, the House, and the Senate, and then further staggered them within the Senate. Consequently, none operates on the same electoral clock. However enthusiastic voters might be for adherents of a given party at a particular time, they are flatly unable to install them in all the key positions in one fell swoop. At least two elections over four years, and possibly three over six years, are required. Second, the Founders assured that each organ would represent "the" people in a somewhat different way. In the House, vox populi arises from the voices of single representatives from 435 small districts. In the Senate, it emerges from a chorus of dual representatives from fifty states. The voice of the people to which the president is most likely to attend is even more complex, since he is chosen in a population-weighted election of the states. For him, "the" people is a plurality of voters in states with a plurality of electoral votes. A faction that might be powerful under one aggregation is unlikely to exert power in all three organs simultaneously.

15

Veto Bargaining

The protections against unitary control are so strong that some observers – usually partisans of the unitary-agent model – portray it as a government at war with itself. This seems too extreme to be really plausible, at least most of the time. Despite the different clocks and the different methods for aggregating voter preferences, the range of disagreement between the branches is probably tightly bounded, provided voters' preferences are neither too heterogeneous nor too mercurial. If voter preferences are such that the median senator is a socialist, the median representative is unlikely to be a libertarian. When key actors in all three branches share a policy goal, law making is remarkably smooth and expeditious. Policy making can occur almost with the speed of a thunderclap (recall FDR's 100 days). If a crisis demands swift and decisive executive action, Congress can allow the president to assume the mantle almost of a dictator, the case of Lincoln providing the most telling example. Even in periods of divided government, Congress regularly produces important legislation (Mayhew 1991). American democracy need not, and frequently does not, end in deadlock. But what can happen – and does with increasing frequency – is that actors with different policy preferences capture different branches of the government. In such a situation, the president's structural incentives to use the veto become important.

Structural Incentives to Use the Veto

The American separation-of-powers system is rarely at war with itself. Nonetheless, the Constitution is an invitation to struggle, in Corwin's memorable phrase. The checks and balances intended to stop the slide into tyranny also provide each organ with tools for bargaining over policy. In the legislative arena, the veto is the president's primary tool. The question is, Does the president have a systematic incentive to use the veto to pursue his policy goals?

A supportive piece of evidence is presidents' consistent use of the veto to further their policy objectives. Even in the earliest vetoes, before Andrew Jackson's presidency, there were clear instances in which presidents used the veto to press raw policy preferences, not merely to block laws of dubious constitutionality. Examples include Washington's veto of a military bill (discussed later) and Madison's veto of a national bank, a proposal whose constitutionality he conceded but whose wisdom he condemned. By the time of the Civil War, vetoes based on "expediency" – that is, preference without any pretense of a constitutional issue – were common.[8]

---

[8] Edward Campbell Mason suggests that the greater reliance on constitutional arguments in early veto messages probably reflected the issues that arose in an era

Interbranch Bargaining

What is the source of the president's structural incentive to veto? One possibility, clearly stated by James Bryce more than a century ago, is the public's hope that the president will counteract institutional pathologies to which Congress is particularly susceptible: "The people regard him [the president] as a check, an indispensable check, not only upon the haste and heedlessness of their representatives, the faults that the framers of the Constitution chiefly feared, but upon their tendency to yield either to pressure from any section of the constituents, or to temptations of a private nature" (1888:75–76). In modern parlance: Congress is prone to excessive pork-barreling, special interest sellouts, localistic parochialism, and sectional logrolling (Ferejohn 1974; Arnold 1979; Shepsle and Weingast 1981; Mayhew 1974). The presidency is much less prone to these particular pathologies. Accordingly, a president can seek electoral advantage by using the veto to limn his own virtue against the pitch of congressional vice. As Bryce noted,

So far from exciting the displeasure of the people by resisting the will of their representatives, a President generally gains popularity by the bold use of his veto power. It conveys the impression of firmness; it shows that he has a view and does not fear to give effect to it. The nation, which has often good grounds for distrusting Congress, a body liable to be moved by sinister private influences, or to defer to the clamor of some noisy section outside, looks to the man of its choice to keep Congress in order. (1888:75)

This is powerfully argued, but the case for popularity-enhancing vetoes is not as clear-cut as Bryce supposed. Political scientists Tim Groseclose and Nolan McCarty have shown how, under special circumstances, Congress can tempt the president to veto popular legislation so that he rather than Congress takes the electoral beating (1996). Edward Campbell Mason's judgment is probably the most judicious one: "the veto is a negative power, not popular or unpopular in itself" (1891:132). Nonetheless, presidents have never hesitated to trumpet Bryce's argument when it suited their purposes. "The president is the only representative of all the people" is a cry that dates back at least to Andrew Jackson. From the perspective of the multiple-agent design, it is a claim that is entirely bogus since both the House and the Senate also represent all the people. But it is an attractive rhetorical device for contrasting presidential responsibility with congressional pathology, as highlighted by a veto.

In addition, consider the strong converse of the structural incentive view: if the policy preferences of the president's electoral coalition conflict with bills passed by Congress, what incentive would restrain the veto pen? What would stop a president from pursuing his supporters'

when many fundamental constitutional questions had yet to be decided (1891:130–31).

17

objectives even in the teeth of congressional opposition? One force might be public opinion. For example, even Roosevelt's ardent supporters found his court-packing plan hard to stomach. Thus, widespread subscription to a Whig conception of the presidency, in which the executive owes the legislature strong deference, might inhibit presidents from exercising the veto. Jeffrey Tulis has argued that nineteenth-century presidents in fact adhered to a different "norm" of the presidency (1987). Yet the (at least nominal) Whig Tyler was one of the greatest vetoers in history, and the decidedly Whigish William Howard Taft displayed a deft hand with the veto.[9] The man known to his contemporaries as the "veto president" was not George Bush or even Gerald Ford. It was Grover Cleveland. As Edward Corwin noted in his 1940 appraisal of the presidency, a restricted notion of the office could never be maintained after Wilson and the two Roosevelts. When policy preferences differ, Congress cannot assume a compliant president. Quite the opposite.

Heading Off Vetoes

I have argued that the American Constitution sets up an institutional framework in which presidents often disagree with Congress over policy goals and have a strong incentive to use the veto. Doesn't this reasoning founder on the simple fact that presidents just don't use the veto very often (putting aside Cleveland's and FDR's vetoes of hundreds of private bills)? No. First, as I suggest later, vetoes are not as rare as they initially appear, at least under specific circumstances. But even if they were, the point would still be misdirected. Alexander Hamilton, in *Federalist 73*, explains why:

A power of this nature in the Executive [i.e., the veto] will often have a silent and unperceived, though forcible operation. When men, engaged in unjustifiable pursuits, are aware that obstructions may come from a quarter which they cannot control, they will often be restrained by the apprehension of opposition, from doing what they would with eagerness rush into, if no such external impediments were to be feared. (Hamilton et al. 1787:480)

Hamilton is here invoking what contemporary political scientists call "the second face of power," power based on anticipated response (Bachrach and Baratz 1962; Nagal 1975).[10] (The so-called first face is outright compulsion.) As has often been pointed out, actor A can influence actor

---

[9] In what is usually regarded as the most extended Whig interpretation of the presidency, published in 1916, Taft wrote with genuine enthusiasm about the veto as a vehicle for expressing the executive's legislative preferences (1916: esp. 16ff.).

[10] Hamilton's apparent restriction of this argument to "unjustifiable pursuits" was probably disingenuous.

B even though A takes no visible actions. The reason is that B anticipates the unpleasant response of A if B takes certain actions. Accordingly, B comports herself so as to head off A's response. It is a principle perfectly familiar from everyday life. The concept of the second face of power clearly suggests that *the veto* (a capability) can shape the content of legislation even if *vetoes* (uses of the capability) are rare.

Beyond pure theory, however, is there any reason to believe the second face of power has practical application to vetoes? Roderick Kiewiet and Mathew McCubbins are perhaps the only political scientists who have tried to test this idea directly. Using measures of policy preferences and fluctuating appropriations in various areas, they find evidence that Congress indeed tries to prevent vetoes by modifying the content of money bills (Kiewiet and McCubbins 1988). In Chapter 6 I provide additional evidence on the second face of power by examining the effect of the veto power on Congress's legislative productivity.

Despite this intriguing evidence, the argument from the second face of power is clearly too powerful, at least in its simplest and most extreme form. In simple models of the veto power (reviewed in Chapter 4), vetoes never occur because Congress is so good at anticipating the president's preferences. In these models, the legislature calibrates bills with razor sharp precision to escape vetoes. But, of course, vetoes do occur.

Something must be wrong with the simple models, or at least missing. What the missing component might be is shown by the case studies that opened this chapter. In both instances Congress appeared to misestimate what the president would tolerate, bringing on a veto. In other words, what these cases show to be missing from the simplest version of the second face of power is *congressional ignorance about what the president will tolerate*. This type of ignorance is an example of what game theorists call *incomplete information*. It assumes a central role in the analysis in this book.

If Congress operates under incomplete information, it is hardly surprising if we observe actual vetoes. But in addition – and this point is essential for understanding the politics of the veto – incomplete information creates rich opportunities for presidents to engage in strategic behavior.

A particularly interesting form of strategic behavior is the veto threat. If Congress is quite sure what the president will accept, there is no room for threats to affect congressional behavior. But if Congress is not sure how far it can push the president before provoking a veto, a veto threat may warn Congress that it is close to or over the line. Perhaps Congress responds to the threat by modifying the proposed legislation before sending it to the president. Or perhaps not: the president may be bluffing and talk is cheap, so why should Congress actually respond?

19

Veto Bargaining

This puzzle occurs in many guises in politics: why should mere rhetoric – just intangible words – induce a very real, tangible response? When will threats, and threats alone, work? At least in the context of veto threats, the puzzle has real empirical bite, for presidents have employed veto threats, with real consequences, for over a century. Remarkably, though, it is possible to untangle this puzzle using modern game theory. When one does, some very stark predictions emerge, predictions that are substantially confirmed by systematic empirical evidence. I examine veto threats in Chapter 7.

In short, the veto does not need to be used to have an effect. Anticipation is sometimes enough. Presidents help anticipation along by making veto threats, which, somewhat amazingly, do shape legislation and head off vetoes.

Using Vetoes to Shape Legislation

Incomplete information has the potential to turn legislating into a high-stakes poker game between the executive and legislative branches. As the game progresses through several rounds – passage, veto, override attempt, repassage, reveto, and so on – vetoes become potent gambits. In sequential veto bargaining, vetoes – actual vetoes, not simply the veto as a presidential capability – shape legislation.

There are three ways vetoes can shape legislation. First, an intransigent president can try to kill a bill. He uses the veto to force its repassage, hoping outside events derail the legislation. Second, the president can force Congress to craft a new, veto-proof version of the bill, one he may still find objectionable but nonetheless preferable to the original version. Third, the president can force Congress to rewrite the vetoed bill, offering enough concessions so he will sign the repassed bill. The president may do this even though he would have been willing to sign the first bill if it were a one-shot offer. In each of these cases the veto is a form of strategic holdout intended to shape the outcome of the interbranch bargaining. Skillful presidents can use sequential veto bargaining to impress their preferences on policy much more than static conceptions of the veto would suggest.

Welfare Reform Revisited. Consider again the story of Clinton and the welfare vetoes. A bargaining perspective suggests viewing the process as a high-stakes poker game. Congress made repeated bids, weighing the value of concessions against the risk of a veto. The president exploited the fear of a veto, with his veto threats. However, extracting substantial concessions required him to go beyond threats to actual vetoes, even at

20

the risk of killing the bill. His vetoes powerfully shaped the content of the final bill.

Given the president's campaign statements about welfare reform during 1992 and in light of their landslide victory of 1994, the Republicans began the bargaining believing the president would accommodate their plans. "Essentially they [the Republicans] thought the president would sign anything," Representative Sander Levin explained in April 1996. "They misread him." The Republicans' initial expectations about the president were reflected in statements at the passage of the Reconciliation Bill. Declared Republican firebrand Senator Rick Santorum, "This is a bill that the president has no reason not to sign. This is well within the parameters he set for welfare when he ran for president." Representative Bill Archer (R-Texas) suggested "Either he can be the New Democrat he claims to be and sign this welfare bill or he can be the last defender of the failed welfare state and veto this historic legislation" (*CQ Weekly Report*, November 11, 1995:3459; November 18, 1995: 3545).

The veto that followed gave pause to some in Congress. But because the principal reason articulated for the veto was health care cuts, not welfare changes, many continued to believe the president would bend to their plans. Hence, the passage of a tough proposal with H.R. 4. To make their hardball offer more persuasive, key Republicans suggested the bill would die after a veto. "We've come a long way. I don't know that we can move any further," declared Representative Clay Shaw, chairman of the Ways and Means Human Resources Subcommittee. Representative Gene Taylor was even blunter. "It's this or nothing."

The second bill thus presented the president with a tough decision. In his own balanced budget plan, he had indicated a willingness to support block grants and $46 billion in cuts. Should he swallow $64 billion in cuts and tough provisions in order to avoid the risk of killing welfare reform? Would welfare reform really die if he vetoed H.R. 4? If not, how many more concessions would a veto extract – enough to make the risk of killing the bill worth the gamble? Clinton decided to find out.

The president's second veto dashed the hope of the Republicans that the president would be a pushover on welfare reform. What would it take to make the president sign a bill? Their third try began by linking welfare reform and Medicaid cuts. It drew an immediate veto threat, now quite credible. They dropped the link with Medicaid cuts. Perhaps the president was utterly recalcitrant and would sign nothing. But Clinton continued to signal support for welfare reform; for example, he praised Wisconsin's far-reaching plan during a radio address. The Republicans responded with a third bill with considerable concessions. "Mr. President, we are calling your bluff," declared Archer. Even here, though, Clinton continued to try to extract more concessions. For example, during the House's initial passage of H.R. 3734 he maximized the uncertainty about his likely response to the plan: he requested House Democrats to vote against the bill but nonetheless issued no veto threat. The result was further concessions in the Senate. Presented with the third bill, Clinton considered the possibility of yet a third veto. But the roll call votes in Congress indicated that the bill was approaching the override point. Another veto would probably extract only modest concessions and ran the risk of killing reform, thereby handing the Republicans a damaging campaign issue. The president accepted Congress's third try at welfare reform.

The president's vetoes forced the Republicans to write a bill that appealed not just to Republicans but to a *majority* of Democrats in Congress, who voted for final passage. During the course of this bargaining, from the Reconciliation Bill to H.R. 3734, Clinton compelled reductions in cuts from $81 billion to $55 billion, some $26 billion in concessions from the Republican Congress. He forced many policy changes that softened the impact of welfare reform on children. *Congressional Quarterly Weekly Report* noted the differences between the initial proposals and the final ones:

Republicans, especially in the House, had previously sought to give states almost complete control over Medicaid, foster care and adoption programs, school meals, and nutritional assistance for pregnant women and children. They also wanted to give states the option to control their food stamp programs and to sharply reduce the number of people eligible for the earned-income tax credit, which provides tax relief to the working poor. In the end, the legislation did none of that. (August 3, 1996:2195)

In short, the president's repeated gambits preserved billions of dollars of welfare expenditures and forced massive changes in Congress's policy proposals, with profound consequences for millions of people. What poker game can offer stakes like that!

Is Sequential Veto Bargaining a Fluke? Is the welfare reform case a fluke? In Chapter 2 I present systematic evidence on sequential veto bargaining in the postwar era. In Chapter 8 I provide case studies of many of the most notable examples from this period. However, it is easy to find dozens of examples of sequential veto bargaining throughout the history of the presidency. Here are a few examples from earlier periods:

- In the very first veto in American history, George Washington refused to assent to an apportionment bill passed in May 1792 that would have redistributed representation away from the southern states. Viewing the bill as unconstitutional, but also fearing its effects on sectionalism, Washington vetoed it in early April. Congress attempted to override the bill but failed even to gain majorities in the House or Senate. Within a week, Congress repassed a new version of the bill, one that met Washington's objections. He readily signed it into law (Jackson 1967:1–3).

- Four days before the end of his second term, George Washington issued his second veto, this time of a bill that included a provision disbanding two dragoon companies in the army, a measure the president opposed. No constitutional issue was involved. After failing to override the veto, Congress repassed the bill, dropping the offending provisions. Washington signed the bill into law on his last day in office (Jackson 1967:3–4).

- In 1812, Madison cast the first pocket veto. Congress passed a bill regulating the naturalization of aliens during the War of 1812. Madison believed the bill's provisions were subject to abuse and vetoed it. When Congress reconvened, the bill's authors modified it along the lines suggested by the president. Congress repassed it and Madison signed it (Jackson 1967:8–9).

- In 1841, Tyler vetoed a bank bill. In 1842, Congress repassed it, making considerable compromises, attempting either to gain the president's approval or beat the veto. But to no avail: Tyler vetoed it again, and his veto was sustained a second time. The bargaining had wrung concessions from Congress but not enough to circumvent the president's opposition (Spitzer 1988:40–45; Jackson 1967: 57–65).

- Following the election of 1876, the Democratic Congress attempted to reduce federal control of elections, attaching to a series of five appropriations bills "riders" that would have removed federal officials from southern voting places. Republican President Hayes, undeterred by the necessity of passing the appropriations, vetoed the bills and kept doing so until Congress stripped them of the riders. Only then were the appropriations enacted (Jackson 1967:289; Spitzer 1988:60; Mason 1891:47–49).[11]

- Reflecting the rise in nativist sentiments, Congress in 1882 passed a bill prohibiting Chinese immigration as "a breach of our national faith." President Chester Arthur vetoed the bill, noting its unfairness and detrimental effects on relations with China. After the veto was sustained, Congress repassed the bill, this time merely suspending

---

[11] Taft also used the veto to force Congress to remove extraneous riders from appropriations bills (1916:25–26).

immigration from China for a few years. Arthur signed the revised bill (Ford 1919:31; Jackson 1967:147).

These examples cut across different eras, different party systems, and different presidents. Despite these differences, sequential veto bargaining was a constant. The conclusion seems inescapable: the possibility of sequential veto bargaining was latent in the rules established by the Constitution. Presidents had a strong incentive to exploit this possibility and almost immediately learned how to do so.

The Frequency of Veto Bargaining

The question remains, though, Does veto bargaining occur *frequently* for *important* legislation? The answer is a resounding yes. However, it takes some work to prove this point.

The biggest problem is identifying important legislation. In an average Congress in the postwar period, lawmakers added 707 new statutes to the books. The bulk of this legislation consisted of relatively inconsequential bills. Here are some examples from the 89th Congress, the postwar Congress most productive of landmark legislation:

- PL 89–783: Strike medals in commemoration of Seabees 25th anniversary and the U.S. Navy Civil Engineer Corps 100th anniversary
- PL 89–784: Change name of Rolla Jewel Bearing Plant to William Langer Jewell Bearing Plant at Rolla, North Dakota.
- PL 89–785: Clarify responsibility of the Veteran's Administration with respect to training and education of health service personnel.
- PL 89–786: Erect a memorial to General John J. Pershing in the District of Columbia

And so on and on. These examples are not unusual. They are *typical*. The mass of Congress's legislative output is of a triviality that can scarcely be believed.

The point of this observation is not to denigrate Congress or downplay its importance as a policy-making institution. Congress passes important legislation and does so regularly. Rather, the point is: at any given time the majority of legislative activity of genuine significance is concentrated in a relatively small number of important bills. It is there that veto bargaining is likely to be concentrated, and of any real consequence. Unless one separates the legislative wheat from the chaff, one's picture of veto politics will be seriously distorted.

In the following chapter I present a method for sorting bills by legislative significance; I defer methodological details until then. However, Figure 1.3 presents the distribution of public laws and vetoes across four

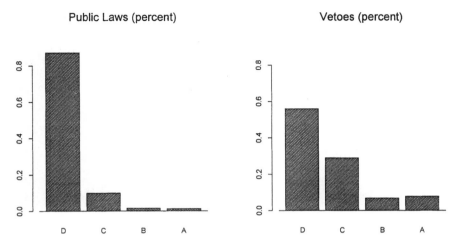

Public Laws (percent)   Vetoes (percent)

Figure 1.3. Distribution by Significance: Public Laws and Vetoes, 1945–1992

classes of legislative significance from 1945 to 1992. Group D comprises "minor" bills, group C "ordinary" legislation, group B "important legislation," and group A exceptionally important or "landmark" bills. As shown, by far the bulk of all public laws are minor (87%); very few public laws are important or landmark. Among vetoes, vetoes of minor legislation still predominate but the distribution shows a much, much greater concentration in the higher significance categories.

Figure 1.4 shows why. The figure shows the percentage of initially passed bills that were vetoed, by significance category and by unified and divided government. The data thus exclude bills repassed after a veto. During unified government, the probability of a veto was very low regardless of the bill's legislative significance. But a remarkable change occurred under divided government. For minor legislation, the probability of a veto was as low as during unified government. But the probability increased dramatically with legislative significance. For landmark legislation, the probability of a veto of initially passed legislation was 20% – one chance in five. This category includes the most important legislation of the postwar period. For landmark legislation during divided government, vetoes are not rare events at all.

To summarize the argument: divided government has become a signature of modern American government. During divided government the president and Congress frequently find themselves at loggerheads over legislation. In the system constructed by the Founders, the president's principal legislative tool is the veto, and he has every incentive to use it in a struggle with Congress over policy. This fact injects the veto into

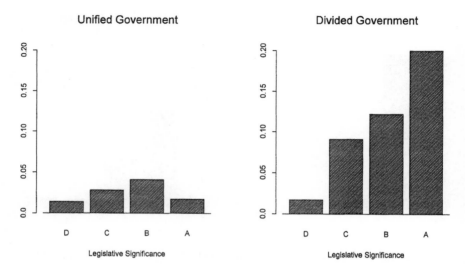

Figure 1.4. Probability of Vetoes by Significance Class, Unified versus Divided Government, 1945–1992

Congress's calculations as it fashions legislation, altering the content of some bills and leaving others stillborn. But anticipation will not head off every veto. Under conditions of incomplete information, the president can use vetoes and veto threats in a very strategic way to extract policy concessions and shape legislation. This type of veto bargaining is concentrated among particularly important legislation, where it is actually rather common. Its consequences may be profound.

In these opening pages this argument remains a sketch. But it does provide a rationale for studying the veto (and for you to invest your time reading this book), for if it stands up to close scrutiny – theoretical and empirical – the presidential veto is much more consequential than is commonly believed. Moreover, the argument points toward a new, institutionally grounded conception of divided government and the separation-of-powers system.

What We Need to Learn

I quickly targeted a key question: Can the president use vetoes and veto threats to gain strategic leverage over important legislation? The bargaining perspective that leads to this question quickly leads to others: Under what circumstances do presidents veto bills? Do vetoes kill bills, or are they just a step in sequential bargaining? Are vetoes more likely to be bargaining ploys rather than fatal bullets under some circumstances than others? If vetoes do not always kill bills (exclusive of successful overrides), when does a veto extract large concessions in successor bills and when doesn't it? When does the president use veto threats? Do they work – or rather, when do they work? Are there differences across presidents in their use and success with veto bargaining? How many important bills remain stillborn, due to the president's veto power? Above all, what is the causal mechanism or mechanisms that explain how and why the process of veto bargaining takes its distinctive shape? The remainder of this book is devoted to answering these questions.

A BRIEF TOUR OF WHAT FOLLOWS

In the next chapter I present a "natural history" of the veto. Without bringing much theory to bear I identify some clear and interesting patterns in the politics of the veto in the postwar period. I begin by outlining a simple but very general framework for thinking about veto bargaining. The framework supplies a vocabulary for discussing episodes of veto bargaining. I then turn to the numbers: the number of episodes of bargaining, the probability that initially passed bills were vetoed, the repassage rate for vetoed bills, the probability of override attempts, their likelihood of success, and a rough measure of congressional policy concessions during veto bargaining. With the basic facts about veto bargaining in hand we can see what minimally acceptable models must explain.

Chapter 3 provides an extended discussion of the philosophy behind the theory that follows. Why so much emphasis on models? Why insist on rational choice models? Is the study of the presidency a reasonable place to use rational choice theory? What criteria are appropriate for judging the success of rational choice models, and their failure? This chapter addresses these questions. In the next chapters, I turn from a general discussion of modeling to its actual practice.

In this book I examine a sequence of models of veto bargaining, as shown in Figure 1.5. In most cases the models are not competitive but complementary, each picking out and examining in greater detail one aspect of veto bargaining.

The first model, the basic take-it-or-leave-it (TILI) bargaining model, analyzes the fundamental ultimatum game in political settings.[12] It examines a situation in which one party, the *proposer* or *setter* (in this case Congress) makes a single take-it-or-leave-it offer to a second party, the *chooser* (in this case the president). The chooser may accept the offer or

---

[12] Other kinds of ultimatum games, especially in economic settings, are discussed in Roth 1995.

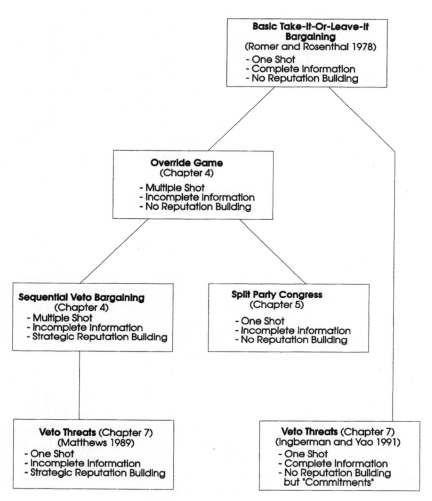

Figure 1.5. Models of Veto Bargaining

may decline it in favor of the status quo. The model assumes complete and perfect information. Consequently there is no reputation building. What the model does provide, however, is a careful analysis of the second face of power. This model was developed in the late 1970s by political economists Thomas Romer and Howard Rosenthal (1978) and is sometimes called the Romer-Rosenthal model in their honor. It has become a workhorse in the new theorizing about the separation-of-powers system.[13] I present no new results concerning this well-known game. But since it provides the analytical core or theme on which all the subsequent models are variations, I review it carefully. I use the presentation of the basic model to introduce, step by step, the apparatus deployed in the later models.

The basic TILI model provides the starting place for thinking about vetoes but it cannot be the ending place. The problem is the "Hicks paradox," which holds that bargaining failures like strikes, vetoes, or wars are irrational in a setting of complete and perfect information (Kennan 1986). The second model, the override game, illustrates how incomplete information resolves the Hicks paradox. The critical element studied in this model is uncertainty about what constitutes a veto-proof bill. The uncertainty affects both Congress and president. The novel feature of the model is the way this uncertainty plays itself out over several rounds of veto bargaining. Thus, we can explore the logic of overrides over extended veto bargaining.

Uncertainty about veto-proof bills is hardly the most important type of uncertainty in veto bargaining. Instead, as the case studies suggested, arguably more central is uncertainty about the president's policy preferences. The third model, the sequential veto bargaining model, studies the consequences of this type of uncertainty. This type of uncertainty propels the strategic elements of the models to greater heights, for it is asymmetric: unlike the uncertainty studied in the override model, it affects only Congress, not the president. This may seem a small difference but it radically transforms the character of the situation. In particular, it allows the introduction of *presidential policy reputation*.

Since the publication of Richard Neustadt's classic analysis of the presidency, *Presidential Power* (1960), nearly four decades ago, political scientists have seen the president's reputation as central to his effectiveness in Washington. But "reputation" is an elusive concept. Only recently has it become possible to bring the tools of analytical social science to bear on the idea. Many of these tools are on display in the sequential veto bargaining model. In the model, Congress learns more about the president's preferences by observing his actions over the course of play. But the president is a fully strategic actor who anticipates Con-

---

[13] The Romer-Rosenthal model is often called the "monopoly agenda setter" model to distinguish the game it studies, where the proposer faces no competition from other proposers, from games in which proposers compete to make proposals. The distinction is helpful in thinking about the choice of games – for example, in considering the difference between "closed rules" and "open rules" in Congress. That distinction buys little here though, since the game is specified by the Constitution. The language I employ emphasizes instead the fundamental character of the bargaining in an ultimatum game.

gress's learning. He deliberately uses vetoes as a tool to shape Congress's beliefs – his reputation – and thus extract policy concessions. And, of course, Congress anticipates the president's strategic maneuvers. The result is a subtle and complex situation that presidents can turn to their advantage.

In Chapter 5 I return with the models in hand to consider again the patterns uncovered in the natural history of Chapter 2. I try to see whether, and how, the models explain the data. As part of this analysis, I examine more closely the case of split party Congresses, when one party controls the presidency and one chamber of the legislature; the other party controls the remaining chamber. I very briefly sketch a model that helps untangle the logic of veto bargaining in this situation.

The models provide a powerful way to understand patterns in veto bargaining. But powerful models do more than explain "stylized" facts; they even do more than explain real patterns in complex data. They also make distinctive predictions about what is not known but is knowable. In Chapter 6 I use the models to generate novel predictions that lie outside the natural-history-oriented data of Chapter 2. In particular, I examine some subtle predictions about concessions and a deadline effect. I then present additional data to test the predictions, a strong challenge for the models. As part of the testing, I take a closer look at vetoes and the second face of power, estimating how the veto power affects the legislative productivity of Congress.

Chapter 7 examines veto threats. Veto bargaining affords a nearly ideal venue for studying political rhetoric, since the situation involved is both repetitious and rather tightly defined. In fact, rational choice theorists have devised two quite different models for studying rhetoric in veto bargaining. The first views rhetoric as a commitment device, one that boxes in the speaker and thus actually strengthens her hand with adversaries. The second views rhetoric as strategic information transmission, aimed at manipulating the beliefs of the listener. In Chapter 7 I review these models, present some of the first systematic evidence on veto threats, and compare actual patterns with the predictions of the models.

Theories, models, and data are the meat and potatoes of analytical social science. But the spice that gives the work savor is understanding specific cases. In Chapter 8, I use the models as a lens for viewing some of the outstanding cases of veto bargaining in the postwar era. I also try to understand the broader contours of veto bargaining across entire administrations, focusing on the Truman, Eisenhower, Ford, and Reagan administrations. In Chapter 9 I undertake the same exercise for the Clinton administration, through the end of President Clinton's first term.

Interbranch Bargaining

I bring the book to a close by speculating about the future of veto bargaining. I draw some lessons about the study of the presidency, and hazard some guesses about new directions for understanding American government.

Appendix to Chapter 1

This appendix derives the probabilities given in the text for the simple two-step Markov portrayal of constitutional design. Let P_{ij} be the one-step transition probability from state i to state j. So, for example, the one step transition probability from V to V (i.e., of staying in the virtuous state) is P_{vv}. The matrix of transition probabilities is $\left\| \begin{matrix} P_{VV} & P_{VT} \\ P_{TV} & P_{TT} \end{matrix} \right\|$, which in the example of the unitary design is $\left\| \begin{matrix} .98 & .02 \\ .002 & .998 \end{matrix} \right\|$. In the multiple-agent design it is $\left\| \begin{matrix} .999992 & .000008 \\ .002 & .998 \end{matrix} \right\|$. Let P_{ij}^{n} be the n-step transition probability, that is, the probability of being in state j, given a start in state i, after n periods. We wish to calculate $\pi_j = \lim_{n \to \infty} P_{ij}^{n}$, the limit of the n-stage transition probabilities, as n goes to infinity. Ross 1993 provides a convenient theorem concerning these limits (theorem 4.1). The theorem indicates that these limits are independent of i (so it doesn't matter which state the system begins in). Moreover, to calculate the limits one need only solve the following system of simultaneous equations:

$$\pi_V = P_{VV}\,\pi_V + P_{TV}\,\pi_T$$
$$\pi_T = P_{TV}\,\pi_V + P_{TT}\,\pi_T$$
$$\pi_V + \pi_T = 1.$$

Solving this system yields

$$\pi_V = \frac{P_{VV}}{1 + P_{TV} - P_{VV}}, \; \pi_T = \frac{P_{VT}}{1 + P_{TV} - P_{VV}}.$$

Simple substitution yields the probabilities given in the text.

2

A Natural History of Veto Bargaining,
1945–1992

> It is a capital mistake to theorize before one has data.
> Sherlock Holmes, in "A Scandal in Bohemia"

Following Holmes's advice means plunging into a sea of data: more than 17,000 enactments and over 400 vetoes. Each veto is unique. Many have fascinating stories. How can one deal with this overwhelming complexity?

It is possible to approach a data set in the spirit of a natural historian. Exploratory data analysis becomes the social scientist's equivalent of a collecting jar, magnifying lens, and scalpel. These tools, along with some simple pretheoretical notions, allow us to search for structure in the data, to reduce the enormous complexity in hundreds of events to a few memorable, reliable patterns that capture much of the variation in the data. The goal of this chapter, in short, is to transform bewildering complexity into bewildering simplicity.

THE DATA

Veto bargaining is a dynamic process. You can no more study veto bargaining by counting the aggregate vetoes per time period, than you can study price bargaining by counting the customers who leave a shop without purchases. What is needed is a different kind of data, *event histories*, longitudinal data in which discrete events (vetoes, override attempts, and repassages) may occur repeatedly.[1] Such data identify episodes of veto bargaining and track what happens in each episode.

---

[1] Tuma and Hannan make a strong case for event histories in their book *Social Dynamics* (1984). The models they advocate are continuous-time semi-Markov models while those used here are discrete-state Markov models. But many of their general points apply.

Veto Bargaining

Constructing a set of event histories of veto bargaining means, in practice, identifying each bill in a bargaining episode and detailing its fate.

Identifying the Bills

I start with the 434 vetoes of public bills cast between the beginning of the Truman administration in 1945 and the end of the Bush administration in 1992. I exclude vetoes of so-called private bills – bills for the relief of some specific individual – as they have negligible policy consequences. Existing sources make compiling a list of public vetoes a simple matter (Senate Library 1992). This list inevitably contains all the initiating vetoes in bargaining episodes (of course, some of the vetoes are not initiating vetoes, but vetoes of successor bills). Identifying successor bills, many of which are not vetoed bills, is more difficult. Fortunately, Congress is the best-documented political institution in the world. Particularly helpful for identifying successors bills is the coverage of the *Congressional Quarterly*. Since 1945, it has offered detailed, comprehensive coverage of congressional law making. Its annual volume, the *CQ Almanac*, contains careful descriptions of introduced bills and enacted laws, detailed legislative histories of major bills, and brief legislative histories for bills of even modest importance. The material is compiled by subject area and extensively indexed. Starting with a description of each vetoed bill, my collaborators, research assistants, and I searched each of the succeeding issues of *CQ Almanac* in the administration of the vetoing president to find successor bills. For each vetoed bill, these searches were conducted at least three times by independent coders. While it is possible we failed to identify some successor bills, I am confident the number of such bills is small and certainly confined to minor legislation.

An important part of my definition of a bargaining episode is the requirement that the same president act as the "chooser" throughout the episode. To see the logic, consider price bargaining. At the weekend bazaar at the corner of Columbus and 76th Street in New York, a buyer and seller may haggle over the price of (say) an antique fountain pen. Their interchange constitutes an episode of price bargaining. When one buyer leaves the shopkeeper's stall, having failed to reach an agreement with the proprietor, and is replaced by another who newly enters the stall and begins to haggle over the same pen, it is not a continuation of the same bargaining episode. It is a new episode. The key is not the identity of the specific buyers and sellers but rather the informational footing on which they stand: what the seller learned about the old buyer's willingness to pay simply does not apply to the new buyer. She must begin learning again. Similarly, when Gerald Ford replaces Richard

Nixon as president, Congress must begin again to learn what the new president will tolerate about particular policies.

This definition has some disadvantages. Some cases of repassed laws stretch across administrations. For instance, President Bush vetoed a family leave bill whose successor was signed into law by President Bill Clinton early in the 103rd Congress. Under the continuity restriction, the bill signed into law does not count as part of the earlier episode of veto bargaining, which is scored as taking place only between Congress and President Bush. From the perspective of veto bargaining, this accounting seems correct. But it means that one cannot use the data on veto bargaining to identify *every* case in which a vetoed bill was repassed by some Congress, only those cases in which a vetoed bill was repassed during the same administration as the vetoing president.

The definition also has some advantages. Because the data were collected for entire administrations, they do not contain instances of unfinished, ongoing bargaining within an administration. So they do not contain what statisticians would call "censored" observations. Censoring can distort the patterns in event history data, since ongoing episodes appear to be cases in which action has terminated. Although there are statistical fixes for censored data, I do not need to employ them.

Once all the bills in all the episodes were identified, we coded many variables. Among these were whether the bill was an authorization or an appropriation (a money bill). To provide denominators for veto rates of appropriations bills, we compiled a list of all appropriations bills passed by Congress in this period. We compiled the list from the appropriations sections of the *CQ Almanac*, summary descriptions of all enacted bills in *CQ Almanac* and *Congressional Index*, and occasional lists in the *Daily Digest* portion of the *Congressional Record*.

We also coded whether the government was unified or divided at the time of each bill's passage. In most periods of divided government in the postwar era, both chambers of Congress have been controlled by the same party. For example, when government became divided under Truman, in the 80th Congress, the Republicans gained control of both the House and the Senate. When the Republicans seized the presidency under Richard Nixon, the Democrats continued to control both chambers of Congress. But during the first six years of the Reagan administration, the Republicans controlled not only the presidency but the Senate. Only the House remained in the hands of the Democrats. During this period (the 97th, 98th, and 99th Congresses), Reagan vetoed fifty-three bills. These vetoes offer the opportunity to study the effects of this unusual configuration – divided government with a split party Congress – on the politics of the veto.

As a first cut at identifying the frequency of concessions, we used the descriptions in the *CQ Almanac* of adjacent bills in chains (Chapter 6 takes a much more detailed look at concessions). Contested portions of vetoed bills were invariably indicated in the *Congressional Quarterly* write-ups, except for a few exceptionally obscure bills. The write-ups also indicated the direction of the president's preferred position, generally as stated during the legislative process or in the veto message itself. For example, if the initial bill included a provision singled out in the veto message as objectionable, and Congress made the provision less objectionable in the second passage of the bill, we scored this as a congressional concession. In many cases, the *Congressional Quarterly* itself explicitly noted concessions. We did not try to assess the relative significance of concessions.

The timing of bills was also coded from information in the *CQ Almanac*. We noted the date of a bill's final passage by Congress and the date of the presidential veto. Information on override attempts was taken from standard sources (Senate Library 1992) and the *CQ* write-ups.

All these data are quite straightforward (an assertion that may ring a little hollow to the research assistants who gamely slogged with me through tens of thousands of pages of *CQ Almanac*). However, some of the most important data used in this book are *not* straightforward, so it is important to describe them more carefully. These data measure the "legislative significance" of bills, a variable that is critical for understanding the politics of the veto.

Scoring Legislative Significance

There is a little secret about Congress that is never discussed in the legions of textbooks on American government: the vast bulk of legislation produced by that august body is stunningly banal. Renaming federal buildings in small towns; tinkering with the boundaries of national parks; commemorating humble members of the vegetable family; increasing per diem reimbursement rates for participants in an obscure advisory group; altering the technical provisions of a minor subsidy program: these are the typical products of the world's greatest legislative body. Congress can and does turn out extraordinary legislation – Medicare, the Voting Rights Act, the national highway program, the Marshall Plan. And it does so year after year, regardless of which party controls the presidency or Congress and whether the government is unified or divided (Mayhew 1991). But it also produces in staggering profusion boatloads of what can only be described as legislative rubbish (though presumably important to someone).

Whatever else might be said about this ocean of minor bills, one fact is obvious: very few of these bills can be in any serious danger of a presidential veto, for the obvious reason that the president, like almost everyone else, couldn't care less about them. Of course there are exceptions – recall Carter's veto of an obscure bill regulating the processing of rabbit meat. However, the basic fact remains, the chance of a veto for a randomly selected minor bill is very small – in a few pages, I estimate it to be about 1.5%. Yet even with such a low veto rate, minor bills dominate summary counts of vetoes simply because Congress passes so many minor bills. We care little about such vetoes simply because the bills *are* so unimportant, whether vetoed or not.

The situation is completely different for the important bills that gleam like sparkling jewels amid the mountains of dreary slag produced by Congress. For legislative gems, the probability of a veto is much greater than for minor legislation. And it is really only these bills and these vetoes that we care about.

Any attempt to find patterns in vetoes will come to grief unless we sort the jewels from the gravel.[2] Any attempt to understand what happens *after* an initial veto will also come to little, unless we can distinguish important vetoed bills from unimportant ones. But how can we do this?

To begin, what do we mean by "legislative significance"? If we take an encompassing view, then legislative significance can be achieved in many different ways. Medicare seems so important because it created a new role for government in an important market and improved the welfare of millions of citizens. The Voting Rights Act is such a huge milestone because it opened the doors to political participation of millions of citizens, transforming the American party system in the process. Laws that dramatically reduce the presence of government in some arena of life, or remove preexisting rights from some group, could also be significant (Derthick and Quirk 1985).

Significance can be achieved without pathbreaking policy innovation, however. Increases in the minimum wage involve no innovations but are nonetheless important because they profoundly affect labor markets, and thus the lives of many. But touching the lives of many is still not a sine qua non. Orphan drug legislation affects a relatively small group (people with exotic diseases), but it does so in a very powerful way: without the orphan drugs the afflicted may die or suffer cruelly. Laws of this type take on significance. Other laws can be seen as significant simply because

---

[2] This insight is hardly original. Two excellent studies, Watson 1993 and Wooley 1991, employ measures of the importance of vetoed bills. What distinguishes the analysis that follows is the attempt to score all bills at risk of being vetoed, in order to generate estimates of veto probabilities.

they involve so much money. When the bulk of the federal government is funded through one mammoth continuing resolution, as occurred in 1987, that bill takes on real heft in terms of significance.

Finally, some laws achieve significance because they help define contemporary partisan divisions. For instance, in the 1940s bills concerning the Tennessee Valley Authority achieved greater prominence than their policy content would seem to warrant, partly because they symbolized the parties' divisions on a salient issue, government intervention in markets. Other examples include the tidelands oil bills in the 1950s, bills concerning abortion policy in the 1980s, and bills regulating family leave policy in the early 1990s.

Changing people's lives, redistributing wealth, creating or destroying rights, limning partisan differences – these are all pathways to legislative significance. They are so many and so varied that a tired but apropos phrase is irresistible: legislative significance is hard to define but easy to recognize.

If significance is hard to define but easy to recognize, then perhaps the best way to score laws is to allow knowledgeable observers to indicate which ones are significant and which ones aren't. David Mayhew, in his 1991 book *Divided We Govern*, pioneered this approach to scoring legislative significance. Mayhew's innovative study utilized two distinct measures, the first tapping into an enactment of contemporary political significance, the second tapping into its retrospective policy significance. The "Sweep One" evaluation employed the annual roundup stories in The *New York Times* and *Washington Post*, stories that summarize the most important legislative accomplishments of the session, in the opinion of the newspapers' Washington correspondents and editors. This approach thus relied on the contemporary judgments of sophisticated "inside the beltway" political generalists. In order for a law to make it onto the Sweep One list, the roundup authors had to declare it an outstanding legislative accomplishment, not merely of that session but of any session. The second measure, the "Sweep Two" evaluation culled policy histories to identify landmark enactments in different policy arenas. This method relied on the retrospective judgments of academic issue experts. In most cases the two evaluations correspond quite closely, suggesting that policy significance weighs heavily in political significance.

Working together with some talented young scholars, I have extended Mayhew's Sweep One approach to include *all* legislation passed by Congress between 1945 and 1994 (Cameron et al. 1996). We extended Mayhew's sources to include the annual roundup section in the *CQ Almanac*, examined *all* bills mentioned in the newspaper roundups, and supplemented those mentions with data on their coverage in the body of the *CQ Almanac*. After extensive statistical analysis, we distinguished four classes of bills:

A. "Landmark" legislation: the same laws identified in Mayhew's "Sweep One" (Mayhew 1991) – that is, statutes hailed in the annual legislative roundups of the *Washington Post* or the *New York Times* as the most important legislative accomplishment of the Congress, comparable with the most important accomplishments of any Congress. This category, however, excludes (almost all) appropriations bills. Between 1945 and 1992, 216 enactments fell into this category.
B. "Important" legislation: legislation of sufficient importance or newsworthiness to warrant discussion in the legislative roundups of either the *Washington Post* or the *New York Times*, and generate six or more pages of coverage in the *Congressional Quarterly Almanac*. Between 1945 and 1992, 283 enactments fell into this category.
C. "Ordinary" legislation: legislation with sufficient policy impact to warrant note in the annual summary section of *CQ Almanac* but not significant enough to warrant six or more pages of discussion in the body of the *Almanac*. Examples include appropriations for noncontroversial agencies, noncontroversial recurrent authorizations, and some controversial authorizations with limited policy impact. Between 1945 and 1992, 1,727 enactments fell into this category.
D. "Minor" legislation: legislation not deemed worthy of notice in the annual summary section of *CQ Almanac*. This includes commemorative legislation, minor bills, and many routine reauthorizations or minor appropriations bills. Between 1945 and 1992, 14,972 enactments fell into this category.

To get a feel for the laws in the first three groups, examine the sample laws in Table 2.1. These laws were drawn at random from the top three categories. The group A sample indeed comprises shining jewels. One, the War Powers Act, is arguably among the Hope diamonds of postwar legislation. The group B sample contains semiprecious stones, laws of genuine noteworthiness in their day but no jewels and certainly no Hope diamonds. The group C sample is clearly composed of ordinary legislation. The group D legislation is gravel.

In our detailed analysis of the laws, we show that several independent measures confirm the groupings. For example, Mayhew's Sweep Two laws load disproportionately into the upper groups. The coverage in *CQ Almanac* of the upper groups is lengthier than that afforded the lower groups, despite the truncation of lengths in group B. Discretionary authorizations tend to be disproportionately represented in the higher groups. The groups seem to make sense.

Table 2.1. *Representative laws by significance class*

Public law	Year	Description
Group A: Landmark legislation		
85-686	1958	Trade Agreements Extension Act of 1958: strengthened presidential authority to make agreements with other countries, extending that authority for 4 years
93-148	1973	War Powers Act: asserted congressional authority over war making
103-322	1994	Omnibus Crime Act of 1994: $30 billion crime bill with ban on assault weapons
Group B: Major legislation		
87-61	1961	Highway Act of 1961: increased highway-use taxes to assure completion of 41,000 miles of the interstate highway system
90-575	1968	Extended all major higher-education acts including NDEA, Higher Education Act of 1965, and National Vocational Student Loan Insurance Act of 1965
103-325	1994	Established community development banks to aid economic development in distressed areas
Group C: Ordinary legislation		
84-864	1956	Raised the borrowing power of the CCC, for farm prices supports (second increase in the 84th Congress)
93-182	1973	Established daylight savings time for 1974–76
103-403	1994	Reauthorized the Small Business Administration
Group D: Minor legislation		
86-656	1960	Authorized medals and decorations for certain chaplains
95-67	1977	Made it clear that members of Congress may not, for purposes of state income tax laws, be treated as residents of any state other than the state from which they were elected

One problem in using these data to study vetoes is that they cover only enacted bills. Vetoed bills without successful override attempts are not included. Mayhew also excluded them from his Sweep One data. Accordingly, we coded each vetoed nonenacted bill using the procedures just indicated, with two provisos. We showed in our statistical analysis of legislative significance that a simple coding rule selects a group of enactments that appear very similar to Mayhew's Sweep One enactments: coverage in two of the three sources (the roundups of the *New*

York Times, those of the *Washington Post*, and the annual summary section of *Congressional Quarterly Almanac*) and at least ten pages of coverage in the *CQ Almanac*. We used this scheme to code significance for vetoed bills. Second, some vetoed bills are listed in the summary section of *CQ Almanac* only in charts of all vetoes. To count as a mention, we required vetoed bills to be mentioned "in their own right" and not simply mentioned in a summary list of all vetoed bills.

Table 2.2 contains a random sample of vetoed bills by significance category, as in Table 2.1. The same pattern of diminishing significance from the highest to the lowest category is again evident.

UNDERSTANDING THE DATA

The event histories provide a wealth of information on vetoes. Making sense of it requires special tools. I employ some from the analysis of stochastic processes, particularly Markov chains. The reader encountered a simple Markov process in the previous chapter, when I discussed the theory behind the separation-of-powers system. I use the same general method here, but elaborate the stochastic process further and then apply it to real data. Although this approach is somewhat unusual in political science, it has long been used by other social scientists, particularly sociologists (Coleman 1973; White 1970; Tuma and Hannan 1984). The point of using these tools is not their novelty, however, but the fact that they allow a simple and intuitive way to understand patterns in complex data.[3]

An Empirical Framework

Figure 2.1 provides an overview of veto bargaining, considered as a Markov process. The figure illustrates the *regular* veto process, rather than the *pocket* veto process (I return to the pocket veto process momentarily).[4] Each "state" is denoted by a circle. Possible "transitions" between states are shown with arrows. The vertical dimension corresponds to the "ordinary" sequence of events in the enactment of a bill (passage,

---

[3] Readers with an aversion to mathematical notation can skip this section without seriously impairing their understanding of the empirical patterns, if they are willing to accept concepts like "veto chain" and "singleton" without precise definition.

[4] Under the provisions of Article I Section 7 of the Constitution, a bill presented to the president becomes law within ten days (not counting Sundays) unless he vetoes it or Congress adjourns in the meantime. The latter possibility allows the president to "pocket veto" bills – hold them until Congress adjourns, thereby killing the bills. In this case, Congress cannot override the veto. For an excellent discussion of the history and constitutional status of the pocket veto, see Spitzer 1988:105–19.

Table 2.2. *Representative vetoes by significance class*

Bill number	Year	Description
Group A: Landmark legislation		
H.R. 12	1956	Agricultural Price Supports of 1956: the major farm legislation of the period
H.J. Res. 542	1973	War Powers Act (see Table 2.1)
S. 2104	1990	Civil Rights Restoration Act: reversed Supreme Court rulings in discrimination law
Group B: Important legislation		
H.R. 9883	1960	Wage adjustments for federal workers
H.R. 8069	1975	Appropriations for Departments of HEW and Labor
S. 5	1992	Family Leave Act
Group C: Ordinary legislation		
S. 1864	1951	Finance purchases of cars by handicapped veterans
H.R. 13918	1972	Authorization for the Public Broadcasting Corporation
H.R. 2699	1991	FY 1992 appropriation for the District of Columbia
Group D: Minor legislation		
H.R. 3087	1953	Gas station improvements in the District of Columbia
H.R. 13895	1972	Revise pay structure of U.S. marshals
H.R. 5061	1992	Dry Tortugas National Park

signing, enactment), while the horizontal extension captures the distinctive elements of veto bargaining.

The process begins in the initial Congress state C_0, whose exit requires the initial passage of a bill for presentation to the president. The process then moves to the first presidential action stage P_0 (the subscripts indicate the *round* of bargaining). The president may accept the bill, sending the process to the A state. Or the president may veto the bill. If the president vetoes the bill at the first presidential action stage, the stochastic process constitutes an *episode* of veto bargaining.

Following an initial veto, the process moves to the congressional action state C_1. At this state, Congress may attempt to override the veto or repass the bill without attempting an override. Or the bargaining process may end without either a repassed bill or an override attempt so the bill enters the "quit" or Q state. If Congress attempts to override the initial veto, the process moves to the override state O_1. Three transitions are possible from this state. First, the override attempt may succeed, sending the process to the A state. Second, the override at-

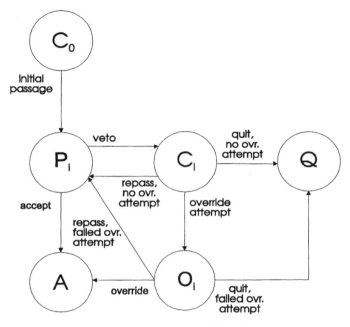

Figure 2.1. Markov Model of Veto Bargaining

tempt may fail and Congress may not repass the bill, sending the process to the Q state. Third, the override may fail and Congress may repass the bill, sending it back to the president, that is, to the P_1 state. If the president revetoes the bill, the process moves to the C_2 state, and so on.

A few additional terms are useful. If an episode of veto bargaining terminates before the president is presented with a second bill, the episode is a *singleton* since there was but one bill and one veto. On the other hand, if Congress repasses the bill at C_1, the episode constitutes a *veto chain*, for more than one bill or veto was involved. The *length* of the chain is given by the number of enactments that occur during the chain. Movement from one enactment to the next constitutes a round of bargaining. Because I require chains to lie in their entirety within a single administration, and because passing bills does require time, the number of rounds in an episode of sequential veto bargaining is necessarily finite. Because the process must exit from the P, C, and O states, they are "transient." But A and Q are "terminal" or "absorbing" states. A key part of the empirical analysis will be estimation of the *transition proba-*

bilities for each transition from a transient state.[5] Occasionally I refer to the transition probability between state x and state y as π_{xy}. Insofar as the data allow, I examine whether particular transition probabilities are constant over rounds of bargaining, that is, whether the process is "stationary" ("time homogeneous"). I also examine how different covariates (e.g., the presence of divided party government) affect the transition probabilities.

The pocket veto process is similar to the regular veto process. However, the process lacks the override state O because Congress has no opportunity to override a pocket veto. Of course, Congress may repass a pocket-vetoed bill.

Finally, the concept of a "state" can include the policy content of a bill at each stage of the bargaining. A change in the content of a bill between C_i and C_{i+1} in a fashion favored by the president is a *policy concession* by Congress.

Conjectures about Veto Bargaining

I have outlined a general framework that allows measurement of many aspects of veto bargaining. But a framework for measurement is not a theory. A *theory* of veto bargaining, like that detailed in Chapter 4, generates a set of testable propositions about transition probabilities as a function of specific covariates, and the size of policy concessions at each round of bargaining. Even absent an explicit theory, however, several preliminary conjectures seem reasonable.

First, the nature of veto bargaining is apt to change as the preferences of Congress and president diverge from one another. Accordingly, one might expect to find large differences in transition rates between periods of unified and divided government, for in the former presidential and congressional preferences are likely to be close together, whereas in the latter they are apt to be far apart.

Second, veto bargaining is apt to vary with the significance of the legislation under consideration. This conjecture extends earlier empirical work by Wooley and Watson, who found differences in the aggregate number of "major" versus "minor" vetoes per time period (Wooley 1991; Watson 1993). The basis for the conjecture involves congressional policy agendas and per period quit rates. The "policy window" for any given unimportant bill is quite likely to close abruptly, as numerous case studies of the legislative process attest (Kingdon 1984). If so, the quit rate π_{CQ} will be high for such bills. When Congress passes such a bill it

---

[5] Some readers may be more familiar with hazard rates than transition probabilities. The two are closely related. The per-round transition probability is equivalent to a discrete-period hazard rate (Lawless 1982).

tends to resemble a one-shot offer since a veto virtually assures the bill's demise. In contrast, the policy window for an important bill is less likely to close abruptly. If so, the quit rate π_{CQ} is likely to be much smaller for such bills. So important bills should strongly resemble sequential offers.

Ad hoc conjectures about vetoes and policy concessions can take almost any form. On the one hand, Congress may simply see vetoes as symbolic gestures or bluffs. If so, it may just repass the same bill, which the president might accept, his bluff having been called. On the other hand, the literature on sequential bargaining in economics strongly suggests that "haggling" should take place: vetoes should wrest policy concessions from Congress. The models in Chapter 4 lead to rather precise hypotheses about concessions.

A Note on Statistical Methods

In the following sections I show helpful tabulations of the data and calculate relevant percentages. But there is a limit to how far such methods can go. They can even be deceptive. For instance, when I calculate that an event occurred 56% of the time in a category with 100 bills at risk, but 80% of the time in a category with 20 bills at risk, are the two rates really different? Or does the apparent difference merely reflect the kind of variation one might expect in fairly small samples? (Under the normal standards for inference, the two percentages do not differ significantly.) When I see an apparent relationship between two variables in a table of data, how can I be confident the association is really there, and how can I determine its magnitude? Even if I calculate simple measures of association between the two variables, how can I possibly know what happens to the apparent association as other variables change?

To overcome these problems I estimate explicit multivariate models. I use statistical techniques that parse changes in a dependent variable of interest – for example, the probability of a veto – into effects due to other variables, such as the presence of divided government or whether the bill is an appropriations bill. The results of the parsing indicate the size of the effects, including whether a given effect is actually present at all. Because most of the dependent variables of interest are actually *probabilities* – for example, the probability a bill is vetoed; the probability Congress repasses a bill without an override attempt; or the probability an override attempt succeeds, given an attempt – I employ a variant of the general linear model that is widely used for such problems, the logit model. The result of a logit estimation is a set of coefficients that relate changes in independent variables to changes in the probability of the event. Unfortunately, the coefficients in logit models are difficult to interpret directly. I report them in the accompanying tables for the benefit of statistically knowledgeable readers.[6] However, the best way to understand the results is visually, in simple graphs showing the impact of key variables on the probability of the event (e.g., the probability of a veto). I supply such figures for the more important models. I have yet to discover how to discuss statistical results without using some statistical jargon, but I banish most technical matters to footnotes. Readers who wish to understand the patterns in the data without worrying about how they were uncovered can focus on the figures. The principal results are summarized and gathered together in Table 2.12, at the end of the chapter.

THE INITIAL PROBABILITY OF A VETO

The logical place to begin is the initial probability of vetoes, that is, the probability following a bill's initial passage by Congress. Only bills that are initially vetoed are candidates for extended veto bargaining.

Overall, vetoes are rare events. As shown in Table 2.3, of the 17,428 public bills initially passed during the period 1945 to 1992, only 434 or 2.3% were vetoed. However, this figure is seriously misleading. As Table 2.3 indicates, it masks differences between unified and divided government and across bills of different legislative significance. I undertake a logit analysis of vetoes of all initially passed legislation between 1945 and 1992. In other words, the analysis is based on more than 17,000 observations, one for each bill passed by Congress and presented to the president.[7] The data exclude bills repassed after a veto.

The results are shown in Table 2.4. In model 1, the legislative significance covariates that are not interacted with "divided" establish a baseline for unified government; those interacted with "divided" capture additional effects specific to divided government. Given this specification, the variable "divided" represents a contrast between group D legislation under unified and divided government. The lack of significance of the group A unified government baseline variable probably reflects the paucity of observations in this category. There is no evidence of a difference in veto probabilities between unified and divided government for minor legislation, nor evidence of a special appropriations effect.[8] The absence of an appropriations effect is worth noting, for overall

---

[6] Liao 1994 is a monograph entirely devoted to the interpretation of coefficients from logit and related models.

[7] The model is estimated on grouped data, hence the indicated degrees of freedom. Like most of the models in the chapter it was estimated with the statistical program S-Plus.

[8] Neither variable was ever significant in any of the specifications of this model I investigated. An analysis of deviance (not shown) indicates that neither variable contributes significantly to the fit of the models (McCullagh and Nelder 1989).

Table 2.3. Vetoes of public bills, 1945–1992

	Total vetoes			Vetoes in chains			Vetoes in singletons		
	No.	Col. %	Row %	No.	Col. %	Row %	No.	Col. %	Row %
Total	434	100	100	176	100	41	258	100	59
Divided	310	71	100	139	77	45	171	66	55
Unified	124	29	100	37	21	30	87	34	70
Appropriations	34	8	100	28	16	82	6	2	18
Authorizations	400	92	100	148	84	37	252	98	63
Group A	34	8	100	22	12	65	12	5	35
Group B	29	7	100	19	11	66	10	4	34
Group C	126	29	100	79	45	63	47	18	37
Group D	245	56	100	56	31	23	189	74	77
Truman	86	20	100	19	11	22	67	26	78
Eisenhower	79	18	100	30	17	38	49	19	62
Kennedy	9	2	100	1	0	11	8	3	89
Johnson	15	3	100	5	3	33	10	4	67
Nixon	41	9	100	23	13	56	18	7	44
Ford	59	14	100	27	15	46	32	12	54
Carter	29	7	100	15	9	52	14	5	48
Reagan	71	17	100	34	19	48	37	14	52
Bush	45	10	100	22	13	49	23	9	51

Note: Column percentages are by category, e.g., percent unified + percent divided = 100%.

Table 2.4. *Vetoes of initially passed legislation: Logit analysis*

Variable	Model 1	Model 2
Intercept	−4.22*	−4.13*
	(.11)	(.06)
Group A	0.71	—
	(.60)	
Group B	1.11*	—
	(.47)	
Group A or B	—	0.82*
		(.36)
Group C	0.69*	.56*
	(.25)	(.23)
Divided: Group A	1.96*	1.92*
	(.64)	(.42)
Divided: Group B	1.03	1.33*
	(.53)	(.43)
Divided: Group C	1.09*	1.25*
	(.27)	(.24)
Divided	0.17	—
	(.13)	
Appropriation	−0.22	—
	(.21)	
Residual deviance (df)	9.7 (7)	12.8 (10)

Note: Standard errors in parenthesis below coefficients.
*$p < .05$.

appropriations bills were more likely to be vetoed than authorization bills (3.3% versus 2.3%). The multivariate analysis reveals this apparent difference to be an artifact of the mix of significance classes among appropriations bills.

Model 2 drops the terms that were clearly not statistically significant, and estimates more precisely the unified government baseline effect for more significant legislation by combining the group A and group B enactments. All the variables are highly statistically significant, while the overall fit declines very modestly.

Figure 2.2 plots the fitted curves from model 2 along with the actual values in each category (the latter are shown by the lowercase letters *u* and *d*, for "unified" and "divided," respectively). As can be seen, this simple model fits the data remarkably well. The estimated probability of a veto under unified government is about 2% across all significance categories (it rises very slightly with greater legislative significance). The estimated probability of a veto of minor legislation is the same during unified and divided government (less than 2%). However, during divided government the estimated probability of a veto rises dramatically with legislative significance. Under divided government, the veto rate more than quintuples with the move from minor to ordinary legislation (from 1.6% to 9%); increases by one-third again with the move to important legislation (from 9% to 12%); and increases by two-thirds again with the move to landmark legislation (from 12% to 20%). Thus, during divided government the probability of a veto of initially passed nonminor legislation ranges from over three to almost six times that during unified government, depending on the significance of the legislation. *Vetoes of initially passed legislation are not rare events at all, provided the government is divided and the legislation is not minor.*

THE FREQUENCY OF SEQUENTIAL VETO BARGAINING

Although vetoes occur regularly for nonminor legislation during divided government, veto bargaining may still be a rarity. Table 2.5 addresses this point. Recall from Table 2.3, that of the 434 vetoes of public bills in the period 1945–92, most (258, or 59%) were singletons. However, as shown in Table 2.5, there were 147 veto chains during this period, an initiation rate of more than three veto chains per year. Overall, 41% of all vetoes were members of chains.

Differences between unified and divided government are very apparent. The bulk of vetoes – 71% – occurred during divided government. Among the vetoes that did occur during unified government, the overwhelmingly majority (70%) were singletons. In contrast, nearly half (45%) of all vetoes that occurred during divided government were members of chains. More than three-quarters of all veto chains occur during divided government.

Differences across significance categories are also very apparent. Most vetoes (56%) involve minor legislation, and most vetoes of minor legislation are singletons (77%). So sequential veto bargaining is relatively rare for minor legislation. The picture is quite different for vetoes of more important legislation. The *majority* of such vetoes are members of chains (over 60% for each of categories A–C versus 23% for category

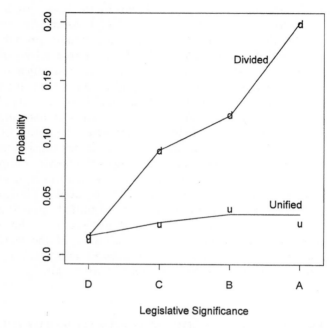

Figure 2.2. The Probability of a Veto for Initially Passed Legislation

D). Figure 2.3 indicates the percentage of vetoes in various categories that were members of veto chains.

In summation, simple event counts show the following:

- Sequential veto bargaining is not a fluke but a common occurrence in the American separation-of-powers system.
- Most vetoes involve minor legislation and, when they do, are very likely singletons.
- When vetoes do involve important legislation, they are likely to be members of chains.
- Sequential veto bargaining is largely a phenomenon of divided government.

A TOUR OF THE BARGAINING PROCESS

Summary event counts hardly capture the subtlety and complexities of veto bargaining. Using the microlevel data, we can follow the process of veto bargaining, step by step. Throughout this section, the reader may

Table 2.5. *Veto chains, 1945–1992*

	Veto chains	
	Number	Percentage
Total	147	100
Divided	113	77
Unified	34	23
Appropriations	23	16
Authorizations	124	84
Group A	15	10
Group B	16	11
Group C	62	42
Group D	54	37
Truman	13	9
Eisenhower	23	16
Kennedy	1	1
Johnson	4	3
Nixon	21	14
Ford	21	14
Carter	15	10
Reagan	31	21
Bush	18	12

Note: Chains classified by significance according to the significance level of the first bill in chain.

find it helpful to refer back to Figure 2.1 as a kind of roadmap for the tour.

Congressional Response to Regular Vetoes

Following a regular veto, the bargaining process enters the C state, from which Congress may attempt an override, repass the bill, or let it die. Overall, between 1945 and 1992 there were 254 regular vetoes of public bills. Of these, Congress attempted to override 50%. Among those it did not attempt to override, Congress repassed 41% and allowed 59% to die. Again, however, these figures mask important differences between unified and divided government and across different types of bills. In order to uncover statistically significant differences, I fit sequential logit

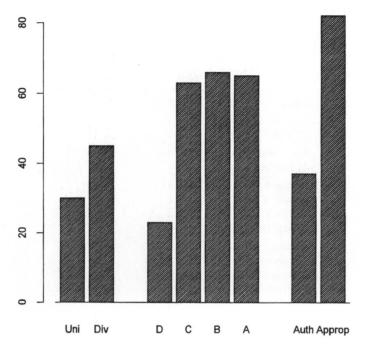

Figure 2.3. Percentage of Vetoes in Chains, by Category

models to the microlevel data. I follow the natural chronological sequence: attempt to override or do not attempt; if no attempt, repass or let die.[9] Results are displayed in Table 2.6 and the first row of Figure 2.4.

Attempting to Override.   First consider the decision whether to seek an override. As shown in model 1, presented in the first column of Table 2.6, there were statistically significant differences between bills of different legislative significance (I again combine groups A and B to assure sufficient observations for precise estimates of effects). Not surprisingly, there was a pronounced divided government effect in override attempts: override attempts were much more likely during periods of divided government. In addition, override attempts were more likely for bills in later

---

[9] I also estimated multinomial logit models in which all three choices occur simultaneously, with results that are broadly similar to those reported here. However, the absence of variation in the no-attempt appropriations bills (discussed later) is much more easily handled in the sequential logit models, which also allow a more flexible estimation of different effects at the two chronologically distinct decisions. Accordingly, I emphasize the sequential logit analysis.

Table 2.6. *Congressional response to regular vetoes: Sequential logit analysis 1*

Variable	Attempt override			Repass absent override attempt [a]		
	Model 1	Model 2	Model 3	Model 4	Model 5	Model 6
Intercept	-1.98*	-2.00*	-1.93*	-1.64*	-1.64*	-1.43*
	(.35)	(.35)	(.31)	(.37)	(.37)	(.29)
Group A or B	2.41*	2.39*	2.42*	2.21*	2.31*	2.53*
	(.43)	(.44)	(.44)	(.86)	(.86)	(.87)
Group C	1.39*	1.44*	1.49*	1.74*	1.73*	1.78*
	(.34)	(.34)	(.36)	(.48)	(.49)	(.49)
Round 2 or 3	1.77*	1.72*	1.78*	—	—	—
	(.67)	(.67)	(.67)			
Divided	1.04*	—	—	0.74	—	—
	(.36)			(.44)		
Split 1	—	.19	—	—	1.64*	—
		(.54)			(.68)	
Split 2	—	1.21*	1.16*	—	.45	—
		(.37)	(.31)		(.48)	
Split 1 and group C or D	—	—	—	—	—	1.38*
						(.65)
Appropriation	0.24	.27	—	—	—	—
	(.67)	(.44)				
Residual deviance (df)	266.0	261.3	261.9	128.5	125.3	126.6
	(248)	(253)	(249)	(113)	(112)	(113)

Note: Standard errors in parenthesis below coefficients.

[a] Authorizations only (see text).

* $p < .05$.

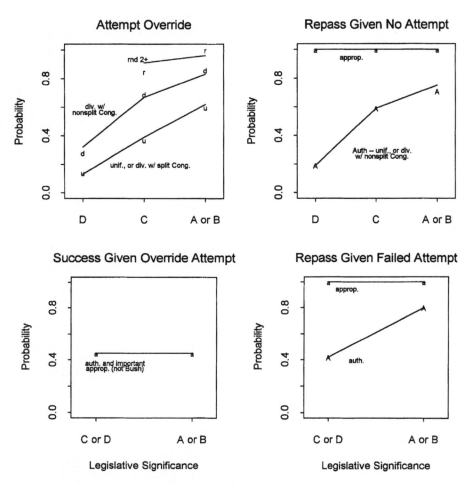

Figure 2.4. Congressional Response to Regular Vetoes

rounds of bargaining, that is, those that were vetoed, repassed, and vetoed again. Finally, Congress was no more likely to attempt overrides
of appropriations bills than of authorization bills.

Model 2 further investigates the divided government effect. The model
uncovers a sensible but hitherto unnoticed institutional pattern: the divided government effect in override attempts was restricted to periods
in which *both* chambers of Congress were controlled by a party different
from the president's (indicated by the variable "split 2"). When only *one*
chamber differed in control from the president (indicated by the variable

"split 1"), override attempts were no more frequent than in unified government. The president's copartisans in the other chamber were apparently able to block many attempts to override.

The upper left-most panel in Figure 2.4 presents these results in an easily interpretable form, using model 3, which drops the insignificant variables from model 2. The three lines plot the estimated probability of an override attempt at round 1 during unified government or during divided government with a split Congress; at round 1 during divided government with a nonsplit Congress (the usual divided government configuration); and at rounds 2 or 3 during divided government with a nonsplit Congress. The number of cases that reached round 2 during other periods or among group D is negligible, hence, estimated probabilities for these cases are not shown. Actual frequencies are shown by the corresponding letters.

In round 1 during unified government, the probability of seeking an override quintupled with the move from the least to the most significant legislation. It almost tripled with the same move at round 1 during nonsplit divided government, reaching a remarkable 84%. The divided government effect was large: the difference between unified government and nonsplit divided government in the probability of attempting an override was 20 percentage points or more at every level of legislative significance. If a bill reached a second round of bargaining – a phenomenon almost exclusively of nonminor legislation during nonsplit divided government – an override attempt was almost certain (over 95%).

Repassing or Quitting without an Override Attempt.   Now consider the decision to repass vetoed legislation without an override attempt. Presumably the veto in such cases was unlikely to be successfully overridden. Among bills without override attempts were thirty appropriations bills, all of which were repassed, and three bills that went beyond round 1, all of which were repassed. This absence of variation precludes statistical estimation of a repassage rate for such bills (i.e., it was 100%). Accordingly, models 4 through 6 in Table 2.6 are estimated only for authorization bills and the variable "round 2 or 3" is excluded. As shown, significant differences exist across the significance classes. However, the variable "divided" does not achieve significance at conventional levels. Parsing it into "split 1" and "split 2," as earlier, to account for split party congresses, reveals that "split 1" is statistically significant; but further investigation reveals an effect only for less significant legislation (see model 6). Since only fifteen bills fell into this category, the "split 1" effect, though statistically significant, may represent overfitting of the data.

Veto Bargaining

These results are shown in the upper right-most panel in Figure 2.4. Based on the observed frequencies, repassage of a vetoed appropriations bill was virtually certain, even absent an override attempt. Estimated probabilities of repassage for vetoed authorization bills with no override attempt, based on model 6, are shown by the lower line in the figure (because of the small number of bills involved, I do not show estimated probabilities for groups D and C authorizations under divided government with a split party Congress).[10] Actual frequencies are again indicated with the corresponding characters. Overall, the actual rate of repassage for authorization bills for which no override was attempted was 36%. However, the estimated repassage rates range from 19% for group D, to 59% for group C, to 75% for groups A and B.[11]

Success or Failure in Override Attempts. Given an override attempt, what are the prospects for success? The short answer is: about 45%, across almost all categories. Models 1–3 in Table 2.7 examine the probability of success, given an override attempt. Model 1 mimics the model of override attempts; however, none of the covariates are statistically significant (nor are "split 1" and "split 2," not shown). Investigation reveals one strongly significant covariate: a dummy variable for the Bush administration. As was widely remarked at the time, that administration enjoyed amazing success in thwarting veto overrides (only one of twenty-two override attempts succeeded). In model 2 the variable "group A or B" approaches statistical significance, hinting at an effect due to legislative significance. In fact, however, the override success rate is nearly constant across legislative significance levels for authorization bills, but very low (about 13%) for less important appropriations bills. As shown in model 3, the latter bills account for the apparent effect due to legislative significance. Although this effect is statistically significant, the small number of bills involved – only sixteen – may suggest overfitting of the data. The results of this analysis are shown in the lower left-hand panel of Figure 2.4.[12]

What accounts for the failure of the covariates to reliably pick out bills that will be successfully overridden, once an attempt is made? This is a mystery I return to in Chapter 5.

[10] The estimated repassage rates for these groups are 45% and 85%, respectively.
[11] For authorizations during unified or nonsplit divided government.
[12] Because of the small number of bills involved I do not show the estimated override success rates for the following groups: groups C and D appropriations other than the Bush administration (15%); authorization and groups A and B appropriations during the Bush administration (5%); groups C and D appropriations during the Bush administration (1%).

Table 2.7. *Congressional response to regular vetoes: Sequential logit analysis 2*

Variable	Succeed in override attempt Model 1	Model 2	Model 3	Repass given failed override attempt[a] Model 4	Model 5
Intercept	−.42	−.64*	−.20	−0.07	−0.33
	(.59)	(.26)	(.21)	(.72)	(.31)
Group A or B	0.59	.74	—	1.83*	1.71*
	(.53)	(.40)		(.81)	(.59)
Group C	−.028	—	—	0.09	—
	(.54)			(.72)	
Round 2 or 3	0.19	—	—	−.60	—
	(.48)			(.67)	
Divided	−0.43	—	—	−0.24	—
	(.56)			(.80)	
Appropriation	0.11	—	—	—	—
	(.52)				
Appropriation and group C or D	—	—	−1.53*	—	—
			(.79)		
Bush	—	−2.70*	−2.73*	—	—
		(1.01)	(1.01)		
Residual deviance (df)	158.3	145.8	144.3	82.6	83.5
	(120)	(123)	(123)	(63)	(66)

Note: Standard errors in parenthesis below coefficients.
[a] Authorizations only (see text).
*$p < .05$.

The probability of a successful override is the product of the probability of attempting an override and the probability of success given an
attempt. So the probability of a successful override, contingent on unified
or divided government and legislative significance, may be read from the
upper left-hand panel in Figure 2.4 simply by multiplying the probabilities there by .45 (the rates for bills vetoed during the Bush administration and for less important appropriations bills are, of course, lower).
Legislative significance and divided government thus emerge as important variables in the probability of a successful override, but manifest
their effects through the decision to attempt an override.

Repassing or Quitting after a Failed Override Attempt. What happened after a failed override attempt? Overall, 56% of authorizations were repassed following a failed override attempt. Fourteen appropriations bills failed an override attempt and, like the appropriations bills for which no override was attempted, all were repassed. Consequently, the additional logit models in Table 2.7 are estimated for authorization bills only. As shown, there appears to be no divided government effect, although the small number of bills in this category under unified government – only ten – makes finding such an effect problematic. Again, more important legislation was repassed at a significantly greater rate than less important legislation (groups C and D are grouped together to facilitate precise estimates). Estimated and actual repassage rates are shown in the lower right-hand panel in Figure 2.4. Among groups C and D, the estimated repassage rate was 42%; among groups A and B the rate was almost twice as high, 80%.

One might expect repassage rates for bills after failed override attempts to be higher than that for bills with no override attempts at all. After all, the support in Congress for the former was sufficiently high to warrant the override attempt. However, even among authorization bills the rates were comparable. For groups A and B the rates were 80% after a failed override versus 75% after no override attempt (under unified and nonsplit Congress government). In groups C and D the repassage rate after a failed override was 42%; if the same mix between groups C and D had prevailed among bills for which no attempt was made, the comparable rate would have been 48%.[13] This finding suggests that breakdown rates are determined largely by the tortuous process of repassage itself, with more important legislation being less likely to suffer a breakdown in the legislative process.

Congressional Response to Pocket Vetoes

There were 181 pocket vetoes of general public bills between 1945 and 1992. Overall, Congress repassed 29% of these bills during the administration of the vetoing president. This repassage rate is much lower than the comparable rates following regular vetoes. However, bills that were pocket-vetoed rarely had much legislative significance: 77% of pocket-vetoed bills belonged to group D, while only 43% of regularly vetoed bills did so. Some 21% of regular vetoes belonged to groups A or B, in contrast with only 3% of pocket vetoes. Is the lower repassage rate of pocket-vetoed bills due to a special effect of pocket vetoes or only to the

---

[13] Among failed overrides, 72% of the C and D authorizations were group C; 28% were group D. The relevant repassage rates after no override attempts were .59 and .19 respectively, thus: $(.72)(.59) + (.28)(.19) = .48$.

Table 2.8. *Congressional response to pocket vetoes:*
Logit analysis of repassage rates

	Repass	
Variable	Model 1	Model 2
Intercept	−1.40*	−1.19*
	(.35)	(.24)
Group A or B	3.23*	3.46*
	(1.14)	(1.27)
Group C	2.17*	1.95*
	(.42)	(.43)
Round 2 or 3	−0.35	—
	(1.19)	
Divided	−0.23	—
	(.35)	
Last year	—	−2.42*
		(.81)
Residual deviance	179.6	164.8
(df)	(175)	(176)

Note: Standard errors in parenthesis below coefficients.
*$p < .05$.

heavy concentration of less significant legislation among pocket vetoes? The logit models in Table 2.8 help provide an answer.

First, as shown in Table 2.8, no divided government effect manifests itself in repassage over a pocket veto. In addition, repassage probabilities appear to be constant across rounds (the variable "round 2 or 3" is not significantly different from zero). Although there are strong effects due to legislative significance, an additional effect of pocket vetoes requires investigation. Because pocket vetoes occur at or after the close of a congressional session, it would seem that repassage of pocket-vetoed legislation must await the next congressional session. Consequently, one might reason, veto bargaining as defined in this book is impossible for bills pocket-vetoed by a president who does not return for the following Congress (an "outgoing" president). As it turns out, however, this line of reasoning is not always true. On several occasions Congress has passed two versions of the same bill, deliberately allowing the president to choose the second (or neither) through a pocket veto – an extremely accelerated form of veto bargaining. Thus, even bills that are pocket-

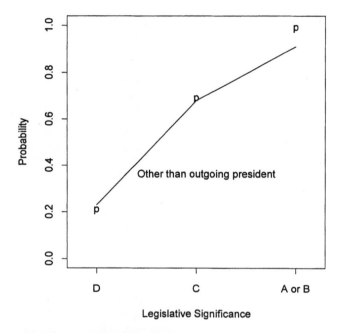

Figure 2.5. Probability of Repassage after a Pocket Veto

vetoed can be, and have been, "repassed" in the same session of Congress. Nonetheless, this event is a rarity. Hence, we define a new variable "last year" that singles out pocket vetoes by an outgoing president. As shown in model 2 in Table 2.8, this variable is statistically significant, acting to depress the probability of repassage.

Figure 2.5 presents estimates of repassage probabilities based on model 2 in Table 2.8. Because all but four of the pocket vetoes by outgoing presidents were in group D, I do not show estimated repassage rate for bills pocket-vetoed by outgoing presidents (the estimated repassage rate for group D was 3%). For pocket vetoes *other* than those cast by outgoing presidents, the estimated repassage rates for groups D, C, and A or B were 23%, 68%, and 91% respectively. (Actual frequencies are denoted by the letter *p*.) Only five bills belonged to groups A and B so the latter estimate needs to be interpreted with caution. However, note that the estimated repassage rate for authorization bills without override attempts was 19% for group D bills and 59% for group C bills, slightly lower than the pocket veto repassage rates. The combined C and D repassage rate for bills after a failed override attempt was 42%. If the same mix of groups C and D had existed in the pocket vetoes as did for bills after a failed override attempt, the combined groups C and D repassage rate for pocket-vetoed bills would have been 54%.

In sum, two points stand out concerning pocket vetoes: first, pocket-vetoed bills tend to be less important than regularly vetoed bills; second, taking into account the heavy concentration of less important legislation, repassage rates for pocket-vetoed bills are not lower than those for regularly vetoed bills, unless the pocket veto is cast by a president who is leaving office (thus making repassage as defined in this book very difficult).

Frequency of Concessions

When Congress repassed a bill, did it usually make policy concessions to the president, or did Congress merely repass the same bill until the president accepted it? Although the content coding provides at best a coarse measure of concessions, the data in Table 2.9 answer this question quite clearly. The data come from 160 pairs of bills in veto chains and indicate whether the content analysis revealed congressional concessions between successive bills. Overall, Congress appeared to make concessions in 80% of repassed bills. This remarkably high rate of concessions is surely one of the most important facts about veto bargaining.

Several other patterns also bear mention. First, the rate of concessions among group A legislation appears to be somewhat lower (67%) than in the other categories, where the rates are all above 85%. The rate of concessions during unified government (87%) is higher than during divided government (78%). And the rate of concessions during the Truman administration (71%) is lower than during all other administrations, where the rate is usually about 80% or higher.

Presidential Response to Repassage

From 1945 to 1992, presidents were presented with 160 repassed versions of bills they had previously vetoed. About one-third of these bills were minor but the remainder dealt with matters of genuine policy significance. About one-fifth (34) were important or landmark bills. How did presidents respond to these repassed bills?

Table 2.10 presents two logit models that address this question. For purposes of comparison, model 1 repeats the earlier model of veto decisions concerning initially passed bills (groups A and B are combined to assure sufficiently large cell counts). The data decisively reject this model – revetoes are quite different from initial vetoes. In fact, however, the data have a very simple structure, captured in model 2. As shown, the reveto rate was almost constant across most categories of bills, with a

Table 2.9. Frequency of concessions during veto bargaining, 1945–1992

	Number of pairs of bills in veto chains				Percentage			
	Total pairs	With concessions	Without concessions	Unclear	Total (column)	With concessions	Without concessions	Unclear
Total	160	128	25	7	100	80	16	4
Unified	30	26	3	1	19	87	10	3
Divided	130	102	22	6	81	78	17	5
Appropriations	32	26	5	7	20	84	16	0
Authorizations	129	102	20	0	80	79	16	5
Group A	18	12	4	2	11	67	22	11
Group B	16	15	1	0	10	94	6	0
Group C	71	62	9	0	44	87	13	0
Group D	55	39	11	5	34	71	20	9
Truman	14	10	4	0	9	71	29	0
Eisenhower	26	21	3	2	16	81	12	8
Kennedy	1	1	0	0	1	100	0	0
Johnson	5	5	0	0	3	100	0	0
Nixon	23	19	2	2	14	83	9	9
Ford	24	19	5	0	15	79	21	0
Carter	15	12	2	1	9	80	13	7
Reagan	33	26	7	0	21	79	21	0
Bush	19	15	2	2	12	79	11	11

Table 2.10. *Presidential response to repassed legislation:*
Logit analysis of reveto rates

Variable	Model 1	Model 2
Intercept	−2.30	−2.25*
	(.47)	(.33)
Group A or B	.69	—
	(1.19)	
Group C	−0.10	—
	(1.16)	
Divided: Group A or B	1.02	—
	1.16	
Divided: Group C	1.41	—
	(1.08)	
Divided: Group A or B: Round 2: Previous pocket of failed override	—	2.05*
		(.56)
Same, Group C	—	1.85*
		(.48)
Residual deviance (df)	151.3	140.7
	(155)	(157)

Note: Standard errors in parenthesis below coefficients.
*$p < .05$.

very specific exception: the reveto rate was much higher if government was divided, the legislation was important or landmark, the bill repassed only once, and the previous bill had failed of an override attempt or had been pocket-vetoed.

Figure 2.6 displays the results of this analysis. As before, the lines indicate estimated probabilities and letters actual frequencies. As shown, the fit of the model is quite good.[14] The estimated reveto rate was 10% for most categories of repassed bills. Included are all repassed minor bills (group D), all nonminor bills repassed during unified government, all nonminor bills repassed during divided government after Congress failed to make an override attempt, and all bills vetoed twice and passed yet a

[14] The only discrepancy of note concerns other bills in groups A and B. However, the actual rate, 14%, was not statistically significantly different from the baseline rate of 10%.

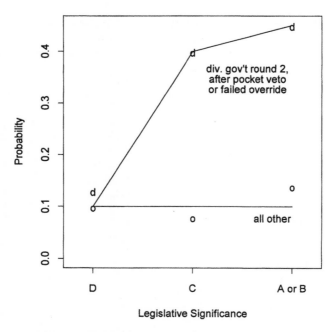

Figure 2.6. Probability of Reveto Following Repassage

third time.[15] However, the reveto rate for group C bills repassed during divided government after either a pocket veto or a failed override attempt was much higher, 40%. The reveto rate for similar bills in groups A or B was even higher, 45%.

Some of these patterns seem, at first glance, somewhat puzzling. For example, why should the veto rate for important bills repassed after a failed override attempt be so high, since one might expect presidents to be less inclined to reveto bills that had sufficient support for an override attempt? Why should the reveto rate for bills passed a third time be so much lower than that for otherwise similar bills passed twice? What feature of previously pocket-vetoed bills makes them a target for further vetoes? I return to these questions in Chapter 5.

Duration

Table 2.11 shows sojourn times for repassage, that is, the length of time in weeks between the veto of a bill and its repassage (the figures are only

---

[15] There were thirteen such bills, all but one of which were accepted by the president upon their third passage by Congress.

Table 2.11. *Time in weeks to repass vetoed bills, 1945–1992*

	Minimum	Median	Mean	Maximum	Standard deviation
All bills	−3.9	17.5	28.3	215.1	34.7
Divided	−3.7	15.6	27.5	215.1	35.9
Unified	−3.9	25.0	31.6	102.4	29.3
Appropriations	−3.7	1.4	4.1	27.1	7.0
Authorizations	−3.9	24.8	33.8	215.1	36.1
Group A	2.9	20.7	28.2	90.9	24.5
Group B	−.2	12.7	22.6	115.9	30.1
Group C	−3.7	14.0	22.7	144.4	26.9
Group D	−3.9	18.7	37.1	215.1	45.1
Second passage	−3.9	18.7	29.6	215.1	35.5
Third passage	−1.4	7.3	13.2	59.0	17.7

Note: Negative times result from vetoes whose official date occurs after the passage of a successor bill.

for bills that were repassed). The median length for all bills was 17.5 weeks. The maximum time was 215 weeks. "Negative" times are recorded when the veto of a bill is officially recorded as occurring after the successor bill was already presented to the president, as sometimes occurred with pocket vetoes. The most striking pattern in the data is the difference in sojourn times for appropriations versus authorizations. When appropriations bills are vetoed and repassed, the median time required for repassage was only 1.4 weeks; for authorizations, the median time was almost 25 weeks.

WHAT HAVE WE LEARNED? A SUMMARY

The statistical analysis in the preceding pages is dense with facts, which are gathered together in Table 2.12. I have arranged the findings into seven categories, plus a "miscellaneous" category. This list provides a concise, simple, yet detailed and reliable description of veto bargaining in the postwar period. I return to it in Chapter 5.

Stepping back from the blur of detail, though, what stands out? In my view, two findings are central. First, when government is unified, vetoes do not appear to be an important phenomenon. Second, when government is divided and legislation is important, this conclusion is

Table 2.12. *Summary of major patterns in veto bargaining, 1945–1992*

1. *Probability of a veto of initially passed legislation*

1a. Irrespective of unified or divided government, the probability of a veto for minor legislation is very low (under 2%).

1b. The probability of a veto for nonminor legislation is much higher under divided government than under unified government (up to ten times higher).

1c. Under divided government, the probability of a veto increases steadily with the significance of the legislation (the probability at the highest level is over ten times that of the lowest level). It does not under unified government.

2. *Chains and sequential veto bargaining*

2a. Most vetoes involve minor legislation and, if so, are usually singletons.

2b. If a veto involves minor legislation, the veto is likely to be a singleton; if it involves more important legislation, it is likely to be part of a chain.

2c. SVB occurs regularly: overall, there were 147 veto chains.

2d. SVB is largely a phenomenon of divided government – singletons prevail during unified government.

2e. Most veto chains are short.

3. *Breakdown and repassage rates*

3a. Breakdown rates do not differ between unified and divided government; and this is true whether the bill was pocket-vetoed or regularly vetoed, and whether an override attempt failed or was not even attempted.

3b. Among authorization bills, breakdown rates fall (and repassage rates rise) with legislative significance. Again, this occurs regardless whether the bill was pocket-vetoed or regularly vetoed, whether an override attempt failed, or whether no attempt was made to override.

3c. Controlling for legislative significance, breakdown rates (and repassage rates) for authorization bills appear similar across bills that were pocket-vetoed (except by outgoing presidents) and those that were regularly vetoed, both for those with a failed override attempt and those for which no attempt was made.

3d. Repassage of a vetoed appropriations bill was virtually certain, even absent an override attempt.

4. Override attempts

4a. Override attempts after a veto are much more likely during periods of divided government.

4b. However, this is true only when both chambers are controlled by the same party. If only one chamber differs from the president, override attempts are no more frequent than during unified government.

4c. Override attempts are more likely for bills in later rounds of bargaining (95%+ for second round, nonminor legislation during nonsplit divided government).

4d. The probability of an override attempt increases dramatically with legislative significance, under both unified and divided government (80%+ for landmark legislation during nonsplit divided government).

5. Probability of success given an override attempt

5a. Given an override attempt, neither divided government nor legislative significance nor authorization versus appropriation predict the probability of success.

5b. The probability of a successful override was unusually low during the Bush administration.

6. Probability of reveto after repassage

6a. The reveto rate following repassage was much higher if government were divided.

6b. It was higher if the previous bill had failed in an override attempt or had been pocket-vetoed.

6c. It was also higher if the bill had been repassed only once.

6d. It increased with legislative significance.

7. Congressional policy concessions in repassed bills

7a. Congress almost always made concessions in repassed bills, across all categories of legislation, unified and divided government, and presidential administrations.

7b. Concessions appear less likely for very important bills, for bills during divided government, and during the Truman administration.

8. Miscellaneous

8a. Pocket-vetoed bills tend to be less important than regularly vetoed bills.

reversed. More specifically, when government is divided and legislation is important (i.e., not minor):

- Vetoes are not rare events.
- Sequential veto bargaining is common.
- Presidents routinely and successfully use vetoes to extract policy concessions from Congress.

Also notable in these circumstances is the importance of override politics.

Veto politics and interbranch bargaining are more frequent and more consequential than suggested by standard theories of American government that implicitly assume unified government. In fact, if we are truly living in the greatest age of divided government in the nation's history, as I suggested in Chapter 1, *veto politics is one of the central features of legislative policy making in contemporary American government.*

Holmes's advice, quoted at the beginning of this chapter, was to *begin* with the data. It was not to *end* with the data. To stop with the findings summarized in Table 2.12 is to risk the fate suggested by Ronald Coase's wickedly amusing evaluation of the early institutional economists: "they had nothing to pass on except a mass of descriptive material waiting for a theory, or a fire." Regardless of the justice of Coase's comment about the early institutionalists, the historical experience distilled in Table 2.12 does await a theory. Without it, the findings in Table 2.12 remain at the level of natural history, fascinating to devotees but ultimately signifying little. How can we build theory to explain the patterns?

3

Rational Choice and the Presidency

Reviewing a conference called to evaluate the state of presidential studies, George Edwards, John Kessel, and Bert Rockman note with somewhat acerbic wit,

> *Theory* and *rigor* were the watchwords of the conference. These are values to which all participants could subscribe, so long as they remained undefined. . . . We have been conditioned to salivate at certain symbols of scientific progress – *theory* and *rigor* are words that appeal to these glands. But behind our operant conditioning (who gets rewarded for saying they are atheoretical or impressionistic?) we have different images of what these words mean. (1993:34)

It is plainly true that there are many ways to do good social science. Those who assemble data, those who conduct case studies, those who analyze others' data, those who produce creative insights, those who take stock of what we know, and those who build theoretical models all make valuable contributions. "Theoretical" and "rigorous" are hardly synonyms for "good social science."

Nonetheless, one of the goals of this book *is* to produce useful and interesting theory about the presidency in an age of divided government. The approach I take is characteristic of the new analytical or rational choice institutionalism. I focus on a specific, repeated, important phenomenon: veto bargaining. Then, I use rational choice theory to build several interrelated models of different aspects of the phenomenon. This approach is sufficiently novel – and controversial – in presidential studies to warrant an extended *apologia*.

WHY MODELS?

Solving puzzles is central to science. We see phenomena like those explored in Chapter 2, and ask why. Solving a puzzle means explaining it. Explaining it means finding and elaborating a causal mechanism for it.

69

But elaborating a causal mechanism is exactly what I mean by model building. So, building models is integral to answering why. The point is general: the solutions to social scientific puzzles characteristically take the form of *models*.

A model is a structure of logical inferences, proceeding from fundamental assumptions, that establishes a causal link between the assumptions and the phenomenon of interest. Given the deductive structure, we can say the assumptions *explain* the phenomenon. From this perspective, it is worth drawing a sharp distinction between *theoretical* and *statistical* models. The latter provide summary descriptions of patterns in data sets, and *that is all they do*. In contrast, a theoretical model does not summarize structure in data but establishes a logical (not an empirical) claim about causal mechanisms. Hence, a theoretical model is not a register of effects; it is an intellectual construction that forms an *explanation* for effects (Bronowski 1977:89–90).

As a (nonsocial) example, if I say that lightning causes thunder, I may assert an empirical regularity but I have not offered a theoretical model because I have not explained how lightning causes thunder: I have not elaborated a causal mechanism that links the two phenomena. It is the causal explanation, carefully spun out, not the empirical regularity itself, that I am talking about when I say a "theoretical model."

Theoretical models do more than supply explanations for puzzles. They also create the baseline or background against which we perceive unsolved puzzles. For example, if we approach American presidential elections with notions of "responsible party government" derived from British politics, we expect to find parties that adopt distinct policy positions. If we find parties that regularly adopt similar positions on important policy matters, we perceive an anomaly. Conversely, if we approach presidential elections with a Downsian spatial model in mind, we expect to see convergence on similar party positions.[1] What stands out as anomalous are parties that obstinately persist in holding different positions. For this reason, facts, like texts, never speak for themselves. They assume meaning only within the context of possibly contending models (Fish 1989).

In fact, to some extent, what we choose to regard as facts depends on our existing models.[2] For example, if our mental framework only allows vetoes to be fatal bullets, the discovery of an episode like Clinton's welfare vetoes is not disconfirming evidence to the "bullet model." It is not even a disturbing anomaly. It's just random noise of no real interest

---

[1] Downsian spatial models have become a standard tool for analyzing American elections. See Downs 1957 and Shepsle and Bonchek 1997.
[2] See Carr 1961 on the contingent nature of historians' "facts."

or significance. However, once our mental image allows bargaining as well as bullets, the hitherto meaningless freak suddenly evokes rich possibilities.[3] Then if we discover that sequential veto bargaining occurs frequently and predictably, a serious anomaly confronts our bullet view of the veto.

In short, our models supply us with our solutions *and* our puzzles, and to some extent determine which world we perceive. It is for these reasons, along with the restricted scope of experimental methods, that models occupy such a prominent place in recent social science, and in this book.

WHY RATIONAL CHOICE?

Even granting a central role for models in social science – a point of view that is hardly controversial anymore – it is still a long stretch to insist on the modeling perspective known as "rational choice theory." What does that perspective entail, and should it be adopted in studies of the presidency?[4]

Broadly speaking, rational choice theory consists of a few guiding assumptions, plus a toolbox for building models. Evaluating rational choice approaches to the presidency requires deciding whether the guiding assumptions seem sensible or wrongheaded for that very special setting, and whether the tools are capable of building models that are interesting and useful or only boring and misdirected.

Rational Choice: The Basic Idea

The guiding assumptions in rational choice theory are threefold. First, the aggregate behavior of social systems reflects the behavior of individual actors. This follows from the obvious fact that someone or something had to do (or did not do) the phenomenon of interest. For instance, voting requires voters; abstentions require abstainers; vetoes require vetoers. Hence, accounts of aggregate behavior – often the object of interest for social scientists – should be grounded in the behavior of individual actors. Call this the *actor assumption*. Second, the behavior of

[3] This seems to occur with some frequency in the natural sciences. For example, certain anomalous observations about radio emissions from distant stars were widely known to astronomers but explicitly rejected as measurement error. Reinterpretation of the "measurement errors" as pulsars led to a revolution in astronomy and a Nobel Prize for the scientist whose conceptual innovation remade the universe that astronomers perceive (Woolgar 1988).

[4] The discussion that follows is highly schematic. Readers who wish to pursue these matters in greater depth might consult the first half of Elster 1983, and Ferejohn and Satz 1995.

individual actors is to be understood in terms of their goals, opportunities, incentives, and constraints. In other words, they are to be understood as intentional actors. This is a charity principle, since without it most of human life, including language, culture, and politics, would be impossible (Ferejohn and Satz 1995). Call this the *intentions assumption*. Third, aggregate behavior results from the interaction of intentional actors (though not exclusively so). This principle allows the recovery of the aggregate behavior from the behavior of individual actors. Call this the *aggregation assumption*. Thus, a rational choice account bottoms an aggregate phenomenon on intentional actors, and shows how their interactions produce the aggregate phenomenon.

Return to veto bargaining. The actor assumption directs attention to presidents and congressmen: vetoes occur because members of Congress pass bills and presidents veto them. They do not occur, at least in a rational choice account, because the zeitgeist was working itself out, or because social forces distinguishable from any human agency somehow compelled the political system to produce vetoes. In turn, the intentions assumption requires us to explain the behavior of presidents and congressmen by reference to their goals and constraints. We assume the president had a reason for vetoing a given bill. He may have been pursuing a policy objective. Perhaps he was trying to bolster his chances for reelection. Or maybe he just wanted to send a message to Congress, reminding it not to take him for granted. Many such imputations are possible. But we would not assume the president vetoed the bill in a fit of absentmindedness, or in a compulsive spasm triggered by a deeply repressed childhood trauma, or in the inexorable grip of a historical cycle far outside his merely conscious awareness. Perhaps a nonintentional explanation is actually correct in a specific instance, but it seems absurd to build a general theory of vetoes on such foundations. Finally, the aggregation assumption requires us to link president and Congress together. It takes two to veto. As president and Congress swirl in the dance of legislation, how does the syncopation of their steps lead to vetoes?

One has only to state the guiding assumptions of rational choice theory – social phenomena require actors, actors are understood by their intentions, aggregate phenomena result from the interplay of individual actors – to see them as obvious. To a large extent, rational choice theory is nothing more that our everyday method for understanding the social world around us, elevated to a method of systematic research.

Despite these roots in common sense, the guiding assumptions often engender misunderstanding. For example, the actor assumption does not require all entities in rational choice models to be people. They can also be aggregates like firms, interest groups, social classes, or "Congress," provided there are good grounds for believing the entity acts *as if* it were intentional (Ferejohn and Satz 1995). Intentionalism does not imply that actors are omniscient or inevitably choose the "best" action, as specified by some outside observer. Instead, actors may be severely constrained in what they can do or imagine they can do. They may understand the situation in which they find themselves only poorly. They often have expectations about others that shape their notions of what they can or should do. Consequently, the relationship between goals and choices may be complex. Nor does intentionalism imply that all outcomes are intended. The collision of two intentional actors may yield outcomes neither intended, anticipated, or desired. The inextricable randomness of human existence may throw a monkey wrench in the best laid plans of intentional actors (whether mice or men). Finally, the whole rational choice approach is sometimes seen as morally suspect, since some rational choice models call into question the platitudes of civics classes, and others provide an understanding rather than a condemnation of evil. I pass over this objection: readers can decide for themselves who had the better case, Galileo or the cardinal who refused to examine the moons of Jupiter through Galileo's telescope lest the sight undermine his faith.

The Reach of the Tools

Putting red herrings aside, there still remain some serious issues that require careful thought. These involve not the philosophical soundness of the guiding assumptions but the reach of the tools currently available. At present, the principal tools in the rational choice toolbox are utility theory (decision theory), which is supposed to supply a psychology for decision makers, and game theory, which is supposed to aggregate individual actions into social outcomes. But does decision theory provide a credible "psychology" for individual actors or organizations? Does game theory allow accurate inference of aggregate behavior from individual action? The strongest answer I am willing to muster is a qualified maybe.[5]

Folk Psychology. First consider decision theory as psychology. Aside from its tractability, the appeal of decision theory to rational choice theorists is well captured in the comment of philosopher David Lewis:

Decision theory (at least if we omit the frills) is not esoteric science, however unfamiliar it may seem to an outsider. Rather it is a systematic exposition of the consequences of certain well-chosen platitudes about belief, desire, prefer-

[5] A serious problem arises when in some context the answer seems to be a definite no. What then? See Chong 1995.

ence, and choice. It is the very core of our commonsense theory of persons, dissected out and elegantly systematized. (Pettit 1991:147)

In other words, decision theory is just folk psychology in fancy dress.

There are good reasons for taking folk psychology seriously. At the level of brute empiricism, it seems to yield sensible results much of the time. For example, if you prefer ten to five dollars, and five dollars to a punch in the nose, utility theory says you should prefer ten dollars to a punch in the nose – and most people seem to. The fact that decision theory really works much of the time explains its status as the psychology of everyday life.

Yet there is a mystery here worth thinking about, for, despite its rough-and-ready practicality, folk psychology is not real psychology. Real people involved in individual decision making systematically depart from what folk psychology predicts; the evidence is so overwhelming that further dispute is really pointless.[6] Moreover, applying the folk psychology of individuals to complex organizations or entities seems absurd on its face. What then explains the attractiveness of folk psychology, in everyday life and in rational choice theory?

Several phenomena are at work. First, some environments are so powerfully structured that even weakly rational decision makers perform just like ultrarational ones. For example, if I wish to buy a house in an expensive neighborhood but have so little money that only the cheapest house is affordable, it doesn't really matter what mental process I employ in choosing among the houses. I end up owning the same one regardless, the house immediately indicated by decision theory. More interesting is the situation in which the environment provides strong feedback tied to rational (i.e., decision theoretic–like) behavior. In such an environment, subrational or even arational players can soon be indistinguishable from extremely clever decision theorists. A graphic demonstration is laboratory experiments in which rats obey the law of demand.

Another mechanism is suggested by the parable of the money pump. Suppose a particular decision maker has intransitive (irrational) preferences – for example, prefers A to B to C, but also prefers C to A. Suppose this person begins by holding C and a wallet stuffed with cash. Then such a person would be willing to pay to trade C for B; pay to trade B for A; but then pay again to trade A for C. He or she would thus return to holding C but with a lighter wallet. A few more spins of this cycle and the money pump – for such is the irrational person to an unscrupulous exploiter – will be dry.

The point of this story is not to attack irrational behavior on logical grounds. Sometimes people or organizations *are* irrational. Rather, the

---

[6] Camerer 1995 provides a convenient review.

lesson is: when people or organizations find themselves systematically exploited because of their irrationality, they have a strong incentive to do something about it. They construct mechanisms to protect themselves from their own preferences (Elster 1979). On a personal level, this may involve self-reflection or use of maxims like "sleep on it." It may involve delegation to parties less likely to be exploited, for example, lawyers, brokers, or investment bankers. It may involve deliberately restructuring one's incentives, for example, joining a twelve-step program or avoiding temptation. Similarly, organizations in harsh environments try to reduce their irrational behavior by constructing a hierarchy, instituting standard operating procedures, or building a corporate culture (Sah and Stiglitz 1986; Kreps 1990b). When such mechanisms work tolerably well, the person or organization looks *as if* it were a decision theorist, even though the true decision-making procedure (involving real people with real psychologies) is quite different from what a literal interpretation of decision theory might suggest. In short, some situations provide actors with *structural incentives* to behave the way decision theory suggests. The actor's true psychology simply doesn't matter. The actor looks pretty much like a decision theorist.

Life as a Game. The question remains, Even if individual actors achieve the kind of consistency envisioned in decision theory, at least in a specific context, does game theory provide a reasonable way to recover aggregate behavior from individual action? At a purely nominal level, if game theory is to be relevant, then a social phenomenon must be a strategic situation, a "game." Two conditions define such situations. First, the fate of each actor must depend at least in part on the decisions of other actors. Second, the actors must realize their interdependence. The confluence of both factors creates a strategic situation.

Although there are important exceptions – economists are interested in perfectly competitive markets, for instance – social scientists are mostly interested in strategic situations. Vetoes certainly take place in a strategic setting. Presidents and congressmen both care whether a proposed law is enacted. The bill's fate depends on both their actions: if the bill is to become law, Congress must pass (and keep repassing) the bill; the president must not successfully veto and reveto the bill. Finally, president and Congress are quite aware of their interdependence, as numerous case studies demonstrate.

Given a strategic situation, the power of game theory hinges critically on the appropriateness of its "solution concepts." A "solution concept" systematically highlights one or more of the multitude of possible outcomes that might occur in a given strategic situation. In other words, it predicts which outcome will actually occur. As an example, in the next chapter I use a specific solution concept, "subgame perfect Nash equilibrium," to analyze the second face of power. This solution concept, which tries to capture the idea of foresight, picks out a unique outcome from among four possible ones. Different solution concepts have different behavioral motivations; some may not have any (Aumann 1985).[7]

The past two decades have seen enormous advances in the development of solution concepts. Largely as a result, game theory has undergone a radical transformation, from a branch of mathematics of little practical use to social scientists into a supple, subtle, complex constellation of ideas with great practicality. Its current frontiers lie deep within some of the most challenging and interesting areas in the human sciences. The possibility of communication, the evolution of shared meanings, the role of expectations in creating culture, and the meaning and consequences of bounded rationality are research concerns at the frontier. Few areas in social science have proved so exciting or fruitful.

As part of this intensive development, game theorists have been willing to pursue the white rabbit of "rationality" wherever it leads, including places that resemble Wonderland more than our landscape. This is completely appropriate for pure game theory. Theorists should follow their ideas wherever they lead. But it can be disturbing when *applied* models employ assumptions about knowledge and beliefs that seem pretty unlikely or even absurd.

Consider the workhorse solution concept in noncooperative game theory, the Nash equilibrium (all the solution concepts used in this book are variants of the Nash equilibrium).[8] A Nash equilibrium refers to a situation in which no player unilaterally wishes to change his or her strategy, given what the other players are doing. It seems quite clear that if the actors in a strategic situation correctly perceive an obvious way to play, the players' strategies must form a Nash equilibrium. If not, some actor would deviate to another strategy and the "obvious way to play" would not describe what actually happens. Thus, if the players correctly perceive an obvious way to play in a strategic situation, they seem to need very strong (and *correct*) notions of what each other is going to do.[9] In fact, the informational assumptions supporting the Nash equilib-

---

[7] The behavioral foundations of, say, stability or universal divinity are quite unclear, at least to me.

[8] This solution concept is named for its discoverer, the Princeton mathematician John Nash. The discussion in the next few paragraphs draws heavily on Kreps 1990a, sec. 12.6; Osborne and Rubinstein 1994, sec. 5.4; Brandenburger 1992; and Taylor 1987. An accessible introduction is Kreps 1990a.

[9] Some games have a dominant strategy equilibrium – each player has an action that is a best response to *any* action of the other players. When such solutions exist they provide an obvious way to play a game. But most situations of interest to po-

rium are much stronger. This branch of game theory rapidly becomes quite abstruse. However, typical results are that all the players must have a deeply shared understanding of the game they are playing, all must know each other to be rational, and all must know what the other players expect to see as actions. In short, the players must share an enormous amount of information about their world and each other.

Game theory is sometimes criticized for assuming atomistic actors who meet in a kind of social desert but, as the foregoing discussion suggests, this criticism is wildly off the mark. What is striking about many solution concepts is not that they assume actors who share so little social knowledge but that they assume actors who share so much. Suppose a dense web of information and mutual understanding were *not* available to the players. Suppose, for example, the players simply do not see an "obvious" way to play a game. Then standard solution concepts don't apply and game theory, at least in standard versions, won't have much to say about what the players will do.[10]

From this perspective, the most disturbing feature of contemporary game theory is not that it assumes so little social glue or that it assumes so much, but that it is silent on where the glue comes from. How do the players arrive at a situation where the solution concepts make sense? Without some tools for thinking about this, we can't know whether a solution concept is likely to apply or not.

Several (informal) answers are often offered for this disturbing puzzle. Perhaps the players already share a common language and can use it to build the necessary web of expectations in a new setting. Or the players may have a history of interaction to draw on. Perhaps they have personal experience with a situation or have observed others. Past play may somehow have established a social convention. Or some apparently unrelated but shared cultural experience allows the players to coordinate their expectations. All these answers seem plausible but remain at too high a level of generality to be very useful in practical modeling. At present, deciding whether and how game theory applies to a specific strategic setting requires intuitive judgments about what is sensible and plausible.

When Is Rational Choice Theory Likely to Work?

Let me summarize and conclude this argument. If the current tools of rational choice theory are to afford much leverage on a strategic situa-

---

litical scientists do not have dominant strategy equilibria (though some do – e.g., the one-shot prisoners' dilemma). The veto games studied in this book do not have dominant strategy equilibria.

[10] A currently active research program in game theory seeks to replace rationality and common knowledge with evolution as the basis for standard solution concepts. The relevance of this work for applied modeling in political science is not yet clear.

tion in politics, the situation should be one in which the players (1) tend to act approximately like decision theorists, and (2) collectively play so as to create a social equilibrium as conceived in game theory. These conditions seem more likely to be met when (a) the players have a good understanding of the situation in which they find themselves, (b) there are substantial rewards for consistent, game theoretically motivated play, or (c) there are substantial penalties for inconsistent, nongame theoretically motivated play. Condition a seems reasonable when the situation is not too complex and the players have a chance to think about what they should do. It is also plausible if the actors have played the game many times in the past and thus learn from personal experience. It could hold if the actors have the chance to observe others play, or can otherwise learn from history. It is also more attainable if the actors share a broader culture. Conditions b and c are more likely to hold if competitive pressure or natural selection is at work. In short, the actual reach of contemporary rational choice theory depends heavily on the presence of structural incentives and shared history and culture.

RATIONAL CHOICE, THE PRESIDENCY, AND VETO BARGAINING

If the argument in the preceding section holds water, we can think of a continuum of strategic situations in politics. At one extreme (call it the "low" end of the applicability scale) are confusing, one-shot, trivial decisions made by relatively atomistic actors. In such situations the analytic leverage offered by game theory is likely to be quite modest. An example might be casting a ballot on a minor bond referendum or voting in a race between unfamiliar candidates for some obscure and unimportant lower office. In such a situation I would expect to see a large role for the cognitive effects so well documented by experimental psychologists. For instance, the order in which propositions or candidates are listed on the ballot might have a discernible effect on the vote. At the other extreme (the "high" end of the applicability scale) are important, familiar, well-understood, and well-considered decisions taken by actors who share a common culture. Examples might include congressmen's decisions about how much constituency service to provide their districts or how to vote on important bills. At the high end of the scale the tools of rational choice theory seem not only appropriate but compelling.

"The Presidency" Is Not a Dependent Variable

Where does presidential politics fall on the applicability scale? The obvious answer is, it depends on what we are talking about. This is not a trivial point. A general theory of "the presidency" is like a theory of "the world": there can be theories of weather, theories of physical geology, theories of planetary formation, but no theory of "the world." Or rather, one begins by asking, Why does the weather change? Why are there earthquakes and volcanoes? and Where did the Earth come from? and one ends up with a set of interconnected models that constitute as much of a "theory of the world" as we shall ever have. And so it is with the presidency.

This perspective on what constitutes interesting theory goes hand in hand with a perspective on empirical work that emphasizes the "small n problem."[11] The small n problem arises when one wishes to summarize structure in a data set: if there aren't many observations, there simply can't be much structure to summarize. This is a famously tricky problem in presidential studies, in which scholars have sometimes treated individual presidents as single observations. But there haven't been many presidents and so there isn't much one can say at this level of analysis. In contrast, in Chapter 2 I examined more than seventeen thousand instances in which Congress passed legislation and presidents responded with a signature or a veto. Each presidency supplied hundreds of observations. Even the analysis of veto bargaining rested on many observations.[12] In short, once one moves from "the presidency" to specific types of decision making, observations abound.

The move to avoid the small n problem is also the right move to build useful theory. If one takes a step back from inchoate entities like "the presidency," "presidential performance," and "presidential decision making," one can consider *specific* strategic settings that present *real* puzzles. Examples are constructing a legislative program, overseeing and managing the bureaucracy, mobilizing public opinion, making Supreme Court nominations, selecting and organizing presidential staff, negotiating and receiving approval for treaties, and choosing between treaties and executive agreements as policy instruments. All these are examples of what might be called the institutional presidency. It is here, if anywhere, that analytical social science including rational choice analysis may have something interesting to say about the presidency.

Veto Bargaining and the Applicability Scale

If vetoes are to fall at the high end of the applicability scale, presidents and Congress need structural incentives to behave like consistent, inten-

---

[11] For a powerful expression of this viewpoint, see King 1993.

[12] When it did not (e.g., for events deep in veto chains), I tried to be very cautious with inferences.

tional actors and must be bound by webs of shared understanding and expectation. Both requirements are met.

First, the veto game is not played for penny ante stakes. Years of effort may have gone into the crafting and passage of a piece of legislation. Hundreds of millions of dollars and passionately held beliefs may be at stake. Under these circumstances, congressmen and their staff will bring intense thought, deliberation, and exacting calculation to bear. Moreover, between them, they are likely to draw on decades of legislative experience. At least on the congressional side, it is hard to imagine a better setting for strategic calculation.

What about presidents? Again, the stakes will often be substantial. Presidents like Gerald Ford or Lyndon Johnson, who have vast experience in Congress, bring an in-depth understanding of veto bargaining with them into the Oval Office. Other presidents – Eisenhower may be an example – may not have a deep personal understanding of the nuances of interbranch bargaining themselves. Nonetheless, the growth of the institutionalized presidency has made it possible for even less experienced presidents to have deep reservoirs of legislative talent in-house. Moreover, the president's party lieutenants on the Hill, themselves masters of the process, will often be willing to advise him on veto strategy. Consequently, there is every reason to believe even relatively inexperienced presidents can use the veto in a knowledgeable and sophisticated way, if they want to – and the constitutional design insures they will often want to.

In short, the Constitution drives the players into a game whose rules are clearly specified and, after two hundred years of shared experience and history, well understood by the players. If any part of presidential politics falls at the high end of the applicability scale, it must be the politics of the presidential veto.

CRITERIA FOR SUCCESS . . . AND FAILURE

What makes a model *good*? How can we tell success or failure when we see it? Closer to home, what standards am I willing to apply to the models in this book? In my view, the best answer is the most straightforward one: rational choice models, including the ones in this book, should be judged with the same criteria social and natural scientists use to judge their models.

So, what are those criteria? What they *should* be is perhaps the central issue in contemporary philosophy of science (Kuhn 1962; Feyerabend 1978; Laudan 1977). But it is important to see that in the present context the issue is not what they should be but what the criteria actually *are*. The question is an empirical one. Science is a social activity with its own kinds of rules (Hull 1988). Among these are standards for appraising the value of models.

A great deal of research has gone into investigating the criteria scientists actually use in evaluating scientific theories. There are a set of reasonably clear findings (Donovan, Laudan, and Laudan 1988). These can be summarized fairly neatly:

- Good models solve empirical puzzles.
- Good models solve empirical puzzles they were not designed to solve.
- Good models solve empirical puzzles that lie outside the domain of their initial success.
- Good models solve puzzles their rivals cannot.
- Good models turn apparent counterexamples into solved problems.

In addition,

- Good models are not required to make novel, counterintuitive predictions.
- Models are judged relative to the competition.

Some of these criteria stand in stark contrast to what well-known philosophers of science have claimed or advocated. As one example, consider the supposed requirement that good models produce stunning, novel, nonobvious predictions. In other words, not only must a model explain what is known and produce valid predictions beyond that, but also deliver a prediction no one has previously conceived of or that strikes many people as wrong. This criterion is a staple of positivist approaches to science and is uncritically adopted by Green and Shapiro (1994), who make just such a demand of rational choice models. But, in fact, working scientists do not make such demands of models and this criterion seems to play no role in actual theory appraisal (Donovan et al. 1988:33).

Also striking is the apparent importance of a quality some philosophers of science call richness or unity (Bronowski 1977; Ferejohn and Satz 1995). Rich theories unify and connect hitherto unrelated problems. They show, in Jacob Bronowski's phrase, that "the world can be understood as a unity, and that the rational mind can find ways of looking at it that are simple, new, and powerful exactly because they unify it" (1977:101). The importance of this feature of scientific theories is shown by the necessity for good models to go beyond what they were designed to explain to show how other, sometimes apparently contradictory, phenomena actually are understandable in terms of the same causal mechanism.

Finally, there is an additional criterion that I believe important for social science. It is omitted from the preceding list, which is derived from studies of natural scientists. The criterion is: good models deliver a substantial normative kick. They deal with matters we care about. For instance, Mancur Olson's (1965) "logic of collective action" is an arresting model because it implies that democracies often will not reflect even the deeply felt interests of citizens. Models of congressional turnover received enormous attention in the 1980s because low levels of turnover seem to violate standard conceptions of democratic accountability and control (Cain, Ferejohn, and Fiorina 1987). Good models need not confirm our normative biases, perhaps just the opposite. But they often speak to our values.

These are very, very tough criteria. They demand theory that operates at a high intellectual level. More than that, they demand models that are rooted in observable phenomena, that take data and empirical findings seriously, and that deal with matters we care about.

4

Models of Veto Bargaining

This chapter develops three models of veto bargaining. I begin with the second face of power, introduced in the first chapter, and develop it into a model of the veto as a presidential capacity. This model, the famous Romer-Rosenthal model of take-it-or-leave-it bargaining, supplies the theme on which all the subsequent models in this book are variations. The first variation examines the politics of veto overrides. The second explores full-blown sequential veto bargaining.

Each model in this chapter tells a story, the story of a causal mechanism. The mechanism in the first model is the *power of anticipated response*. The model explores how the president's veto power affects the balance of power in a separation-of-powers system. The mechanism in the second model is *uncertainty*. The model shows how uncertainty tempers congressional action, allows actual vetoes to take place, and shifts the balance of power somewhat toward the president. However, this model misses an important part of the politics of the veto for it cannot explain how vetoes wrest policy concessions from Congress. The mechanism in the third model is *strategic reputation building*, the deliberate manipulation of beliefs through vetoes. This model addresses the veto and congressional policy concessions.

Why do I present three midlevel models of veto bargaining rather than one grand model encompassing everything? To tell its story, each model isolates one or two elements of veto bargaining and then examines them extremely carefully. I could yoke several of these stories together into a kind of megamodel, much as a writer might do in a novel. But whether in literature or social science, this is worthwhile only if the juxtaposition creates a whole that is greater than the sum of the parts – for instance, if the different causal mechanisms interact in a substantively interesting way. Otherwise, forcing the different parts together creates pointless, confusing interactions that disrupt the flow of the separate stories. In such a case, the writer should let the separate parts remain as crystalline short stories; the theorist should build a few models, each with a clear point, rather than a single one with so many that none can be understood.

Throughout this chapter I try to keep the exposition simple, without becoming simplistic. Nonetheless, the models draw on over forty years of continuous work by political theorists and even conscientious readers may find parts heavy going. To ease the burden, I rely heavily on figures and numerical examples to convey intuition about the results. Additional details can be found in the appendix to this chapter.

THE BASIC MODEL: THE SECOND FACE OF POWER REVISITED

The Logic of Anticipation

In Chapter 1 I introduced the "second face of power." The insight was that power can work through anticipation, so a power relationship may exist even absent visible compulsion. This idea is inherently game theoretic, so it seems natural to express it in a simple game, as shown in Figure 4.1. Though the situation is generic, I tell the story in terms of vetoes.

As shown in Figure 4.1, Congress moves first and has two choices: pass version 1 of a bill or pass a modified version, version 2. (The restriction to two choices is just to keep the example simple; in a few paragraphs I introduce a more flexible way to represent the content of bills.) The president has the next move regardless of which bill is passed. He can either veto the bill or accept it. In this tinker-toy version of veto politics, neither overriding nor repassing is possible, so the game ends after the president's action. Payoffs for each player under the four possible outcomes are shown by the ordered pairs at the tips of the game tree. The first number indicates Congress's payoff, the second the president's. Because a veto enforces the status quo, I scale the payoffs so that both players value the status quo at zero. Also, to keep things interesting, assume the president and Congress potentially could agree on a bill both prefer to the status quo. However, they disagree over the best alternative. In fact, to sharpen the possible disagreement, assume the president prefers the status quo to Congress's most preferred policy. Let us say version 1 of the bill reflects Congress's preferred policy while version 2 better reflects the president's. In accord with this underlying story, then, $0 < c < a$ and $b < 0 < d$.

Will the players see an obvious way to play this game? One argument, based on the solution concept known as "subgame perfection," suggests they should. This solution concept requires each player to maximize his

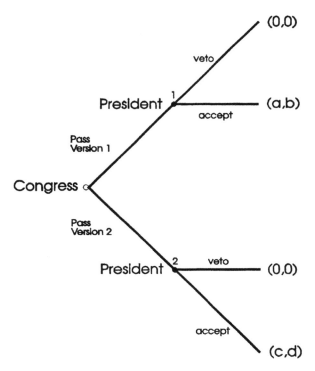

Figure 4.1. The "Second Face of Power" Game

or her expected payoff. It requires the president to take his best possible action for *any* bill passed by Congress. And it assumes Congress can correctly anticipate the president's actions regardless of which bill is passed.

Suppose the president finds himself at the node labeled "1." His choice at that point is either to veto version 1 of the bill, yielding a payoff of 0, or accept it, yielding the inferior payoff *b*. Hence, he will veto. Conversely, suppose he finds himself at the node labeled "2." Since *d* > 0 he will accept version 2 of the bill. *If Congress understands what the president will do*, then it knows that its real choice is between passing version 1 and receiving a payoff of 0, and passing version 2 and receiving a payoff of *c*. Hence, it will pass version 2. The president need not make an explicit veto threat nor even take any action; the truly interesting action is taking place purely through congressional anticipation of presidential actions. Consequently, all we will see is Congress passing bills acceptable to the president and the president signing them. We might mistakenly interpret this placid scene as presidential acquiescence to congressional activism! But in fact the implicit threat of a veto at node 1 compels Congress's choice of bill. This very simple model suggests how *the veto* (a capability) can shape the content of legislation even if *vetoes* (uses of the capability) are rare.

Simple as it is, the model incorporates three of the four building blocks needed to model veto bargaining: actors, sequence, and information. The actors are the president and Congress. Both are actually complex organizations – even the "president" is really an amalgam of the individual and his subordinates. However, the argument from structural incentives, sketched in the previous chapter, justifies their inclusion as single actors. The sequence of play is shown in Figure 4.1: Congress selects a bill, the president vetoes. (I examine much more complicated sequences shortly.) The model's information structure is extremely simple: both players know everything in the game that is worth knowing. The ability of Congress to forecast the president's actions is critical for the proposed solution to the game.

A fourth element is missing from the model, however: *policy*. Policy is central to veto bargaining. To address it, the model needs a device for representing policies. An extraordinarily useful device is the policy space.

Policy and Policy Preferences

Policy spaces are a hallmark of rational choice institutionalism. They are routinely used in models of Congress, the courts, and bureaucracy. Their use is one of the features that distinguish models of political settings from those of economic ones.

The concept of a policy space originated with Columbia economist Harold Hotelling who introduced it in the 1930s to study spatial competition among firms. However, the version used in institutionalist models might better be attributed to Melvin Hinich and his collaborators, particularly James Enelow and Peter Ordeshook, who together pioneered the modern spatial theory of voting, beginning in the late 1960s (Enelow and Hinich 1984).

The basic idea is extremely simple and is best introduced through an example. Consider the unit interval, that is, a line whose origin is zero and whose terminus is one. Points in this unidimensional policy space could correspond to, for example, tax or tariff rates ranging from 0 to 100 percent. More generally, points on a line can represent quantities such as expenditures. In fact, points on a line can even represent more qualitative matters, such as "degree of restrictions on abortion" or "support for human rights."

Occasionally there are bills that deal only with a single ratelike quantity, for example, a routine adjustment to the minimum wage or a simple authorization. But most bills make many changes simultaneously. For example H.R. 12384, a military construction bill passed in 1976 by the 94th Congress, authorized $3.3 billion for military construction. Economy-minded President Ford vetoed the bill, but not because of the bill's authorization level. Rather, the bill contained a provision requiring advance notification of base closings. It was this provision, quite distinct from the dollar levels, that the president found objectionable. (Congress repassed the bill, maintaining the dollar level but modifying the base-closing provision along the lines indicated by the president.) A literal representation of the characteristics of this bill would require several dimensions, one for each qualitatively distinct facet. Literal representations of extremely complex legislation, by no means uncommon on Capitol Hill, would require hundreds or perhaps even thousands of dimensions.

Most models of interbranch bargaining employ only one dimension; none employs thousands. Is this justifiable? On empirical grounds, yes. Abundant empirical evidence indicates that a single dimension acounts for around 85% or so of the variance in roll call voting. This dimension corresponds pretty clearly to "liberalism-conservatism." In other words, most roll call voting in the House and Senate looks almost as if individual bills or amendments came labeled with a liberalism-conservatism index, and that is sufficent information for congressmen casting a yea and a nay.[1]

Why this should be is not entirely clear. Some evidence suggests the public sees political issues in low-dimensional terms. This in turn creates an incentive for politicians to portray policies this way, since doing so helps them maintain simple, clear policy reputations of value in elections. Perhaps, then, the link between the way the public understands issues and the way politicians and experts discuss them is self-reinforcing. However, whatever the mechanism by which inherently multidimensional bills are tagged with one-dimensional labels, I shall assume this structure.[2]

[1] For a clear expression of this viewpoint, see Poole and Rosenthal 1994; in addition, see Smith 1989. The viewpoint is slightly controversial but not terribly so. For an opposing viewpoint see Koford 1994.

[2] There is an extremely interesting puzzle here that has yet to be resolved satisfactorily. But some contributions are Snyder 1992a, Dougan and Munger 1989, Hinich and Munger 1994, and Zaller 1992. A nonstarter appears to be Congress's own internal organization. See Snyder 1992b (Congress's committee structure could create unidimensionality if committees used their gate-keeping powers aggressively) and Poole and Rosenthal's rejoinder (1991). At any rate, models of interbranch bargaining that study signaling or screening invariably assume unidimensional policy spaces, for in this setting these phenomena are tractable using advanced but standard modeling techniques. With the addition of more dimensions, standard techniques are no longer good enough; new technique is required. This is a tall order. In this book I

I still need to define the policy preferences of the president and Congress. Again following the logic of structural incentives, I assume they have the sort of preferences conceived in decision theory. Specifically, I assume their preferences are well represented by "single-peaked" utility functions (see Figure 4.2). Experience has shown this to be a sensible modeling choice in political settings. Actors with single-peaked utility functions have most-preferred policies, with the attractiveness of other policies declining as they diverge more and more from the most-preferred policy. For example, you may have a preferred level of expenditures on defense policy; both underspending and overspending are less attractive.[3] Figure 4.2 illustrates a policy space and associated preferences. The horizontal line X is the unidimensional policy space. The vertical dimension represents "utility," the happiness (as it were) of the players. The utility of any point in the policy space to either the president or Congress can be read from their utility functions. For example, the utility to Congress of a policy located at 0 is just 0, while that of one located at 1 is -1. For any two points a and b on the line, the utility function indicates whether the actor prefers a to b or is indifferent between them.

The utility functions shown in the figure are examples of "tent" utility functions, so-called for the obvious reason. These functions are easy to understand and simple to work with so I employ them consistently throughout this book. However, many of the results given here hold qualitatively for more general utility functions, provided they are single-peaked.[4]

The equation describing Congress's utility function in Figure 4.2 is extremely simple:

$$U(x) = - |x| \qquad (4.1)$$

The absolute value function generates the characteristic tent shape. If we let c denote Congress's ideal point (its most preferred policy) then $c = 0$. In Figure 4.2, the utility function of the president has the same general form as that of Congress, except that the indicated ideal point, p, equals 1.

concentrate on developing state-of-the-art models of interbranch bargaining using the best available technology, and then testing them. Inventing new modeling technique is beyond the scope of the book.

[3] Detailed exegesis of single-peaked utility functions can be found in Ordeshook 1986 and Enelow and Hinich 1984.

[4] In some cases, additional technical requirements are necessary. For example, the veto threats model in Chapter 7 requires the utility functions to display certain properties (e.g., a kind of single-crossing property), which are carefully spelled out in Matthews 1989. The SVB model uses tent utility functions to generate closed form solutions in the form of differential equations, whose iterative solution yields the empirical hypotheses. So the hypotheses in that model are closely tied to these utility functions.

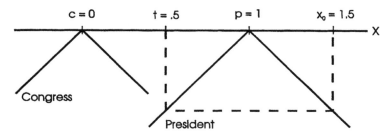

Figure 4.2. Preferences in a Spatial Setting

Also shown in Figure 4.2 is a special point, x_0, the *status quo*. The status quo represents the current policy, which will continue unless the players enact a new one. Not surprisingly, the location of the status quo often has a profound effect on the nature of veto bargaining.

An important feature of single-peaked utility functions is that for any point x, there is another point x' that is *utility equivalent* to x. Of particular interest is the point utility equivalent to the status quo x_0, especially for the president. Consider the president's utility function in Figure 4.2. The point x_0 is located at 1.5. Since $U(x_0) = U(\frac{1}{2}) = -\frac{1}{2}$, the points x_0 and .5 are utility equivalent for the president.

It proves extremely helpful to rescale the president's utility function in terms of the utility equivalent points (just why will become clear in a few pages), an innovation of the economist Steven Matthews. So long as the rescaled function does not alter the preference relationship between different points on the line, the rescaled function represents the president's preferences just as well as the original one.[5] The rescaling works as follows. Without altering its shape, slide the entire function straight upward until one end of the "tent" is anchored at x_0, the status quo (see Figure 4.3).

To avoid confusion with Congress's utility I denote the president's rescaled utility function as $V(x)$. More specifically,

$$V(x;x_0,t) = \frac{|x_0 - t| - |t + x_0 - 2x|}{2} \qquad (4.2)$$

where $t = 2p - x_0$. This appears somewhat complicated but yields the simple form shown in Figure 4.3. This utility function is constructed so the point that is utility equivalent to the status quo is always given by

[5] Matthews 1989 provides a set of sufficient conditions on general utility functions so that this normalization retains the preference ordering of the original function. Tent utility is just a special case, as it satisfies these sufficient conditions.

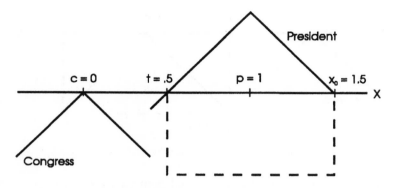

Figure 4.3. Rescaled Utility Function

the point t. Note that $V(t) = V(x_0) = 0$. I assume this utility function for the president throughout the book.

In all the models I consider in this chapter, I normalize Congress's ideal point c to 0 and assume the status quo $x_0 > 0$. This is without any loss of generality since the cases with the status quo to the left of Congress's ideal point are just mirror images of cases I do consider. Focusing on just one set of cases keeps the exposition simple.

The Basic Model

I can now extend the game in Figure 4.1 into a real model of the veto. The sequence of play remains the same: Congress makes a single and final take-it-or-leave-it offer of a bill with a particular ideological tenor (i.e., a given spatial location in X). The president then accepts it or vetoes it. The game ends and the players receive payoffs as specified in equations 4.1 and 4.2. In this extremely simple model, vetoes really are bullets and are purely reactive.

The graphical device in Figure 4.4 is extremely helpful for conveying some intuition about veto bargaining in this setting. Consider all the policies the president considers as good or better than the status quo, that is, all the policies as close or closer to his ideal point than x_0. This set of policies is the president's *preferred set*, $\wp_p$. As shown in Figure 4.4, it is an interval of the line, namely $[t, x_0]$ (this notation is read: the line segment from t to x_0, inclusive). Since this is a one-shot game, the president should accept any offer in this interval, assuming all he cares about is attaining the best possible final policy, that is, if he wants the best payoff according to equation 4.2. The preferred set of Congress,

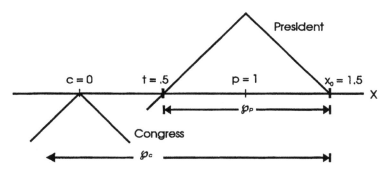

Figure 4.4. Preferred Sets in the Basic Model

$\wp_c$, is defined similarly and is thus $[-x_0, x_0]$. The *intersection* of the two preferred sets, that is, $\wp_c \cap \wp_p$, is just the overlapping portions of the two preferred sets. In the figure, this is the line segment $[t, x_0]$. This set contains all the points *both* players prefer to the status quo. In voting games the intersection of the relevant preferred sets is often called the *win set*. At least under complete and perfect information (as assumed in the basic model), it seems natural to seek the outcome of veto bargaining in the win set since Congress has no incentive to make an offer it prefers less than the status quo and the president has no incentive to accept an offer he likes less than the status quo (excluding veto overrides for the moment). All such points are found in the win set. Moreover, since Congress gets to select the bill while the president can do nothing except accept or veto, a reasonable conjecture is that Congress will pick from the win set the best possible bill from its perspective. Given the specified game and assuming equation 4.1 really does summarize the relevant payoffs for Congress, it is not hard to deduce which bill this will be. However, I will be fairly methodical in working through this deduction.

First, we need to specify *strategies* for the players. A strategy specifies a plan for a player under every conceivable contingency that might arise in a game.[6] Given the information structure and sequence of play in the basic game, a strategy for Congress is simply a point x from the line X. A strategy for the president is a probability distribution over his two actions, accept or veto, *given Congress's offer* (and, of course, the status quo and his own preferences). That is, for any given bill, the president's strategy indicates the probability of a veto. Denote this function as $r(x)$

---

[6] More formally, a strategy is a mapping from information sets into actions. Additional details can be found in standard game theory texts, for example, Myerson 1991 or Osbourne and Rubenstein 1994.

(this can be read, "*r* of *x*" or "the reply to *x*").[7] We also need to specify a *solution concept*. As in the second face of power game, subgame perfect Nash equilibrium captures the notion of anticipation or foresight.

There are three cases which are neatly characterized by the location of *t*. The location of *t* can be thought of as the president's *type*.[8] The president's type *t* may take any value on a continuum, depending on the location of the status quo and the president's ideal point. But each type falls into one of three classes. The first is shown in the top panel of Figure 4.5. The critical feature of this case is that $t \leq c$ so Congress's ideal point lies in the president's preferred set. (Note that the president's ideal point *p* may be greater or less than *c*; it makes no difference so long as $t < c$). Accordingly, presidents of this type are willing to accept a bill located at Congress's ideal policy. In Matthews's evocative terminology, such presidents are *accommodating*. Since Congress can do no better than to offer its ideal policy, which accommodators surely accept, the solution concept specifies $x = c$ as the prediction when $t < c$.

The second case is shown in the middle panel of Figure 4.5. The defining feature of this case is that $c < t \leq x_0$. Congress's ideal point *c* no longer lies within the win set, here the interval $[t, x_0]$. Offering a bill at *c* would be futile since the president would veto it, leaving Congress with the undesirable status quo. From Congress's perspective, the best feasible policy is *t*, which the president would accept.[9] Thus, the solution concept specifies $x = t$. Since presidents of the type $c < t \leq x_0$ are not accommodating but will accept some proposals, Matthews refers to them as *compromising*.

The final case occurs when $c < x_0 < t$, as shown in the bottom panel of the figure. In this case, the win set is composed of a single element,

---

[7] Just to be quite formal, define the set $A = \{$accept, veto$\}$ and let $\Delta(\cdot)$ be the set of all probability distributions over an arbitrary set. Then the president's strategy is a function $r:X \rightarrow \Delta(A)$.

[8] The word "type" has a technical meaning in games of incomplete information: an actor's private information is summarized in his or her "type." Since there is no incomplete information in this game, I slightly abuse the terminology. But what I call the actor's type will be exactly the subject of incomplete information in models 2 and 3.

[9] If a proposal lay exactly at the edge of the president's preferred set, he would be indifferent between accepting and rejecting the bill. But suppose his strategy called for him to reject such a bill. Then Congress would not offer it; it would "shade" the proposal a little toward the president's ideal point so he would accept. But when Congress's pure strategy space is a continuum, "shading" is not well defined (e.g., for any "shade" other than zero, there is a smaller one that is better for Congress). So there cannot be a well-defined equilibrium in this configuration in which the president rejects proposals at the edge of his preferred set with positive probability. In fact, the specified strategies constitute the unique pair of best responses in this configuration.

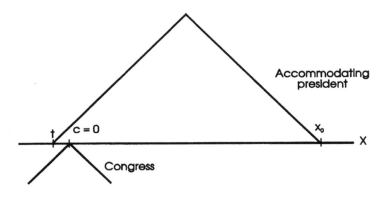

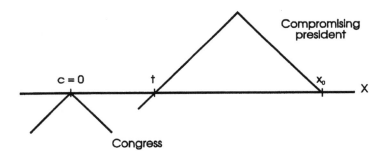

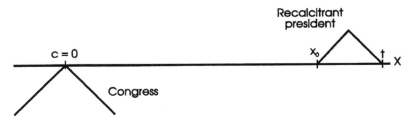

Figure 4.5. Three Cases in the Basic Model

the status quo x_0. It matters naught what Congress offers; policy is deadlocked.

The following proposition summarizes the analysis:

Proposition 1 (Romer-Rosenthal Theorem): A subgame perfect equilibrium to the one-shot veto bargaining game under complete and perfect information is

$$x^* = \begin{cases} c \text{ if } t \leq c \\ t \text{ if } c < t \leq x_0 \\ x_0 \text{ if } c < x_0 < t \end{cases}$$

$$r^*(x) = \begin{cases} \text{accept if } x \in \wp_p \\ \text{veto otherwise.} \end{cases}$$

The asterisks denote optimum or equilibrium strategies. The expression "$x \in \wp_p$" is read, "x is an element of the president's preferred set."

The implications for outcomes are shown in Figure 4.6. Outcomes are shown on the vertical axis; the horizontal axis shows the location of t. When the president is accommodating, the outcome is c. When he is compromising, the outcome is t. When he is recalcitrant, the outcome must be the status quo, x_0.

In the figure, the vertical distance between an outcome and c indicates the impact of the second face of power. The model specifies quite precisely when the second face of power will manifest itself (cases 2 and 3, compromisers and recalcitrants), and when it won't (case 1, accommodators). As the figure indicates, the maximum possible impact of the second face of power depends on the distance between Congress's ideal point and the status quo – not a surprising result but a graphic reminder of the importance of the status quo in politics. More generally, when the second face of power appears, its magnitude depends on the distance between the Congress's ideal point c and the minimum of the status quo and the president's utility equivalent point t – hardly an intuitive result but readily understandable once the model is in hand.

Veto Overrides in the Basic Model

It is extremely easy to expand the model to include the possibility of veto overrides. Simply add a third player to the game, the veto override player (the "v-player").[10] This player occupies a particular place within Congress: precisely two-thirds of the members have ideal points to her left (remember that I consistently assume $c = 0$ and $x_0 > 0$). Conse-

---

[10] The results in the next few paragraphs are due to Ferejohn and Shipan 1990. I present them with a notation consistent with the rest of the chapter.

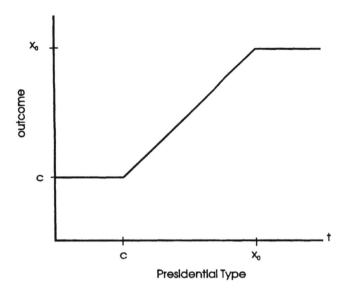

Figure 4.6. How Outcomes in the Basic Model Depend on the President's Type

quently, if the veto override player is exactly indifferent between a bill and the status quo, two-thirds of Congress prefers the bill and one-third prefers the status quo. As a result, veto override attempts succeed or fail according to the vote of the veto override player. If $\frac{1}{3} + 1$ of congressmen lie to the right of the status quo, so does the veto override player. In this configuration, Congress cannot pass a veto-proof bill that it prefers to the status quo. But otherwise it can.

Adding the veto override player to the model is straightforward. First scale the v-player's utility function just like the president's. However, denote the point that is utility equivalent to the status quo for the override player by τ (tau) rather than t (to keep the two points distinct). The veto override player's "type" is thus given by the location of tau. Given this scaling, we can employ exactly the same analysis as in the basic game.

To see the difference imposed by a qualified rather than absolute veto, consider the following scenario: the president is compromising but just barely. But the override player is much more compromising. Imagine, for instance, Truman confronting the Republican 80th Congress over the formation of labor policy. The status quo had been set during the New Deal, establishing a policy strongly supportive of labor unions. The president was a proponent of this policy, though he was willing to put some restrictions on unions' ability to strike. But the Republican Congress, responding to a wave of strikes, was determined to clip the wings of the high-flying labor movement. Figure 4.7 represents this situation, using the basic model with veto overrides.

How much power would the two sides exercise over the outcome? The president's willingness to veto the legislation prevents the hostile Congress from passing its most preferred bill. So $x = c$ is not feasible. Instead, Congress must craft a veto-proof bill if it is to accomplish anything. Thus, the location of the veto override player is critical. Historically, the veto override player in the 80th Congress was often a moderate Democrat. According to the model, then, the Republican leadership and the bill's floor managers will try to pass a bill that makes this member indifferent between the bill and the existing policy. Therefore, they will try to place the bill exactly at τ. If the bill is located at this strategic position, the model predicts, it will be enacted into law even over the president's veto. And, given the definition of the veto override player, the vote for passage should be about 2:1 in at least one of the chambers. (In Chapter 8 I relate what in fact happened.)

This example shows how the qualified veto can shift the balance of power toward Congress, relative to an absolute veto. For if Figure 4.7 fairly represents the situation and the president had an absolute veto, he could block any move from the status quo toward Congress that went farther than t. But the qualified veto would still restrict Congress to a bill at τ rather than c.

The qualified veto does not *necessarily* reduce the power of the president, relative to an absolute veto. For example, consider Figure 4.8, which may reasonably represent the confrontation between President Clinton and the Republican 104th Congress over welfare reform and similar issues. The veto override player was, plausibly, a liberal Democrat, while the president was a more moderate Democrat. Thus, tau (the key location for an override attempt) may have been to the right of t (the key location for presidential approval). If so, Congress could craft a veto-proof bill (if $\tau \leq x_0$) but could do better by finding a bill the president would (grudgingly) sign. The model predicts the outcome here to be identical to that under an absolute veto.

The following theorem summarizes the impact of a qualified veto:

Proposition 2 (Ferejohn-Shipan Theorem): A subgame perfect equilibrium to the basic game with overrides is

$$
x^* = \begin{cases} c \text{ if } \min(t, \tau) \leq c \\ \min(t, \tau) \text{ if } c < \min(t, \tau) \leq x_0 \\ x_0 \text{ if } c < x_0 < \min(t, \tau) \end{cases}
$$

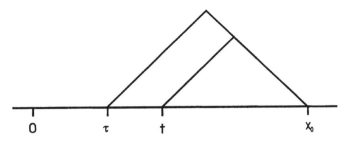

Figure 4.7. Truman Confronts the 80th Congress over Labor Legislation

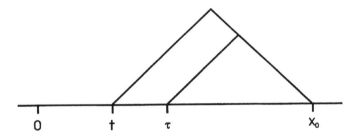

Figure 4.8. The Veto Override Player May Be Irrelevant

$$r^*(x) = \begin{cases} \text{accept if } x \in \wp_p \cup \wp_v \\ \text{veto otherwise} \end{cases}$$

$$w^*(x) = \begin{cases} \text{override if } x \in \wp_v \\ \text{sustain otherwise} \end{cases}$$

In the proposition, "$\wp_p \cup \wp_v$" denotes the union of the president's and veto player's preferred sets. The president "accepts" if the bill lies within either of the two preferred sets but "vetoes" otherwise. The veto override player's strategy is denoted by the function $w^*(x)$. And "min(t, τ)" connotes the minimum of the two values.

Evaluating the Basic Model

The basic model is much more capacious than the elementary second face of power game. Unlike that game, it indicates the policy content of bills during veto bargaining. It identifies conditions when veto power will emerge and conditions when it won't. It specifies the factors that determine the magnitude of veto power, when it does emerge. It extends easily to study the impact of a qualified rather than an absolute veto.

97

Most important, its elaboration of the logic of the veto seems persuasive, at least so far as it goes.

Empirically, however, there is reason for skepticism. First of all, do people really behave this way? More astutely: when people find themselves in a situation like that envisioned in the model, how does their actual behavior diverge from the model's predictions, and what causes the divergence? Economists have studied many ultimatum games in carefully controlled laboratory experiments, which provide arguably the best way to investigate this question. These experiments uncover two situations that lead to systematic departures from the predictions of the models. First, when the proposer fears future retribution from the chooser, she tends to make more generous offers than the model predicts (the action in the model is, after all, strictly one-shot). Second, when the proposer fears the chooser will reject the offer in outrage at its niggardliness – in other words, when the proposer believes the chooser might not obey the logic of the preferred set – she also makes a more generous offer than the really "hardball" offer the model predicts. However, when games are carefully constructed to eliminate those fears, the model's predictions stand up fairly well.[11]

Do these situations frequently arise in veto bargaining? For example, did fear of future retaliation cause Representative Joseph Martin and Senator Robert Taft, the Republican leaders in the 80th Congress, to accommodate Truman's preferences on labor policy? The history of the Taft-Hartley Act, enacted over Truman's veto, suggests otherwise. Did it check the partisan fervor of Speaker Jim Wright, when with a solid Democratic majority in the 100th Congress he tried to face down Ronald Reagan on tariff policy? Did it stay the hand of Newt Gingrich and make him shrink from confrontation with President Clinton as the triumphant majority leader tried to harvest the fruits of the Republican victory of 1994? Very doubtful. At least in periods of divided government, interbranch bargaining is often bare-knuckle politics.[12] Both sides tend to push for maximum advantage. Hardball offers are expected. It would seem, then, that the model might afford a reasonable starting place for thinking about veto bargaining. It certainly seems a useful benchmark for investigating the balance of legislative power in a separation-of-powers system.

Nonetheless, we can reject the basic model *as a model of veto bargaining* without any elaborate statistical tests at all. The problem is, the model predicts we should see no vetoes. But, of course, we do.

---

[11] Roth 1995 provides an extensive discussion.

[12] Though not always. Sam Rayburn and Lyndon Johnson apparently tried to avoid brutal confrontations with Eisenhower in 1955–56, though interbranch politics took a tougher turn prior to the 1960 presidential election.

Models of Veto Bargaining

This problem has long been recognized. In labor economics, for example, it goes under the rubric of the "Hicks paradox." Early models of strikes assumed complete and perfect information, as does the basic model. But if there is really complete and perfect information, then all the players know perfectly well how a strike will ultimately be resolved. And if the strike is at all costly for the players, they should be able to reach an equivalent agreement without bothering with the strike, thus avoiding the costs. The same argument applies to many other phenomena, including wars and vetoes.

The way to resolve this "paradox" is to abandon the assumption of complete and perfect information. I pursue this idea in the next section.

THE OVERRIDE GAME

The move from the basic model – a model of the veto as a *capability* – to a model of active *veto bargaining* requires two new elements: incomplete information, to resolve the Hicks paradox; and repeated play, for, as the data in Chapter 2 show so clearly, vetoes are dynamic phenomena.

Incomplete Information

The model introduced in this section, the override model, incorporates incomplete information by making the president and Congress somewhat uncertain about the location of the veto override player. The source of this uncertainty is the unpredictable identity of the veto override player. Although the party whips work hard to "count noses" and get their members to the floor, it is never entirely certain who will be present, and a few members may unexpectedly change their votes from what was anticipated. The ability of the president to sway undecided voters may not be clear in advance, even to himself. As a result, there can be some uncertainty about just who the critical override player will be. And consequently, there may be some doubt whether a bill is actually veto-proof.

Uncertainty about overrides can produce high drama. In some cases an attempt will hang by a hair. The vice-president may assume his chair in the Senate to cast the tie-breaking vote, if needed. Senators or representatives may arise from a sickbed to make a dramatic, unexpected entrance. No one may be sure of the outcome until the last vote is cast.[13]

[13] As interesting and occasionally important as this type of uncertainty is, I see it as somewhat peripheral to the main themes of sequential veto bargaining, which involve uncertainty about what the president will accept. Nonetheless, uncertainty about overrides provides a relatively simple yet nonetheless significant setting in which to begin studying incomplete information and veto bargaining.

Veto Bargaining

A feasible method for adding incomplete information to models of strategic interaction long eluded game theorists. In the late 1960s, however, the mathematician and philosopher John Harsanyi conquered the technical difficulties. Harsanyi was subsequently awarded the Nobel Prize in Economic Science for his accomplishment, and the key idea is sometimes called the "Harsanyi maneuver" in his honor. The basic idea is to convert a game of radically incomplete information into a much more tractable game of imperfect information.

In the override model the Harsanyi maneuver works like this. In the previous section I introduced the notion of the veto player's "type," indicated by the location of tau, the point she finds utility equivalent to the status quo. Suppose, given the situation, there are several representatives – say, a dozen – who could be the override player, depending on who is actually present. Denote the lowest utility equivalent point among these representatives as $\underline{\tau}$ and the highest as $\overline{\tau}$. There is some probability that each of the twelve representatives with τ's between $\underline{\tau}$ and $\overline{\tau}$ could turn out to be the veto override player, but the probability that a representative with higher or lower τ could be the key player is effectively zero. For a particular potential v-player, call the probability that he is the actual override player $f(\tau)$. The probabilities across the twelve possible "v-players" sum to one. The Harsanyi maneuver involves the addition of a new player, "Nature," who begins the game by drawing one of the possible veto players using these probabilities. The identity of the key player will not be revealed until the critical moment, but if the other players know the drawing probabilities – and it is assumed they do – the players can factor them into their calculations.

To avoid assuming an arbitrary number of override players, I approximate the players' uncertainty with a continuous probability distribution $f(\tau)$ defined over the interval $[\underline{\tau}, \overline{\tau}]$. Nature draws the override player from this interval using this probability distribution. The probability that the v-player's utility equivalent point is lower than τ is denoted $F(\tau)$ (where the capitol "F" indicates the cumulative probability distribution) and the probability that it is higher is $1 - F(\tau)$. To keep things simple, I assume the distribution is uniform over the interval: each possible type has the same probability of being drawn.[14] In this case,

$$F(\tau) = \frac{\tau - \underline{\tau}}{\overline{\tau} - \underline{\tau}} \text{ and } 1 - F(\tau) = \frac{\overline{\tau} - \tau}{\overline{\tau} - \underline{\tau}}.$$

Even without solving the model, we can now see how an actual veto could occur. Suppose the configuration resembles the one I discussed

---

[14] Any given continuous distribution on [0,1] could be approximated with an appropriate beta distribution and the points in this section would go through. But the simplest beta distribution, the uniform, allows the same points to be made.

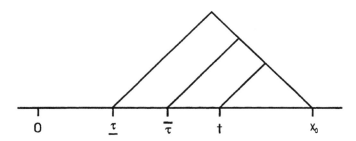

Figure 4.9. Incomplete Information about the Veto Override Player

between Truman and the 80th Congress but with a range of possible override players. This configuration is illustrated in Figure 4.9. If Congress makes a hardball offer, it would pass a bill in the interval $[\underline{\tau}, \bar{\tau}]$, since a lower offer would be futile and a higher offer needlessly accommodating. Because this interval lies outside the president's preferred set he might be inclined to veto the bill, especially since the veto player may sustain the veto (unless the offer is located at $\bar{\tau}$).

Uncertainty about τ does not necessarily imply an override attempt. In some configurations override attempts would definitely not occur. For example, if in Figure 4.9 the president's utility equivalent point t lay to the left of that of the lowest override players (i.e., if $t < \underline{\tau}$), then Congress would not need to pass a veto-proof bill. It could find a better bill (from its perspective) that the president would accept. The logic of theorem 1 would apply. Since I am interested in using the model to study overrides, I assume the configuration in Figure 4.9 in the remainder of this section.[15]

Dynamics

I introduce repeated play in the simplest possible way: an episode of veto bargaining can go through two iterations or rounds. Congress begins by passing a bill; the president can veto it or accept it; then the veto player can override or sustain the veto. The data in Chapter 2 demonstrate that bargaining may break down at this point. I incorporate this possibility by allowing "Nature" to terminate the bargaining, with probability q. Then, if bargaining does not break down, Congress repasses the vetoed bill, altering its content if it wishes. The president may reveto it if he

---

[15] The analysis is not restricted to this case however. Suppose $\underline{\tau} < t < \bar{t}$. Then the effective type space for the override player is $[\underline{\tau}, t]$. Moreover, if the distribution on $[\underline{\tau}, \bar{t}]$ is uniform so will be that on $[\underline{\tau}, t]$. So the analysis below goes through unchanged.

chooses; and the override player again opts to sustain or override. The game terminates with the players receiving payoffs according to the policy in place at the end of the game. This sequence could be extended to any number of rounds, but two is sufficient to illustrate the impact of uncertainty on the dynamics of bargaining. Figure 4.10 shows the sequence of play, taking into account the Harsanyi maneuver.

This players' reward structure requires justification. The model tries to capture the idea of electorally oriented politicians who strive to build a record for the next election. In building the record, it doesn't matter too much whether an accomplishment occurs early in a Congress or presidential term, or late: the important thing is whether it occurs at all (Mayhew 1974). In contrast, economists argue that money earlier is better than money later (since you can invest it and earn interest), and this is surely true of hikes in farm subsidies or Social Security checks. So perhaps hiking benefits early in the electoral cycle brings politicians greater rewards then hiking them later.[16] Or perhaps not: voters seem to have short-term memories for favors (Popkin et al. 1976). In that case, hiking benefits later might actually be better. These notions could be developed into competing models of optimal legislative timing but that would be a distraction from the story of veto overrides. I treat politicians as rather straightforward record builders.

As indicated in Figure 4.10, the two-period game implies two veto override players, one in the first round and one in the second. These two need not, and probably would not, be the same person. Moreover, the first veto player wouldn't know any more about the identity of the second veto player than anyone else. She must factor this uncertainty into her override decision. Should she sustain a veto in round 1 in the hope of getting a better bill in round 2? Perhaps the new override player will sustain a veto of that better bill! She will have to calculate carefully.

Equilibrium Offers

What bills will Congress pass in the two-round game? Given the evidence in Chapter 2, one might suspect that Congress will begin with a "tough" offer. Then, if the first bill is vetoed and the veto is sustained, Congress might make a concession. However, in the override model this intuition is incorrect.

In working out a solution to the game I again need to specify a solution concept. In this game, the actors have beliefs about the probable location of the next or's. A sensible solution concept requires the players

[16] David Baron builds this logic into a dynamic model of entitlement programs (1996).

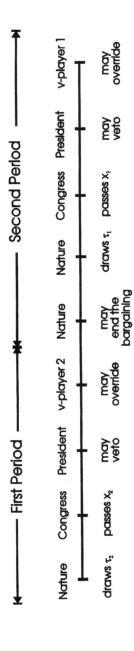

First Period ◀──────▶ Second Period

Nature	Congress	President	v-player 2	Nature	Nature	Congress	President	v-player 1
draws τ_2	passes x_2	may veto	may override	may end the bargaining	draws τ_1	passes x_1	may veto	may override

Figure 4.10. Sequence of Play in the Override Game

always to act in accord with their current beliefs. But where do the beliefs come from? A special feature of this game is that players do not learn anything about the location of the second v-player from what they observe in the first round. This follows from the fact that the two override attempts are really separate events (technically, Nature's draws are independent of one another). So beliefs about the current τ always come straight from the distribution of v-player types.[17]

It is easiest to see what will happen in the second round (if we assume bargaining gets that far), so I begin there. Since the second bill is a take-it-or-leave-it offer, both the second veto override player and the president will act in accord with their preferred sets: the v-player will override only if the second bill is as good or better for her than the status quo, and the president will accept the bill only if it is as good or better for him than the status quo. Given the configuration in Figure 4.9, Congress need never offer a second bill greater than $\bar{\tau}$, since this bill is assuredly veto-proof. Nor will it ever make an offer lower than $\underline{\tau}$, since, if it did, the president would veto and all possible override players would sustain the president's veto. Such a low offer, though attractive to Congress, would surely fail. It is possible to calculate exactly the offer a utility-maximizing Congress would make, though I leave the details to the appendix to this chapter. But, taking into account the uncertainty about the location of the second veto override player, Congress's second offer will be:

$$
x = \begin{cases} \dfrac{\tau + x_0}{2} \text{ if } \dfrac{\tau + x_0}{2} \leq \bar{\tau} \\ \bar{\tau} \text{ otherwise} \end{cases}
\tag{4.3}
$$

In other words, it will "split the difference" between the lowest possible type and the status quo, unless the status quo is quite far away, in which case it will offer a bill that is surely veto-proof (since a sustained veto would yield such an unpleasant outcome.)[18]

Now, what will happen in the first round? The following argument supplies the intuition (I supply a constructive proof in the appendix). Consider the veto override player. Any type who would accept the second offer will definitely accept a similar offer in the first round, since to turn it down is to risk receiving the status quo in the event of a bargaining breakdown, while gaining nothing from the risk. Conversely, any type who would reject the second offer will also reject an identical

---

[17] Technically, the solution concept is a perfect Bayesian equilibrium. However, given the simple information structure and the president's and v-player's strategies in the assumed configuration, optimal offers can be calculated straightforwardly using stochastic dynamic programming.

[18] So far as I know, this elementary result first appeared in Matthews 1989.

offer in the first round, since such a type prefers the status quo to the offer. In other words, type-by-type, the strategy of the first v-player must be identical to that of the second v-player. Similarly, the strategy of the president must be the same in the first round as the second round. Since the strategies of the other players are the same and Congress's information about the veto player is the same in both rounds, if x^* is the optimal offer in the second round, it must also be the optimal offer in the first round. In short, the override model predicts that *Congress passes the same bill twice; it will not make concessions.*

The following proposition summarizes this analysis.

Proposition 3: In the override game, the following is a perfect Bayesian equilibrium in the assumed configuration: each round Congress passes the same bill, which lies between $\underline{\tau}$ and $\overline{\tau}$ (inclusive of the latter). Each round the president vetoes the bill (unless it lies at $\overline{\tau}$). In each round, the v-player overrides the veto if lies above the offer but otherwise sustains it.

Outcomes in the Model

Proposition 3 implies that vetoes can occur: incomplete information has resolved the Hicks paradox. Moreover, successful overrides can occur in this model. The following outcomes are possible:

- A bill is passed and vetoed; the veto is overridden.
- A bill is passed and vetoed; the veto is sustained, and the bill dies.
- A bill is passed and vetoed; the veto is sustained; the bill is repassed and revetoed; and the veto is sustained again.
- A bill is passed and vetoed; the veto is sustained; the bill is repassed and revetoed; and the veto is overridden.

An interesting implication of this range of outcomes is that the uncertainty about the location of the veto override player advantages the president, relative to a world without that uncertainty. Recall from proposition 2 that in the configuration assumed in this section Congress can surely impose a policy on the president that is worse for him than the status quo. But when there is uncertainty about the override player, override attempts will sometimes fail (or so the override model predicts), and bargaining may break down. The president will be able to maintain the status quo where otherwise he would not. Even though the uncertainty is symmetric in the sense that neither Congress nor president has better information than the other, it advantages the president in a conflict with a hostile Congress.

The model assumes Congress always attempts an override after a regular veto, whenever feasible. Ofttimes, however, Congress does not. Suppose there were a cost to Congress if it attempted an override, for instance an opportunity cost in precious floor time. Then Congress would never attempt hopeless overrides and even some that might succeed would not be essayed.

The range of possible outcomes generated by the model resembles that actually observed, at least superficially. In the next chapter I probe the model's empirical implications more thoroughly. Nonetheless, the model is a striking – and interesting – failure in one regard: it predicts zero congressional concessions during veto bargaining. Yet one of the most notable features of real veto bargaining is that concessions almost always occur. The problem in the current model is that a failed override is just a piece of bad luck, and bad luck in the previous round will not wrest a concession from Congress. To explain concessions, I turn to another type of uncertainty, one closely connected to the concept of presidential reputation.

SEQUENTIAL VETO BARGAINING

Presidential Reputation: Neustadt Revisited

There are few truly great books on the presidency. But there is one outstanding exception to this rule: Richard Neustadt's *Presidential Power*. In his 1960 analysis of the Roosevelt, Truman, and Eisenhower administrations, Neustadt set himself the task of identifying the bases of presidential power. He found three: the formal powers of the office, such as the veto; the president's reputation in the Washington community with whom he must deal; and his standing with the public at large (1980: 164). Of these Neustadt emphasized the second, for in his view presidential power is largely the power to persuade others to do what the occupant of the White House wants. And, Neustadt argued, critical to this persuasive ability is the president's reputation for "skill" and "will" in using his power resources.

Although Neustadt's analysis immediately assumed a canonic status among scholars of the presidency, the concept of "presidential reputation" remained as he had left it. The concept was not developed further, for two reasons. First, in the years immediately following the publication of *Presidential Power* political science moved into its behavioral stage. Measurement and quantification became de rigueur. Unlike presidential popularity (for example), which can be measured in a fairly plausible way through public opinion polls, Neustadt's "presidential reputation" seemed too ineffable for hard-nosed study. But perhaps even more important, the conceptual foundations of "reputation" remained murky –

106

and not just in political science. Nowhere in the social sciences was new light shed on the concept. No path could be seen for developing Neustadt's insights. And so they remained largely in the state he left them.

Far removed from presidential studies, however, two developments in game theory promised to break this intellectual stasis. The first was, again, the Harsanyi maneuver, which rendered tractable strategic situations with incomplete information. The second was the formulation of a powerful solution concept tailored to dynamic games of incomplete information, games in which the players operate under uncertainty, learn about each other over the course of play, and change their actions as learning occurs. This solution concept, known in slightly different versions as "sequential equilibrium" or "perfect Bayesian equilibrium," was developed by game theorists David Kreps and Robert Wilson (1987), though earlier work by Roger Myerson (1978) was closely related.

The power and flexibility of the new tools meant the concept of reputation could finally find a new and much more solid foundation, though it took some time for social scientists to realize this. The critical moment came with the simultaneous publication in 1982 of papers by Kreps and Wilson, and Paul Milgrom and John Roberts. These papers were among the most influential in economics during the 1980s.

The basic insight of the Kreps-Wilson-Milgrom-Roberts (KWMR) papers is that reputation and incomplete information are inextricably linked: your reputation *is* the beliefs that others have about your incompletely known characteristic. Those beliefs – your reputation – affect others' actions. Moreover, in a dynamic strategic setting their beliefs will evolve in response to your observed actions. Consequently, by choosing your actions carefully you may be able to manipulate your reputation to your advantage. Conversely, the need to maintain an effective reputation may inhibit your actions. KWMR showed how these ideas could be analyzed very precisely using the Harsanyi maneuver and the new solution concept. Suddenly, it became possible to construct detailed theoretical models of reputation building.

The implications of this work for the study of power are sweeping. Where the concept of subgame perfection made it possible to develop models of the second face of power (like the basic model), perfect Bayesian equilibrium makes it possible to develop models of what political scientists have called the "third face of power." The third face of power has two dimensions. The first involves transformation of values, in which the oppressed take on the values of the oppressor. This idea remains elusive to formal analysis. But the second involves the manipulation of others' beliefs. So, for example, coal miners refuse to strike because the company's reputation makes the miners believe a strike will be futile and self-defeating – a reputation carefully cultivated by the companies (Gaventa 1980). How such a power relationship could come into existence and be maintained, and how it might end, are topics ideally suited to the new tools.

Well within the reach of the new tools is Neustadt's concept of presidential reputation. Exactly the ideas in the KWMR papers appear repeatedly in *Presidential Power*. "A President's effect on them [the men who share in governing] is heightened or diminished by their thoughts about his probable reaction to their doing. They base their expectations on what they can see of him. . . . what these men think may or may not be 'true' but it is the reality on which they act, at least until their calculations turn out wrong" (1980:45). Therefore, "they must anticipate, as best they can, his *ability* and *will* to make use of the bargaining advantages he has. Out of what others think of him emerge his opportunities for influence with them. If he would maximize his prospects for effectiveness, he must concern himself with what they think" (p. 46).

Neustadt illustrates these points with telling examples. For example, Eisenhower diminished his power prospects in 1957–58 by sending contradictory signals that undermined his policy reputation on Capitol Hill (1980:49–60). In contrast, in 1959 he used veto threats, vetoes, and rhetoric to build an effective reputation (pp. 61–62).

Neustadt spells out the necessity for incomplete information about the president in a particularly compelling form:

In a world of perfect rationality and unclouded perception it might turn out that Washingtonians could take the past performance of a President as an exact, precise, definitive determinant of future conduct, case by case. The known and open record, wholly understood, could be ransacked for counterparts to all details of each new situation. His skill, or lack of it, in using comparable vantage points for comparable purposes in like conditions, could be gauged with such precision that forecasting his every move would become a science practiced with the aid of mathematics. In the real world, however, nobody is sure what aspects of the past fit which piece of the present or future. As the illustrations in this book suggest, particulars of time, of substance, organization, personalities, may make so great a difference, case by case, that forecasting remains a tricky game and expectations rest upon perceptions of a most imperfect sort. (1980:46)

Propositions 1 and 2 are precisely the mathematical predictions that Neustadt envisioned. Detailing the "tricky game" of "forecasting" is the subject of the sequential veto bargaining model.

Adding Presidential Reputation to the Models

Before the new analytical tools can be used, a key question must be answered: what is the president's reputation *about*? What entity or variable is the subject of incomplete information? Neustadt states his view in several places: "The men he [the president] would persuade must be convinced in their own minds that he has the skill and will enough to *use* his advantages" (1980:44). It is these "residual impressions of tenacity and skill accumulating in the minds of Washingtonians-at-large" that constitute his reputation (p. 48). From the president's perspective, an effective reputation for "skill and will" must be such as to "induce as much uncertainty as possible about the consequences of ignoring what he [the president] wants. If he cannot make men think him bound to win, his need is to keep them from thinking they can cross him without risk, or that they can be sure what risks they run" (ibid.).

This formulation is helpful and puzzling at the same time. It is helpful because it links the president's reputation to his "advantages," his "vantage points" in Neustadt's phrase. His reputation will concern his willingness to use his powers. This is what his adversaries must predict. So it is in the *confluence* of formal powers and intangible reputation that presidential power lies. It is puzzling because "skill" is analytically intractable and "will" is extraordinarily ambiguous. Good models of strategic skill in politics must await a much deeper understanding of bounded rationality than contemporary social science possesses. But we seem to be waiting for Godot: despite nearly half a century of work, bounded rationality remains one of the philosopher's stones of modern social science.[19] This is not to suggest skill is unimportant in presidential politics: it surely is. But, at least at the end of the twentieth century a political theorist has little useful to say about it.

What then about "will"? Neustadt is rather vague about what he means by a reputation for "will" but sometimes he seems to invoke a quality of character, "grit" or "pluck." But suppose Congress were absolutely certain about the president's policy preferences. Would tenacity, toughness, or grit allow the president to escape the iron logic of propositions 1 and 2? Only if "will" actually means "willingness to behave irrationally." Suppose a president cultivated the image of a hothead who vetoed in a fit of pique, even if it meant cutting off his nose to spite his face (in policy terms). Such a reputation might well strengthen his bargaining position with Congress – recall the laboratory experiments on ultimatum games or game theorist Thomas Schelling's famous arguments about the value of appearing irrational (Shelling 1960). But no president, not Nixon or even Andrew Jackson, has tried to build a reputation as an irrational hothead in matters of domestic policy. As a practical matter, impetuous irrationality meshes poorly with the deliber-

---

[19] On the other hand, see Rubenstein 1998 and Young 1998.

ate pace of legislating. A reputation as a loose cannon is probably electoral poison.

Consider instead how one builds a useful reputation in some other setting, for example when bargaining over a car or in a weekend bazaar. You try to create the impression that the merchandise is worth little to you. For example, you may feign to leave the shop when the merchant announces his opening price. You lament your limited budget. In short, you don't try to create a reputation as a "tough bargainer." You *become* a tough bargainer by creating the impression you have a naturally low "striking price," the highest price you would possibly agree to. If the merchant believes your striking price is truly low, he will come down in price if he wants to sell.

What is the equivalent of the president's striking price in bargaining with Congress? It is the president's reservation policy, the point beyond which he will not go because he would rather veto and retain the status quo. In the spatial framework, it is exactly t, the point utility-equivalent to the status quo. The president's willingness to veto depends critically on the location of the bill relative to t. But for exactly the reasons enumerated by Neustadt – "the particulars of time, of substance, of organization, personalities" – Congress will often be somewhat uncertain where t lies. Over the course of a bargaining episode, the president may be able to turn this uncertainty to his advantage.

The Sequential Veto Bargaining Model

Much of the apparatus I developed for the override game transfers directly to sequential veto bargaining (SVB). Now, however, Congress's uncertainty concerns the president's policy preferences, which, of course, the president himself knows perfectly well. The Harsanyi maneuver provides a method to capture Congress's uncertainty about the president's policy preferences. So at the beginning of the game let t be drawn from the interval $[\underline{t}, \overline{t}]$ using the common-knowledge distribution $F(t)$, the same uniform distribution as in the override game. The president knows his own type t, which remains fixed for the entire game, but Congress does not.

The play of the SVB game depends heavily on the location of $[\underline{t}, \overline{t}]$ relative to the override player's reservation policy and Congress's ideal point $c = 0$. For the moment assume the configuration shown in Figure 4.11, that is, $0 \leq \underline{t}$ and $\overline{t} \leq \tau$. Allow the same type of dynamics as before: the game moves through two rounds of bargaining, with the possibility of a breakdown in bargaining after an initial veto.

All seems similar to the override game, except one thing: the president's true type t is fixed throughout the game, while the identity of the

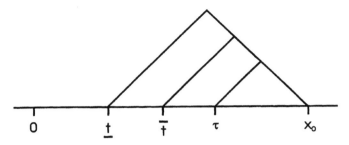

Figure 4.11. Sequential Veto Bargaining: The All Compromisers Case

override player varied from round to round – a seemingly small difference but sufficient to transform the strategic situation. Whatever Congress learns about the president in the first round can and will be used in the second round. The president thus has an incentive to build a policy reputation in the first round, in order to extract a better bill in the second.

To see how this might work, picture Congress in the first round of a bargaining episode. Congress begins with a notion of the range of possible presidential preferences and so bases the content of its initial bill on its expectations about what the president might accept. Congress will not pass a bill every likely type of president would veto – such a bill would be pointless. Nor is it likely (except under special circumstances, detailed shortly) to pass a bill the president would surely sign whatever his true preferences. To do so would be to yield too much. Thus, Congress is likely to pass a tough bill but one with a reasonable chance of enactment. Suppose, though, the president vetoes the bill. How will this affect his policy reputation? If the president had been sufficiently accommodating, he would have accepted the initial bill rather than risk a breakdown and receipt of the status quo. Because the president did not accept the bill, Congress can be quite sure the president did *not* have those preferences. In other words, Congress can screen out some types of presidential preferences after seeing a veto. Given the screening, Congress will see the president as somewhat "tougher" than it did before (in the sense that his policy preferences cannot be very accommodating). The content of the second bill, if Congress gets the chance to enact it, will reflect this new understanding of the president's policy preferences. Accordingly, the second bill will incorporate policy concessions.

In the first round of bargaining the president can anticipate what Congress will offer in the second round, if he vetoes the first bill. Depending on his preferences, the president may find the second bill, if it includes concessions, more attractive than the first bill. In fact, it may be so attractive that he is willing to risk a breakdown in order to alter his policy reputation and thus extract the better bill from Congress. Such a president would engage in a *strategic veto* in the first round. But can this work if Congress knows the president has the temptation to do so? This is indeed a "tricky game," in Neustadt's phrase! But it is possible to untangle.[20]

Optimal Bills and Strategic Vetoes

By this point, the strategies of president and Congress in the second round will be familiar. Since the second bill is a take-it-or-leave-it offer, the president will veto it only if it lies outside his preferred set. Let us say that Congress, based upon its initial bill and a presidential veto, has screened out all types with t's less than a particular value, call it t_2. So in the second round, Congress believes the president's type definitely falls somewhere in the range $[t_2, \bar{t}]$. Using the same methods employed in the analysis of the override game, I show in the appendix to this chapter that Congress's second offer will then be

$$
x = \begin{cases} \dfrac{t_2 + x_0}{2} & \text{if } \dfrac{t_2 + x_0}{2} \leq \bar{t} \\ \bar{t} & \text{otherwise} \end{cases}
$$

Since this is exactly the form of the offer in the override game – an average of the lower bound on types and the status quo, unless the status quo is quite distant (see equation 4.3) – this should not be surprising.

Determining the president's strategy in the first round is straightforward. Call the offer in the first round x_2 (meaning, the offer occurs when two opportunities for vetoes remain) and that in the second round x_1 (meaning, only one opportunity for a veto remains).[21] The president, seeing x_2, is able to estimate that Congress will pass x_1 in the second round in the event of a veto, as long as bargaining did not break down. Then there would be a type who is exactly indifferent between accepting

[20] The first models of this type, focused on economic bargaining, can be found in Sobel and Takahashi 1983 and Fudenberg and Tirole 1983. Subsequently, this type of model has been used to study strikes, settlement in negligence suits, and monopoly pricing by durable goods monopolists. Gibbons 1992 provides a fairly accessible introduction, and Fudenberg and Tirole 1991b a more advanced review. Banks 1991 is a superb review of models in political science in which strategic reputation building is important.

[21] This somewhat unfortunate numbering follows a standard convention, which proves helpful with extensions to any arbitrary number of rounds of bargaining. Because I consider such extensions elsewhere, I maintain it here (see Cameron and Elmes 1995).

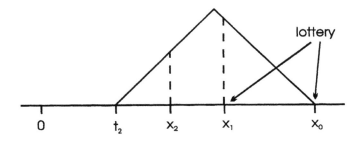

Type t_2 is indifferent between accepting x_2 and rejecting it in favor of a lottery between x_1 and x_0.

Figure 4.12. The Indifferent Type

the bird in the hand, x_2, and the gamble created by a veto, that is, between receiving the unattractive status quo and the quite desirable bird in the bush, x_1. Call this exactly indifferent type t_2.

Figure 4.12 illustrates such an indifferent type. He is presented the first offer, x_2, so if he accepts it he certainly has $V(x_2)$. If he rejects it, he may be offered x_1, which is more attractive. But it is a risky prospect, for with probability q he receives instead the status quo, x_0. Type t_2 is exactly indifferent between the two choices. Critically, all presidential types *lower* than t_2 prefer the first offer and so accept it, while all types higher than t_2 prefer the gamble and so veto the first bill. Hence, the president's strategy in the first round is simple: accept the first bill if $t \leq t_2$ but otherwise veto. If Congress understands this strategy, and can follow the president's reasoning, then it knows that $t > t_2$ if it sees a veto in the first round.

Somewhat surprisingly, the relationship in Figure 4.12, the equation for Congress's last offer, the shared network of mutual expectations, and the logic of utility maximization tie down Congress's twin offers. In the appendix, I calculate the optimal first offer to be

$$x_2^* = \frac{1 + 4q - q^2}{2(1 + 3q)} x_0 + \frac{(1 + q)^2}{2(1 + 3q)} t \qquad (4.4)$$

and the optimal second offer to be

$$x_1^* = \frac{1 + 5q}{2(1 + 3q)} x_0 + \frac{(1 + q)}{2(1 + 3q)} t \qquad (4.5)$$

while the critical value for t, t_2, is

$$t_2^* = \frac{2q}{1 + 3q} x_0 + \frac{1 + q}{1 + 3q} \underline{t} \tag{4.6}$$

These equations may appear distressingly complicated, but note that the quotients in each expression add to one. So in each case, the critical value is just a weighted average of the status quo and the lowest possible type. The forbidding appearance of the equations reflects the complex way the weighting depends on q, the probability of a bargaining breakdown.

A Numerical Example. To get a feel for the model's predictions, it is helpful to work through a numerical example. Suppose Congress begins with the belief that the lowest possible type $\underline{t} = 0$ while the highest possible type is $\bar{t} = x_0 = 1$ (recall that beliefs are assumed uniform over the interval). In other words, Congress is sure the president is a compromiser but is rather uncertain about his exact preferences. Let the probability of a breakdown in bargaining following a veto $q = \frac{1}{2}$. Congress begins by offering x_2^* which equation 4.4 reveals to be .55. The president accepts this bill if his true type t is less than t_2^*, which equation 4.6 reveals to be .4. Types with $t > .4$ veto the initial bill. Having seen the veto, Congress updates its beliefs about the president's type. Its new beliefs are restricted to the interval [.4,1]. Following the veto, there is a 50–50 chance bargaining breaks down. If it does, the status quo remains in place. But if it does not, Congress makes a second and final offer, which reflects the president's new policy reputation. Equation 4.5 indicates this bill will be placed at .7. Congress makes a rather large policy concession. If the president's true type falls below .7, he accepts the second bill. If not, he vetoes it once again.

The process of reputation building in the example illustrates the phenomenon Neustadt discussed in connection with "the new Eisenhower" of 1959. Through miscues and internal dissension, Eisenhower appeared to Congress in 1957–58 as a likely accommodator, or not a very distant compromiser, particularly in fields like education or welfare. Congress moved to take advantage of the policy opportunity. But a stunning set of vetoes in 1959 forced Congress to change its view: the president was indeed committed to a restrictive budget, low taxes, and parsimonious government. His vetoes, along with his rhetoric, recast his reputation.

The example also illustrates the concept of a strategic veto. All the presidential types between .4 and .55 actually prefer the first bill to the status quo. But that does not dissuade them from vetoing the bill. They know that if they do they face a reasonable chance of getting a much more attractive second offer though, of course, bargaining might break down and leave them with the unattractive status quo. Nonetheless, for these types the gamble is worthwhile, so they take the plunge and veto. In fact, types as low as $t = .25$ prefer the second bill to the first, if they could simply choose between the two bills without the risk of a breakdown in bargaining.[22] But for types between .25 and .4, the second offer is not so attractive as it is for the types between .4 and .55. The risk of a bargaining breakdown dissuades them from attempting a strategic veto. Types between 0 and .25 actually prefer the first bill to the second, even neglecting the possibility of a breakdown. They also prefer the first bill to the status quo. Needless to say, they accept the first bill.

Other Cases. Extending the analysis from two rounds to any finite number involves no new principles, only a great deal of tedious calculation. However, there are several other configurations of preferences that deserve mention. All are straightforward extensions of the basic case.[23]

Suppose the top of the type space lies to the left of the status quo – that is, $\bar{t} < x_0$. As Congress screens out the lower types, its offers rise. In no case will Congress offer a bill greater than $\bar{t}$. But Congress may indeed offer a bill at $\bar{t}$, in which case the president surely accepts. Such a *constrained offer* is more likely to occur if the status quo is far from Congress's ideal point and accommodating types have been eliminated.

Suppose the President may be an *accommodator* – that is, $\underline{t} < 0$. If the probability that the president is an accommodator is sufficiently large, Congress may begin the bargaining by offering its ideal policy. If this bill is vetoed, the remaining bargaining proceeds similarly to the all compromisers case.

Suppose the president may be either a *compromiser* or a *recalcitrant* – that is $0 \leq \underline{t} < x_0 < \bar{t}$. Then bargaining proceeds as indicated in the all compromisers case, but offers can never be constrained (since they will never exceed the status quo).

Suppose the reserve policy for the veto override player lies not to the right of the status quo but to the left. Then bargaining proceeds as indicated previously. However, offers never exceed the reserve policy. The following might happen. Congress begins by passing a bill it hopes a compromiser will accept. If the bill is vetoed, Congress knows the president has rather distant policy preferences. Its next offer may then be

[22] Types whose ideal point z lies closer to .7 than .55 prefer .7; those whose ideal point lies closer to .55 than .7 prefer .55. The midway point between .7 and .55 is .625, so .7 is more attractive for those whose $z > .625$. Recall that $t = 2z - x_0$ so types greater than $2(.625) - 1 = .25$ prefer .7. Note that this comparison is between two "birds in the hand"; it neglects the gamble implied by a bargaining breakdown.
[23] For detailed exegesis of these cases, see Cameron and Elmes 1995.

geared for an *override* attempt rather than presidential acceptance, depending on the location of the override player.

These results are summarized in the following proposition:

Proposition 4: In the SVB model, Congress makes concessions in repassed bills; there is a positive probability the president accepts each bill; and there is a positive probability no offer is accepted (unless the final offer equals *ī*) even if bargaining does not break down. In the first period, some types of president are willing to strategically veto, that is, to veto a bill they prefer to the status quo.

What's Missing?

Needless to say, the sequential veto bargaining model omits some factors that may affect the politics of the veto. For example, reputation is sometimes a two-edged sword. The president builds a policy reputation with his vetoes, and if he wants to extract substantial concessions from Congress, he needs to appear somewhat extreme. But appearing extreme may sometimes hurt the president with the voters – after all, it was they who elected Congress as well. If appearing too extreme risks a heavy cost in votes, the president may not be as ready with strategic vetoes as the model predicts. In other words, the underlying dynamics of the model will remain the same but appear in more subdued fashion. An added complexity occurs if Congress tries to use "veto bait" to force a veto in order to make the president appear extreme (Groseclose and McCarty 1996). Rather than continuing to pursue additional strategic complexity, however, I will take the models in hand and bring them to data.

CONCLUSION

We now have a framework for thinking about override attempts, and a framework for analyzing sequential veto bargaining. Although these models are new, they represent rather straightforward extensions of a standard model, the Romer-Rosenthal model of take-it-or-leave-it bargaining, and build on a decades-long tradition of spatial modeling in political science.

The question remains: can the models explain the observed patterns in real veto bargaining? Are they able to bring order to the welter of facts compiled in Chapter 2's natural history of the veto?

Appendix to Chapter 4

Basic Model

Proofs of propositions 1 and 2 are readily available elsewhere so I do not consider them here.

Override Model

Because there are two rounds of play, I distinguish decisions made in one round from those in the other via subscripting. Following a standard convention in stochastic dynamic programming, I denote the *last* period as "$n = 1$" and the *prior* period as "$n = 2$," and subscript relevant variables accordingly.

A more complete version of Theorem 3 is the following.

Proposition 3: A perfect Bayesian equilibrium to the override game is:

$$x_n^* = \begin{cases} \dfrac{\tau + x_0}{2} & \text{if } \dfrac{\tau + x_0}{2} \leq \bar{\tau} \\ \bar{\tau} & \text{otherwise} \end{cases}$$

$$r_n^*(x_n) = \begin{cases} \text{accept if } x_n \in \wp_p \\ \text{veto otherwise} \end{cases}$$

$$w_n^*(x_n) = \begin{cases} \text{override if } x_n \in \wp_v \\ \text{sustain otherwise} \end{cases}$$

$n = (2,1)$, and beliefs are everywhere determined by the common-knowledge distribution $f(\tau)$.

Proof. The proof is by construction. In the second period, the v-player will override if $x_1 \in [\tau_1, x_0]$ but otherwise sustain. The president

117

will definitely veto any non-veto-proof bill not in his preferred set, since there is a chance the v-player will sustain the veto, thus killing the bill. He will be indifferent about vetoing a definitely veto-proof bill not in his preferred set, that is, $x_1 \in [\overline{\tau}, t)$. We can specify any action in such a contingency; I assume the president does not veto such a bill.

Given these strategies, for Congress $x_1 = \overline{\tau}$ dominates any higher offer, since the president will accept both with certainty while the former yields greater utility. Also, offers above $\underline{t}$ dominate those below, since ones above $\underline{t}$ have a chance of enactment while those below do not. So we need only consider offers in $(\underline{\tau}, \overline{\tau}]$. Under the assumed configuration, the president will veto all these bills. Consequently, Congress's problem is to choose the second offer to maximize

$$EU_1 \equiv \frac{x^1 - \tau}{\Delta \tau} U(x_1) + \frac{\overline{\tau} - x_1}{\Delta \tau} U(x_0)$$

$$\Rightarrow \frac{1}{\Delta \tau} \left(-(x_1 - \underline{\tau})x_1 - \left(\overline{\tau} - x_1 \right)x_0 \right)$$

where $\Delta \tau \equiv \overline{\tau} - \underline{\tau}$. The first quotient gives the probability v-player 1 overrides the veto, the second the probability she sustains the veto. An interior maximum requires

$$\frac{\partial EU_1}{\partial x_1} = \frac{1}{\Delta \tau} \left(-2x_1 + \underline{\tau} + x_0 \right) = 0$$

$$\Rightarrow x_1 = \frac{\underline{\tau} + x_0}{2}.$$

Hence, in the second period

$$x_1^* = \begin{cases} \dfrac{\underline{\tau} + x_0}{2} & \text{if } \dfrac{\underline{\tau} + x_0}{2} \le \overline{\tau} \\ \overline{\tau} & \text{otherwise} \end{cases}$$

In the first period, there is the possibility that the v-player will strategically sustain a veto, that is, turn down a bill in order to get a more attractive bill in the second period, albeit risking the possibility of a breakdown. Given some offer in the first period, $x_2 < x_1^*$, there is a type of v-player $\hat{t}_2$ who is exactly indifferent between the two offers:

$$V_2^v (x_2; \hat{t}_2) = (1 - q)\pi(x_1^*)V_2^v(x_1^*; \hat{t}_2)$$

where $\pi(x_1^* = \dfrac{x_1^* - \tau}{\Delta \tau}$ denotes the probability that the second v-player will override the veto of the optimal second offer, and V^v_i denotes the

118

utility of v-player i, which is (using the definition of rescaled utility in equation 4.2)

$$V_i^v (x_i; x_0, \tau) = \frac{|x_0 - \tau_i| - |\tau_i + x_0 - 2x_i|}{2}$$

where $\tau_i = 2v_i - x_0$, letting v denote the v-player's ideal point. Substituting this definition of utility into the indifference relationship and solving for the first offer yields

$$x_2 = \hat{t}_2 + (1 - q)\pi(x_1^*)(x_0 - x_1^*)$$

or more conveniently $x_2 \equiv \hat{t}_2 + k$. In other words, if the first offer is lower than this value, the first v-player will strategically sustain the veto in order to get the chance to enact the second offer. For a given first offer, the probability that the offer is this low is (from Congress's perspective) just the probability that $\hat{t}_2 > x_2 - k$, which is $\frac{\bar{\tau} - x_2 + k}{\Delta\tau}$, while the probability the first veto player will override the veto (thus ending the bargaining) is $\frac{x_2 - k - \underline{\tau}}{\Delta\tau}$. Consequently, the problem facing Congress is to choose the first offer to maximize

$$EU_2 = \frac{x_2 - k - \underline{\tau}}{\Delta\tau} U(x_2) + \frac{\bar{\tau} - x_2 + k}{\Delta\tau} \left(qU(x_0) + (1 - q)EU_1(x_1^*)\right).$$

After using the definition of Congress's utility, equation 4.1, the following describes an interior maximum:

$$\frac{\partial EU_2}{\partial x_2} = \frac{1}{\Delta\tau}\left(-(x_2 - k - \underline{\tau}) - x_2 - EU_2(x_1^*)\right) = 0.$$

In this expression, the expected utility of the optimum offer in the second period is

$$-\frac{x_1^* - \underline{t}}{\Delta\tau}x_1^* - \frac{\bar{\tau} - x_1^*}{\Delta\tau}.$$

Substitution and solution for x_2 then yields

$$x_2 = \frac{\underline{\tau} + x_0}{2}.$$

Hence, in the first period the optimum offer is

$$x_2^* = \begin{cases} \dfrac{\underline{\tau} + x_0}{2} & \text{if } \dfrac{\underline{\tau} + x_0}{2} \leq \bar{\tau} \\ \bar{\tau} & \text{otherwise} \end{cases}$$

119

which is the same as in the second period. Q.E.D.

> *Corollary to theorem 3.* The probability of an override, given an attempt, is bounded by ½ and 1.

Proof. The probability of an override, given an attempt, is the probability that τ lies below x^*, that is

$$\frac{x_1^* - \tau}{\Delta\tau} = 1 - \frac{\overline{\tau} - x_1^*}{\Delta\tau}$$

which, given x^*,

$$\Rightarrow \frac{1}{2} + \frac{x_0 - \overline{\tau}}{2\Delta\tau}.$$

The quotient may be zero (if $\overline{\tau} = x_0$) but otherwise must be positive. The upper bound on the probability is 1 (which occurs at $x = \overline{\tau}$). Q.E.D.

Sequential Veto Bargaining

The key to constructing equilibria is the following observation. Given two bills, x_i and x_{i-1}, with $x_i < x_{i-1}$, and a probability of breakdown q, there will be a presidential type in period i, t_i, who is just indifferent between the two offers. For this type,

$$(x_i;x_0,t_i) = (1 - q)V(x_{i-1};x_0,t_i) + qV(x_0;x_0,t_i). \tag{4.7}$$

This is the relationship illustrated in Figure 4.12. Lemma 1 then follows (recall that z_i is t_i's ideal point).

> *Lemma 1 (cutoff-rule property):* If type t_i is indifferent between two bills x_i and x_{i-1}, with $x_i < z_i < x_{i-1}$, then all types less than t_i prefer x_i to x_{i-1}, while all higher types prefer x_{i-1} to x_i.

The cutoff-rule property has two implications. First, consider an ascending sequence of offers all less than min $\{x_0,\overline{\tau}\}$ (there is no need to be concerned with higher offers since Congress would never make such offers). Then the president's strategy takes the form of a simple cutoff rule in all periods except the last: accept x_i if $t \leq t_i$, and reject otherwise. In the last period $i = 1$, the rule is: accept x_1 if $t \leq x_1$, and reject otherwise, just as in the one-shot game. Second, given this cutoff rule and the sequence of offers, Congress can be certain following a veto that $t > t_i$. This fact allows Congress to update its beliefs about the president's type and make subsequent offers contingent on those beliefs. The

120

progressive winnowing down of possible types as offers are rejected gives the model its distinctive flavor of screening.

I now calculate equilibria in the two-period game. In brief, one finds the optimal last-period offer; then, backwards induction using the indifference relation (equation 4.7) reveals the optimal earlier offer. The cutoff rule used by the president allows updating of beliefs, for example, if priors are uniform on $[\underline{t}, \bar{t}]$ and all types lower than t_2 accept the first offer and all higher types veto, then following rejection of the first offer beliefs must be uniform on $[t_2,\bar{t}]$.

Let $U_i(\kappa)$ denote Congress's expected utility at time i when beliefs are uniform on $[\kappa,\bar{t}]$. In the two-period game, from dynamic programming

$$U_2(\underline{t}) = \max_{x_2,t_2} - x_2\left(\frac{t_2 - t}{\bar{t} - \underline{t}}\right) + \left(\frac{\bar{t} - t_2}{\bar{t} - \underline{t}}\right)\{-qx_0 + (1 - q)U_1(t_2)\} \quad (4.8)$$

Subject to

$$(x_i;x_0,t_2) = (1 - q)V(x_1;x_0,t_2) + qV(x_0;x_0,t_2). \quad (4.9)$$

In equation 4.8,

$$U_1(t_2) = - x_1^*(t_2)\left(\frac{x_1^*(t_2) - t_2}{\bar{t} - t_2}\right) - x_0\left(\frac{\bar{t} - x_1^*(t_2)}{\bar{t} - t_2}\right)$$

where the asterisk on the second-period offer $x_1(t_2)$ denotes the utility-maximizing value given uniform beliefs on $[t_2,\bar{t}]$. Simple optimization indicates that

$$x_1^*(t_2) = \frac{x_0 + t_2}{2}$$

if $\frac{x_0 + t_2}{2} < \bar{t}$ and $\bar{t}$ otherwise. Assume the former "unconstrained" offer case (a detailed analysis of the "constrained" offer case in the n-period game can be found in Cameron and Elmes 1995). Substituting presidential utility (equation 4.2) into the indifference relation (equation 4.7) yields $x_i = t_i + (1 - q)(x_0 - x_{i-1})$, so equation 4.9 may be rewritten as

$$x_2 = t_2 + (1 - q)(x_0 - x_1) \quad (4.10)$$

Substituting equation 4.10 and the above expression for $x_1^*(t_2)$ into equation 4.8 yields an expression for $U_2(\underline{t})$ that is solely a function of t_2 and the parameters $(\underline{t},\bar{t},x_0,q)$. Maximizing this expression with respect to t_2 and solving for t_2 then yields

$$t_2^* = \frac{2q}{1 + 3q} x_0 + \frac{1 + q}{1 + 3q} \underline{t}. \qquad (4.6)$$

Substituting this value into the expression for $x_1^*(t_2)$ yields

$$x_1^* = \frac{1 + 5q}{2(1 + 3q)} x_0 + \frac{(1 + q)}{2(1 + 3q)} \underline{t} \qquad (4.5)$$

and substituting t_2^* and x_1^* into equation 4.8 to solve for x_2 yields

$$x_2^* = \frac{1 + 4q - q^2}{2(1 + 3q)} x_0 + \frac{(1 + q)^2}{2(1 + 3q)} \underline{t}. \qquad (4.4)$$

The expression for t_2^* and x_i^* ($i = 1,2$) are weighted averages of x_0 and $\underline{t}$, that is, the coefficients are nonnegative and sum to one. Extensions to the general n-period game and detailed analyses of the "other cases" noted in text can be found in Cameron and Elmes 1995.

Multiple versus Unique Equilibria and Comparative Statics

In Chapter 5, I use the comparative statics of the SVB model to generate empirically testable propositions about veto bargaining. It is certainly possible to empirically test models with multiple equilibria; Cox 1997 provides an example. However, comparative statics become problematic in the face of multiple equilibria, since changes in parameters may not involve local perturbations in a given equilibrium but shifts across different equilibria. Multiple equilibria frequently arise in signaling and screening models, because Bayes's rule does not tie down beliefs at information sets off the equilibrium path. The looseness of these beliefs can give rise to multiple equilibria.

Multiple equilibria do not arise in the SVB model, as the strong backward induction flavor of the foregoing derivation may have suggested. (Of course, the model displays very different behavior depending on its parameter values.) The intuition for the absence of multiple equilibria is that the president is limited to "veto" or "accept," with the latter ending the game. Hence, there isn't much room to play with beliefs off the equilibrium path. This is a typical feature of bargaining models with one-sided offers and one-sided incomplete information (see Sutton 1986 for additional discussion).

5

Explaining the Patterns

As children, most of us delighted in Rudyard Kipling's "just-so" stories. Kipling began with a simple fact, for example, elephants have long noses. Then he made up a fanciful story to explain it: perhaps a crocodile stretched an elephant's nose and the trait was passed down to other elephants. Just so!

In the previous chapter, I began with some simple facts, and then made up a causal mechanism to explain them. The three facts were: vetoes actually occur, veto chains are relatively common, and concessions often occur over the course of a chain. The first model failed to generate any of these patterns, but it supplied a useful framework for additional thought. The override model can generate the first and second patterns, but not the third. The sequential veto bargaining (SVB) model can generate all three.

Are the override and SVB models merely just-so stories? Or do they capture something real about the dynamics of interbranch bargaining? How can we tell? To answer this question I rely on the criteria outlined toward the end of Chapter 3. As indicated there, a sine qua non for a good model is an ability to explain empirical puzzles it was not designed to explain. Table 2.12, which I reproduce in separate tables throughout this chapter, is filled with empirical puzzles that go well beyond the three "stylized facts." For example, why does the probability of a veto increase with legislative significance during divided government, but not during unified government? Why are veto chains short? Why don't any of the covariates predict the success of an override attempt, once the decision to attempt an override is made? Can the models explain *these* facts? If so, they begin to look less like just-so stories and more like real models of real politics.

Veto Bargaining

Interrogating Formal Models

Seeing how an articulated, internally consistent causal mechanism explains a pattern in data sounds as if it should be easy. Sometimes it is; frequently it is not. The trick is to "deductively interrogate" the model, to show how the pattern is a logical corollary of the model's assumptions (Shepsle 1986).

Three methods are commonly used for deductively interrogating formal models. The first is "comparative statics." The idea is to vary a particular parameter in the model (like the distance between Congress and president) and then deduce an observable consequence (for instance, the effect on the probability of a veto). In the case of dynamic models like the sequential bargaining model, the method of comparative statics extends to "comparative dynamics." Here, the analyst varies a particular parameter and then works out the changes that result in a series of future periods. In other words, the model predicts the path of variables over time, following a specific change.

Comparative statics and dynamics often yield predictions about directions of change without yielding estimates of the magnitudes of change. So they usually take the form of predictions such as: if the distance between the president and Congress increases, the probability of a veto weakly increases (goes up or stays the same but does not decrease). They rarely take a form such as: increasing the interactor distance by 10% will increase the probability of a veto by 6%. This degree of precision requires calibrating the model's structural parameters with real data, something rarely attempted in political science. Nonetheless, even absent such calibration, it is possible to use the third method when a model is sufficiently tied down by specific assumptions. One proceeds by calculating sample equilibrium values given particular parameter values. By varying the parameters and recalculating, it is possible to get a feel for relative magnitudes, at least within reasonable ranges. These three methods – comparative statics, comparative dynamics, and exact calculation of sample equilibria – provide the tools for deductively interrogating a model. I use all three in this chapter.

EXPLAINING BASIC PATTERNS IN VETO BARGAINING

The place to begin is the most basic patterns: the probability of a veto for initially passed legislation, the frequency of veto chains, and their length. I pay close attention to the impact of divided government and legislative significance.

124

Explaining the Patterns

Table 5.1. *Empirical patterns: Veto probabilities for initially passed legislation*

1a. Irrespective of unified or divided government, the probability of a veto is very low for minor legislation (under 2%).
1b. The probability of a veto for nonminor legislation is much higher under divided government than under unified government (up to ten times higher).
1c. Under divided government, the probability of a veto increases steadily with the significance of the legislation (the probability at the highest level is over ten times that of the lowest level). It does not under unified government.

Initial Vetoes

In Chapter 2 I identified three patterns in veto rates for initially passed legislation, which are displayed in Table 5.1. First, the probability of a veto of minor legislation is very low and virtually the same under divided government as under unified government. Second, the probability of a veto is much higher under divided government than unified government. Third, under unified government, vetoes remain rare regardless of the significance of the legislation. But under divided government, the probability of a veto increases dramatically with the significance of the legislation. The probability of a veto of initially passed legislation depends on an *interaction* between control of government (unified versus divided) and the significance of the legislation.

Why Vetoes of Minor Legislation Are Rare Irrespective of Governmental Control (1a). It is easy to see why minor legislation is unlikely to be vetoed, irrespective of unified or divided control. Presidents just don't care whose name graces a federal building in Podunk. They couldn't care less about tiny adjustments to the boundaries of national parks. And whether America celebrates National Artichoke Day is not a pressing concern to the leader of the Free World. In contrast, the congressman who hails from Podunk, whose district contains the park, or whose constituents spend their days cultivating artichokes find these matters important. Congressmen work very hard to pass such localistic trifles. Intervention from the executive, who has bigger (or at least different) fish to fry, is hardly a factor. Legislation of this type just doesn't enter the president's utility function. Of course, he doesn't veto it.

Veto Bargaining

Very occasionally, though, a congressman's bright idea for helping his constituents promises to wreak havoc in some corner of the bureaucracy. Requiring the government to subsidize artichoke prices and then distribute the inevitable glut to poor people may seem a brilliant idea to a congressman from the artichoke belt. But to the bureaucrats who oversee the budget or try to rationalize farm policy it may seem alarmingly expensive and needlessly wasteful. They may take their case to the chief magistrate, urging him to veto the bill.

Examples abound. For example, in 1958 Senator Margaret Chase Smith finagled the passage of a bill (S. 2266) that would tie pay rates for work on U.S. Navy vessels in the Bath Iron Works to those prevailing in the Brooklyn Navy Yard. In other words, the Navy was to use public funds to eliminate a market differential between low-cost, chronically depressed Maine and high-cost, metropolitan New York. The proposal's economic sense was elusive but its political logic was impeccable, at least to the senator from Maine. On the other hand, to the Navy, this raid on its construction budget, once sanctioned, promised to open the door to similar raids on every military construction project in the country. Not too surprisingly, President Eisenhower vetoed the bill.

This sort of veto is easily understood in terms of the model. Senator Smith was unsure whether the president really had any preferences about the subsidies; if he didn't he was de facto accommodating. As it turned out, he did. The president's ideal point was coincident with the status quo, which was set to zero subsidies: he was recalcitrant.

Once legislation takes on any degree of significance, it draws the attention of the men and women in the executive branch. The president is likely to be concerned with all important legislation and intensely concerned about landmark legislation. How then to explain the difference in veto rates between unified and divided government for more significant legislation, and the increase in veto rates with increasing legislative significance *during divided government*?

Why Vetoes Are More Common during Divided Government (1b). An essential difference between unified and divided government is the greater divergence of policy interests between Congress and the president. For example, Lyndon Johnson and the 89th Congress had similar policy preferences. In contrast, Ronald Reagan had profound differences with the leadership and the average floor member of the rather liberal 100th Congress. There are exceptions, of course. The conflict between Truman and the Republican 80th Congress was very bitter over domestic policy but the president and the Republican's lead player on foreign policy, Senator William Knowland, saw eye-to-eye on com-

126

munism. Despite divided government, the president and congressional leaders joined together to enact the Marshall Plan, one of the outstanding legislative achievements of the postwar era. Conversely, despite unified government in the 81st and 82nd Congresses, Truman was far out of step with his fellow Democrats on internal security and immigration. He vetoed landmark bills in both these areas.[1] Nonetheless, the basic equation holds true: different parties, different policy preferences.

It may seem obvious that vetoes will be more likely when policy preferences diverge. As shown in Chapter 4, though, this result does not emerge from the basic model. Calculation of sample equilibria shows that it does in the SVB model. To demonstrate this, I briefly consider three scenarios. The first tries to capture those moments when the president and Congress share a common outlook. Johnson and the 89th Congress might provide an example. The second examines moderate policy divergence. This situation would represent, for example, the early Eisenhower Congresses, when government was divided but a conservative coalition rather sympathetic to the president's views dominated Congress. The third scenario examines extreme policy divergence, such as Truman and the 80th Congress, Ford and the 94th Congress, Reagan and the 100th Congress, or Clinton and the 104th Congress, among others.

Suppose the ideal point of Congress and the *expected* ideal point of the president are the same, a scenario of *policy convergence*. But also suppose Congress is somewhat uncertain about the location of the president's ideal point. Otherwise, the Hicks paradox prevents even the possibility of vetoes.[2] Under these circumstances, given a uniform distribution over presidential types, the president's true ideal point would lie to the left of Congress's ideal point half the time and to the right half the time. Of course, as discussed in Chapter 4, the critical matter is the location of the president utility-equivalent point t relative to Congress's ideal point. As shown in Figure 5.1, all the types whose ideal points lie to the left of $\frac{x_0}{2}$ have t's that lie to the left of Congress's ideal point. In other words, they are accommodators. In fact, unless the ideal point of the highest presidential type is closer to the status quo than to Congress, *all* the presidential types will be accommodators. If so, Congress may be unsure about the president's exact preferences but it can still sure he will accept a policy located at Congress's ideal point. In this configuration,

---

[1] I discuss the immigration veto in Chapter 8. On Truman's 1950 veto of the McCarren Internal Security Act, see *CQ Almanac* 1950: 390–98.

[2] If Congress is more certain about presidential preferences under unified government, then the president's type space $[\underline{t}, \overline{t}]$ would be narrower and the results below would be strengthened.

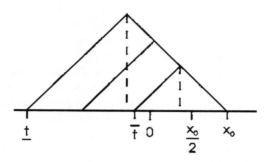

Figure 5.1. Policy Convergence despite Uncertainty

the model predicts that Congress will pass its ideal point, which the president will accept. The model thus predicts no vetoes despite substantial incomplete information.

Suppose instead the policy preferences of the players diverge somewhat, though not in an extreme way. This scenario of *moderate policy divergence* might arise during divided government if the president and Congress did not profoundly disagree. The middle Congresses of the Eisenhower administration provide many examples. Or this situation might arise during unified government when the president was at a substantial remove from many in his party. The Carter administration offers examples.

The following example tries to capture the essence of the situation. Assume the two-period game analyzed in Chapter 4. The probability of a breakdown, q, can be taken as a proxy for the significance of the legislation, with low values associated with highly significant legislation (I return to this point, later). Suppose $q = \frac{1}{2}$ so the legislation has some significance but is not terribly important. In this example, Congress begins the bargaining believing the president's type is uniformly distributed between $-\frac{2}{3}$ and $\frac{1}{3}$. The possible ideal points for the president thus range between $\frac{1}{6}$ and $\frac{2}{3}$. No type shares Congress's ideal point but most are accommodators and all can agree with Congress that there are policies superior to the status quo ($x_0 = 1$).[3]

The sequential bargaining model predicts the following (I detail the calculations in the appendix to this chapter). Congress begins by offering a bill $x_2 = \frac{1}{6}$. Presidential types with $t < 0$ accept the bill; all others veto it. The probability of acceptance is therefore 67% while the probability of a veto is 33%. Types between 0 and $\frac{1}{6}$ veto strategically – they prefer the bill to the status quo but nonetheless veto it in the hope

[3] One could add veto override players to the scenario, but so long as $\bar{t} \leq \tau$, as would be reasonable in the scenario, they will play no role in the veto bargaining.

128

of getting the second offer. After a veto, Congress's beliefs about the president's type are concentrated on the interval $[0, \frac{1}{3}]$. If Congress passes a second bill, it makes a "constrained" offer: $x_1 = \bar{t} = \frac{1}{3}$, and the bill is accepted with certainty. In this case, the chance of acceptance of the initial bill far outweighs its chance of rejection and, even if it is vetoed, the repassed bill is surely accepted.

Now suppose much greater divergence of preferences, a scenario of *extreme divergence*. For example, imagine the president and Congress bargaining over legislation in a highly contentious issue during divided government. The Truman and the 80th Congress, the Ford administration, Reagan and the 100th Congress, and (perhaps) Clinton and the 104th Congress provide examples of president and Congress at loggerheads.

To capture this case, assume presidential types are uniformly distributed between $\frac{1}{3}$ and $1\frac{1}{3}$; again, $x_0 = 1$ and $q = \frac{1}{2}$. Thus, there is no chance the president is an accommodator and a substantial chance – 33% – that he is recalcitrant. In this case, the SVB model predicts that Congress initially passes a bill, $x_2 = .725$. Types less than .6 accept, and higher types veto. So the probability of a veto is 73%. If Congress makes a second offer it is a tough one, $x_1 = .8$. Types above .8 also veto this bill, so the probability of a veto is 53%. The example captures intense, highly conflictual veto bargaining.

In sum, calculation of sample equilibria show clearly how and why the SVB model predicts pattern 1b, the increased probability of vetoes during divided government. Wide divergence in preferences between Congress and the president not only opens the door to vetoes; it also allows sufficient uncertainty about the president's preferences that the repeated screening and learning dynamic of sequential bargaining can come into play.

Why Veto Rates Increase with Significance during Divided Government (1c). One of the most striking findings in Chapter 2 is the interaction between divided government and legislative significance. During unified government, the probability of a veto is low across all significance classes, a fact explained earlier. But during divided government, the probability of a veto increases dramatically with legislative significance. Why?

The key is "q," the probability of a breakdown during bargaining. The probability of a breakdown is much, much higher for minor legislation than for more important legislation. In Chapter 2, I estimated the breakdown rate following a veto to be about 80% for minor legislation; for landmark legislation the rate is only 25%. Minor legislation is "brittle": if vetoed, it is likely to die. Major bills are much less brittle, so a veto checks them temporarily but is not likely to stop them permanently. The resilience of major legislation means the president can anticipate that Congress is apt to repass a vetoed bill. Accordingly, he can be much bolder in using the veto to extract policy concessions.

This is the intuition; the details in the model are easily sketched. In Chapter 4 I showed how the president's veto strategy depends on "t_2^*," the critical presidential type in a two-round game: if the president's true type t lies to the left of t_2^*, he accepts Congress's optimal first offer. But if his true type lies to the right of t_2^* (so the president's ideal point is farther from Congress's), he vetoes the bill. Thus, the probability of a veto following an initial offer is just the probability that t lies above t_2^*. For a given distribution of presidential types, the probability of a veto therefore decreases as t_2^* rises, and increases as t_2^* falls.[4] The issue, then, is the effect of an increase in the breakdown rate on the value of t_2^*. In Chapter 4 I calculated an exact equation for t_2^*, equation 4.6, in a two-period game in which all presidential types are compromisers.[5] Using equation 4.6 it is easy to show that t_2^*, increases as q increases.[6] In other words, the probability of a veto falls as the breakdown rate increases, that is, as significance decreases. Conversely, the probability of a veto increases as significance increases. As an example, using equation 4.6, $t_2^* = \underline{t}$ when $q = 0$: if the legislation is so important a breakdown is impossible, all types veto (in this configuration). Conversely, suppose $q = 1$, so the legislation is so insignificant a breakdown is certain. Presidents usually have no preferences at all about so minor a bill and are happy to accept it. But suppose the president did have preferences about the bill's content and is a compromiser. Then $t_2^* = \dfrac{x_0 + \underline{t}}{2}$, for example, if $x_0 = 1$ and $\underline{t} = 0$ then $t_2^* = \frac{1}{2}$. Even if the president cares about the bill, many types accept rather than veto.

Chains and SVB

Table 5.2 summarizes basic findings about chains and sequential veto bargaining. The first pattern is easy to explain. For any given minor bill

---

[4] If the density of the distribution is everywhere positive on its support, as I assumed in Chapter 4.

[5] The equation is actually somewhat more general. It also holds if the type space contains accommodators, but not so many that Congress opens with its ideal point. It also holds if the type space contains recalcitrants. However, the second offer must be unconstrained by the top of the type space (which is surely true if the type space contains recalcitrants) or by the override player.

[6] $\dfrac{\partial t_2^*}{\partial q} = \dfrac{2(x_0 - \underline{t})}{(1 + 3q)^2} > 0 \; \forall \; x_0 \neq \underline{t}$ (q is bounded by 0 and 1).

130

Table 5.2. *Empirical patterns: Chains and sequential veto bargaining*

2a. Most vetoes involve minor legislation and, if so, are usually singletons.
2b. If a veto involves minor legislation, the veto is likely to be a singleton; if it involves more important legislation, it is likely to be part of a chain.
2c. SVB occurs regularly: overall, there were 147 veto chains.
2d. SVB is largely a phenomenon of divided government – singletons prevail during unified government.
2e. Most veto chains are short.

the probability of a veto is extremely low, since the president simply doesn't care about such bills. But Congress passes an enormous number of minor bills – 14,972 were enacted between 1945 and 1992. Even a low rate yields many vetoes when applied to so many laws. The veto rate for more significant legislation during divided government is much higher, but there are many, many fewer such bills passed by Congress. In short, most vetoes involve minor legislation because Congress passes so much minor legislation.

Most of the remaining patterns in Table 5.2 are consequences of differential breakdown rates and Congress's workload. Given the differing breakdown rates, the patterns emerge directly from the models. (I discuss *why* breakdown rates vary so much in the following section.)

The override rate for minor legislation was very low (about 13% during unified government, 32% during divided government). But, as I pointed out in the previous section, the breakdown rate for minor legislation was over 80%. This enormously high breakdown rate assured that minor vetoes were mostly singletons. Conversely, the breakdown rate for major legislation (level A and level B legislation) was much, much lower, about 25%. Hence, important vetoed bills were likely to be members of chains.

The third pattern, pattern 2c, reflects the fact that Congress passed important bills during divided government (Mayhew 1991). Given the policy differences between the branches that characterize divided government, vetoes of initially passed legislation occur frequently, as discussed in the preceding section. Therefore, given an initial veto and the low breakdown rates for important bills, chains result.

The pattern was very different during unified government (pattern 2d). During unified government, the rate of initial vetoes was low and almost flat across the significance classes (recall Figure 2.3). Since the vast bulk of unified government legislation is minor, flat rates imply that most unified government vetoes are minor. Given the extraordinarily high quit rate for minor legislation, a predominance of singletons was inevitable. In short, the explanation for the pattern is the concentration of low significance vetoes during unified government, coupled with the high quit rate for minor bills.

The most subtle of these five patterns is the last, pattern 2e, concerning the average length of veto chains. The expected length of veto chains – that is, the expected number of rounds in chains – is determined by a complex interaction between the size of concessions between rounds, the probability of a breakdown in bargaining following a veto, the president's optimal veto strategy, and the timing of offers relative to an election. A priori, it is not at all obvious that short veto chains are implied by the models. Are they?

With reasonable parameter values, it is possible to calculate the expected number of rounds in a veto chain, for all breakdown rates.[7] Consider a case that seems likely to lead to a long chain. Suppose all presidential types are compromisers and none are accommodators. Suppose the override player lies beyond the status quo, so an override will not terminate the bargaining. And suppose the status quo is not terribly extreme, so concessions come fairly slowly. How long will the chain be on average? The answer is provided in Figure 5.2. The figure shows the expected length of chains in such a configuration, for all values of q between zero and one.[8] For breakdown rates corresponding to minor legislation (80%), chains are singletons. But for breakdown rates corresponding to major legislation (about 25%) chains are still short, averaging about two rounds. This is the pattern actually seen in the data.

EXPLAINING REPASSAGE AND BREAKDOWN RATES

The analysis in Chapter 2 uncovered four patterns in breakdown rates, summarized in Table 5.3. In considering these patterns, it is useful to distinguish two views about breakdowns in bargaining. In the first, the bargaining process is viewed as entirely self-contained. No outside events interfere at all, so it is somewhat misleading to speak of a "breakdown." Rather, one party may become so pessimistic about the other party's willingness to strike an agreement that it simply walks away from the table. For example, after a bill is repeatedly vetoed, Congress might

[7] For games with at most two potential rounds, one can use equations 4.4–4.6 to do the calculations. But for games with potentially more rounds – the more interesting case here – one needs generalizations of those equations, extending them to any finite number of rounds. This generalization is provided in Cameron and Elmes 1995.

[8] The figure is based on bargaining in a game with potentially five rounds of offers, $x_0 = 1$ and $T = [0,1]$. The calculations generating the figure employ exact numerical solutions to equations similar to 4.4–4.6 but for games of any arbitrary length, as derived in Cameron and Elmes 1995.

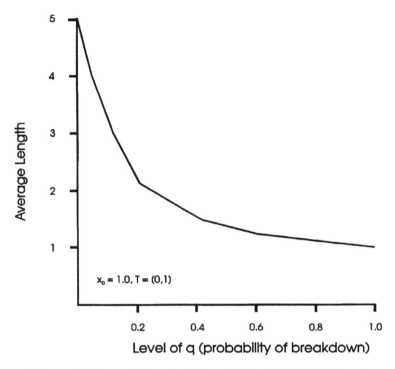

Figure 5.2. Expected Length of Veto Chains (Five-Period Game)

become so convinced the president is recalcitrant and an override impossible that it simply quits repassing the bill. In the second view, legislating is an uncertain process subject to random shocks. Sometimes unexpected outside events abruptly close a "policy window." For example, a sudden crisis may bump a bill off Congress's active agenda, or a key congressman may stumble on a better use for his limited time and effort. Thousands of such random events are imaginable and many are well documented in case studies of the legislative process. In actual bargaining, both processes are probably at work. But a model should incorporate only the most important features of a process, lest it become impossibly complex.

If the first view is the more relevant one, "breakdowns" should be related to the policy distance between the players. If the president is unlikely to be recalcitrant, for example, during unified government, then breakdowns should rarely occur. But if he is, for example, during divided government, they should be more frequent. On the other hand, if breakdowns are due mostly to random shocks, the policy distance between

133

Table 5.3. *Empirical patterns: Breakdown rates*

3a. Breakdown rates do not differ between unified and divided government; and this is true whether the bill was pocket-vetoed or regularly vetoed, and whether an override attempt failed or was not even attempted.

3b. Among authorization bills, breakdown rates fall (and repassage rates rise) with legislative significance. Again, this occurs regardless of whether the bill was pocket-vetoed or regularly vetoed, whether an override attempt failed, or whether no attempt was made to override.

3c. Controlling for legislative significance, breakdown rates (and repassage rates) for authorization bills appear similar across bills that were pocket vetoed (except by outgoing presidents) and those that were regularly vetoed, both for those with a failed override attempt and those for which no attempt was made.

3d. Repassage of a vetoed appropriations bill was virtually certain, even absent an override attempt.

---

the players should make little difference in the breakdown rate. What should make a difference is the bill's significance, since it will take a larger shock to derail an important bill than an unimportant one.

The evidence summarized in Table 5.3 strongly supports the "random shock" view of breakdowns. Breakdown rates are *not* correlated with unified versus divided government (pattern 3a). But they *are* strongly related to legislative significance, and in the expected way (pattern 3b). If breakdowns depend mostly on the size of random shocks relative to legislative significance, then one would not expect to see much difference in breakdown rates following regular and pocket vetoes, once one controls for significance and end-of-term effects. And that is also what one sees (pattern 3c).

The final result, concerning appropriations bills, is hardly surprising. In the event of a disagreement over funding levels for a program, Congress routinely passes a "continuing resolution" funding the program at a level all can agree on. So veto chains involving appropriations bills virtually never end in a bargaining breakdown.

EXPLAINING OVERRIDES – ATTEMPTS AND SUCCESS

The statistical analysis in Chapter 2 indicated the importance of override politics during veto bargaining. In this section I deploy the models to explain the main patterns in override politics.

Explaining the Patterns

Table 5.4. *Empirical patterns: Override attempts*

4a. Override attempts after a veto are much more likely during periods of divided government.

4b. However, this is true only when both chambers are controlled by the same party. If only one chamber differs from the president, override attempts are no more frequent than during unified government.

4c. Override attempts are more likely for bills in later rounds or bargaining (95%+ for second round, nonminor legislation during nonsplit divided government).

4d. The probability of an override attempt increases dramatically with legislative significance, under both unified and divided government (80%+ for landmark legislation during nonsplit divided government).

Override Attempts

Data on override attempts display four distinctive patterns, summarized in Table 5.4.

Why Override Attempts Are More Likely during Divided Government (4a). Given a veto, why are override attempts more likely during divided rather than unified government? The intuition behind pattern 4a is simple: pleasing a president of your own party is usually more attractive than gaining override votes from the opposition. But satisfying an opposition president is another matter. If the president is extreme in his views, gaining override votes from the opposition will be more attractive than satisfying the balky chief executive.

Figure 5.3 clarifies this intuition. The key to the analysis is the likely location of t, the president's reservation policy, relative to the bill best positioned for an override attempt. The top panel depicts a unified government configuration. Congress may not know the exact location of t, but it can be sure a signable bill (which will be located between $\underline{t}$ and $\bar{t}$) is more attractive than a bill written for an override attempt (which will be located between $\underline{\tau}$ and $\bar{\tau}$). After all, the president is likely to share the sentiments of his copartisans. The veto override player, on the other hand, is almost invariably a member of the opposition party and is likely to have more discordant preferences.[9] Accordingly, Congress will offer

[9] In the 89th Congress, the Democrats commanded a two-thirds majority in both chambers (in the first session, 293–149 in the House and 68–32 in the Senate). But such a situation is extremely rare.

135

Unified Government

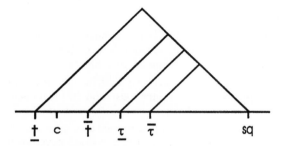

**Congress tries to write a signable bill –
if it is vetoed, an override is hopeless**

Divided Government

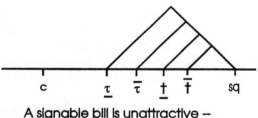

**A signable bill is unattractive –
Congress writes the bill anticipating
an override**

Figure 5.3. Why Override Attempts Are More Common during Divided
Government

a bill in the first range, as indicated by the SVB model. The president
might decide to veto the bill. But given its location between $\underline{t}$ and $\bar{t}$ an
override attempt is hopeless. As I noted in Chapter 4, if there is any
opportunity cost in time and effort for override attempts – as there surely
is – Congress will not waste effort on a hopeless attempt. Thus, override
attempts will not take place in this configuration.

The bottom panel illustrates a divided government scenario. In the configuration shown, it is more attractive for Congress to write a bill positioned for an override rather than concede enough to satisfy the president. The president will veto the bill and Congress will attempt to override, which may succeed or fail.

The configurations in the figure are hardly inevitable. In Chapter 8 I discuss cases in which Democratic Congresses tried to override vetoes cast by Democratic presidents, and cases in which Democratic Congresses declined to contest vetoes cast by Republican presidents. Several examples exist in the Truman and Eisenhower administrations, respectively. Nonetheless, the figure shows configurations that are typical of unified and divided government.

Why Override Attempts Are Rare during Split Party Congresses (4b). Split party Congresses occur when one party controls the lower chamber and another the upper chamber. Three of the four Reagan Congresses were split party Congresses. Because this configuration presents such an interesting case in the American system of separated powers, it is worth examining more closely. I sketch a model here, to suggest some interesting results.

The models in Chapter 4 assumed uniparty control of both chambers, so preferences in the two chambers would not differ much from each other and the legislature could be regarded as effectively unicameral. This assumption is inappropriate for a split party Congress. Bargaining between each chamber, not just between the legislature and the executive, becomes central. The sequence of play now becomes: the two chambers bargain to an agreement, then present it to the president either to accept or veto.

Let h denote the ideal point of the House, s that of the Senate, and x_0 the status quo. Without modeling the interchamber bargaining, assume that if $h < s < x_0$ the two chambers by themselves would bargain to an agreement $\hat{x}$ somewhere between h and s, that is, if the chambers did not have to worry about interference from the president.[10] What effect will a presidential veto have? As a baseline assume complete and perfect information and assume Congress makes a single take-it-or-leave-it offer to the president. In the spirit of the earlier models, assume $h < s < x_0$ and (as in the Reagan cases) the president's ideal point is closer to s than h. In a real split party Congress the critical veto override player would almost certainly reside in the chamber nearer the president. More-

---

[10] For some models that precede somewhat along these lines but provide more detail, see Calvert, McCubbins, and Weingast 1989, and Milner and Rosendorff 1997.

over, it would be a member of the president's own party.[11] Let τ denote the reserve policy for this player.

There are three cases in this elementary game. In the first, either the president or the veto override player is accommodating of the bargain the two chambers would strike by themselves.[12] In that case, the outcome is $\hat{x}$. In this scenario, the presidential veto does nothing to alter outcomes; they are determined solely through interchamber bargaining. In the second case, neither the president nor the senatorial veto override player is accommodating of $\hat{x}$. But t lies closer to $\hat{x}$ than τ.[13] A reasonable prediction is that Congress offers the president t. In this case, the effect of the presidential veto is to strengthen the hand of the Senate in its bargaining with the House. In the third case, neither the president nor the override player is accommodating and the reserve policy of the override player lies closer to $\hat{x}$ than does τ.[14] A reasonable prediction is that Congress offers the president τ. In this scenario, the House must compromise enough to satisfy the veto override player in the Senate. Unless the veto override player in the Senate is quite distant from the average Senator, the presidential veto will again advantage the Senate.

One could imbue each of these scenarios with the feel of the sequential bargaining and override models by adding incomplete information and repeated offers. But rather than pursue this idea in detail, consider instead pattern 4b, the rarity of override attempts during split party Congresses.

Figure 5.4 indicates why override attempts were rare during split party Congresses. The figure shows the configuration in the third scenario, adding some uncertainty about the location of the veto override player. The indicated configuration is impossible unless the president is quite extreme, not only relative to the members of the opposite party but to the bulk of the members of his own party in the Senate as well. In fact, in the indicated configuration the House's preferences are largely irrelevant in determining the bill's placement. The key to override attempt lies in the friendly rather than the hostile chamber. In this sense, the configuration strongly resembles *unified* rather than divided government. Just as override attempts are rare in unified government, so will they be in split party Congresses.

Congressional Quarterly estimated in 1986 that a bill geared for a

---

[11] In the assumed configuration, the override player would lie two-thirds of the way from the left-most senator to the right-most senator. Since $h < s$, the left-most senator would be similar in preference to House members, for example, a Democrat in the Reagan split party Congresses. The two-thirds player in the Senate would thus have the same party affiliation as the average senator, for example, be a Republican.

[12] This case occurs if $t \leq \hat{x} \leq \tau$, $t \leq \tau \leq \hat{x}$, $\tau \leq t \leq \hat{x}$, or $\tau \leq \hat{x} \leq t$.

[13] The case is $\hat{x} < t \leq \tau$.

[14] The case is $\hat{x} < \tau < t$.

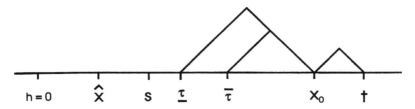

Figure 5.4. Override Configuration for Split Party Congresses

successful veto override would need to gain the votes of eighty senators upon initial passage, due to the president's ability to sway his copartisans in the override vote (*CQ Almanac* 1986:366). Without such massive support, the override would fail; without about this much support, no override would be attempted. For the president to oppose all but twenty members of his own party in the Senate, he would need rather extreme preference. Such situations did occur: Reagan's veto of the Anti-Apartheid Act, discussed in Chapter 8, provides an example. But they were rare events.

Why Override Attempts Are More Likely for Bills in Later Rounds of Bargaining (4c). Override attempts are much more likely after a second veto than the first. Here are the statistics. Some 229 bills were regular vetoed after initial passage. Override attempts were essayed for 103 or 45% of these bills. Twenty-seven round-2 bills were regular vetoed. Congress attempted to override 24 or 89% of these vetoes. Finally, one round-3 bill was regular vetoed, and Congress attempted to override that veto. Thus, the override attempt rate (contingent on a regular veto) rose from 45% to 89% to 100% as bills moved deeper into the bargaining sequence. The statistical results reported in Table 2.6 indicate this pattern persists if one controls for legislative significance.

I offer a more detailed discussion of the dynamics of later offers in the following section, where I discuss reveto rates. However, pattern 4c is very easily explained by the sequential veto bargaining model. If the president is likely to be recalcitrant or a very distant compromiser, Congress may begin its bargaining with a bill geared for an override attempt. But for many initial bills, Congress offers a bill it hopes the president will sign. The bill is not geared for an override attempt for to do so would be to cede too much from the beginning. If the president vetoes the bill, Congress does not attempt to override the veto for the attempt is sure to fail. But having seen the veto, Congress eliminates a range of accommodating or proximal compromisers from its calculation. Its next

Table 5.5. *Empirical patterns: Probability of success given an attempted override*

5a. Given an override attempt, neither divided government nor legislative significance nor authorization versus appropriation predicts the probability of success.

5b. The probability of a successful override was unusually low during the Bush administration.

bill (if it passes one) contains concessions and so the bill moves closer to the location of the reserve policy of the veto override player. In fact, given the exclusion of the more proximal presidential types, Congress may now see the veto override player as more proximal than the president. If so, it gears the second bill for an override attempt. Thus, the rate of override attempts rises following the second veto. In short, pattern 4c is an immediate implication of the concessions predicted by the SVB model.

Pattern 4d is the increasing probability of an override attempt with legislative significance. This pattern is hardly surprising. Legislative floor time is a valuable commodity. More significant legislation is better able to command the requisite time and effort involved in an override attempt.[15]

Success and Failure with Override Attempts

The analysis in Chapter 2 uncovered two facts about success or failure in override attempts, which are reviewed in Table 5.5. First, none of the covariates predicted success or failure. But an unexpected one did: whether the attempt occurred in the Bush administration.

Why the Covariates Don't Explain Success or Failure (5a). The probability of success in an override attempt depends on the placement of the bill. Factors that lead Congress to make a riskier offer should correlate with the probability of failure. But the override model predicts bill placement during override attempts. Equation 4.3 indicates the relevant variables. According to equation 4.3, bill placement depends on the location of the status quo and the lowest possible type for the over-

---

[15] The models do not explicitly incorporate the costs of legislating, as discussed earlier. But at least in the context of override attempts, the concept is partially captured by "q" – more important bills are able to overcome the obstacles to continued bargaining.

ride player. Neither of these factors is observable. Moreover, the model predicts that bill placement will *not* depend on legislative significance: q does not enter equation 4.3. Nor should it depend on unified versus divided government, nor authorization versus appropriation, none of which enter equation 4.3. In short, the override model predicts that success or failure will be uncorrelated with the variables used in the statistical analysis, and this is in fact the case.

The Bush Phenomenon (5b). Contemporary observers noted the remarkable success of the Bush administration in beating override attempts. The statistical analysis corroborated this impression. What explains the pattern? And does this finding invalidate the override model – like q, "Bush" does not enter equation 4.3!

One possibility is that President Bush was unusually circumspect in using the veto. If he vetoed only "sure things," they would not be overridden. However, the data do not support this explanation. Statistically, there is no "Bush effect" in the probability of vetoes: Bush vetoed bills at about the same rate as any other postwar president, if one controls for the significance of legislation and the presence of divided government. His success was not due to timidity in fighting Congress.

Another possibility is that the administration was exceptionally skillful on Capitol Hill. Perhaps the legislative liaison and Republican leadership had much better information than the Democrats about the likely location of the veto override player. If so, they could beat the odds. Two arguments weigh against this possibility, however. First, there is scant evidence of uncanny legislative expertise in the Bush administration. There have been particularly effective legislative liaison teams, at least as scored by knowledgeable contemporary observers. For example, Reagan's first-term team is sometimes given high marks. But no one seems to have viewed the Bush team this way. Second, if the administration really did have superior knowledge or skill, then the Democrats would have soon learned to anticipate it. Thus, when the president vetoed a bill, it would signal that he knew he could beat the override. One would expect to see override attempts drop off. But they did not. Instead, the Democrats kept trying to override and kept losing.

These ad hoc explanations do not stand up to scrutiny. The veto-bargaining models themselves do not afford an obvious way to explain Bush's extraordinary success. Is there any theoretically grounded way to explain Bush's remarkable success? An intriguing model developed by political scientist Keith Krehbiel offers one way (1996, 1998). Krehbiel's model is a spatial model similar in assumptions to the Ferejohn-Shipan model discussed in Chapter 4. Thus, it shares basic assumptions and methods with the veto models. The distinguishing feature of Krehbiel's analysis is its careful attention to factors likely to cause "gridlock" or policy stasis in the separation-of-powers system. Examples are filibusters and a disciplined party system. In addition, the model examines a particularly interesting kind of dynamics. Given a particular configuration of preferences and the institutional rules of the game, the policy window will open for policies located in particular places in the policy space. The players can agree that better alternatives exist and over time will alter those policies, moving them into regions where no further movement is possible. As the configuration of policy preferences change over time, due to congressional and presidential elections, and as the players move to alter policies they find undesirable, policy windows will open and close.

What does the model imply about policy making in the Reagan-Bush years? The beginning of the Reagan administration represented a dramatic shift in the preference configuration, with a conservative Republican president and Senate replacing more liberal Democratic ones. This configuration lasted six years, during which changes were made in most of the policies that could be changed. In 1986, the replacement of the Republican Senate with a Democratic one opened the window for some hitherto blocked changes, though the president's veto and filibusters in the Senate could block others favored by the Democratic majority. Some of the policies that could be moved would require overriding the president's veto and this did happen (recall the increase in successful overrides between the last two years and preceding six years of the Reagan administration). Over the last two years of the Reagan administration, Congress may well have moved most of the policies that could be easily enacted by this route.

The election of George Bush inaugurated a new administration but it did not alter the underlying preference configuration very much. Congress had already passed most of the policies that could be easily enacted through veto overrides. Arguably, the only ones left were the riskier ones, ones less likely to beat the veto. The Bush Congresses tried diligently to move these policies. Risky as they were, they still offered the best chance for legislative success. But the determined president was able to block most of them. Ironically, then, Bush's *success* with overrides was a legacy of Reagan's frequent *failures* after the loss of the Senate in 1986 – just as Bush's "gridlock" was a legacy of the Reagan administration's earlier successes in the long-lasting preference configuration of the 1980s.

This argument suggests an intriguing speculation. Suppose Richard Nixon had won the 1960 election, rather than John Kennedy. If so, his administration might well have been a "gridlock" administration like

Table 5.6. *Empirical patterns: Probability of revetoes*

6a. The reveto rate following repassage was much higher if government was divided.
6b. It was higher if the previous bill had failed in an override attempt.
6c. It was also higher if the bill had been repassed only once.
6d. It increased with legislative significance.

the Bush administration, for few policies would have been alterable after six years of Eisenhower and Democratic Congresses. More over, after the intense veto bargaining of 1959–60, the hypothetical "Nixon administration" of 1961–64 might have run up a remarkable record beating overrides, just as the Bush administration did thirty years later.

EXPLAINING THE PROBABILITY OF REVETOES

Data on veto chains show four patterns (see Table 5.6). Presidents were more likely to reveto a repassed bill if (1) government was divided, (2) if there had been an override attempt after the previous veto, (3) it had been repassed only once rather than twice, and (4) if the bill was more significant. Explaining these findings about the probability of revetoes requires thinking about the dynamics of veto bargaining. What does Congress do when making a second or third offer, and how does the president respond?

Why Reveto Rates Were Higher under Divided Government (6a). Suppose the president vetoes a bill and bargaining does not break down. According to the models, what happens next? Several things, depending on the location of the veto override player and the policy reputation created by the first veto. Consider again the two-period game analyzed in Chapter 4.

First, suppose the political configuration is that shown in Figure 5.5, intended to illustrate they nature of second offers during unified government. Congress is somewhat uncertain about the president's type, but is sure the veto override player is more distant. For example, the Democratic 95th and 96th Congresses may have been somewhat unsure about President Jimmy Carter's preferences in certain matters, but they could be very sure the preferences of the veto override player, a conservative Republican, were quite far away. Suppose such a Congress passed a bill the president then vetoed. By doing so, the president reveals his type

143

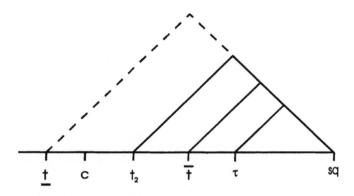

The first veto excludes types between $\underline{t}$ and t_2.
The second offer will fall between t_2 and $\bar{t}$.

Figure 5.5. Second Offers during Unified Government

to be higher than t_2. According to the sequential bargaining model, Congress's second offer will fall between t_2 and $\bar{t}$. As discussed in Chapter 4, if the status quo lies far enough to the right, Congress might well offer $\bar{t}$, a "constrained offer" that the president is certain to accept.

Suppose instead the configuration is like that in Figure 5.6, representing divided government. In this configuration, the veto override player is distant but there is a chance the president is even more distant. For example, in the heavily Democratic 100th Congress, the veto override player was a Republican. But on some issues President Reagan appeared even more conservative than the veto override player (I discuss several cases in Chapter 8). If such a president vetoed an initial bill, Congress could again exclude types below t_2. Depending on the location of the status quo, Congress would place its second bill between t_2 and τ, but it would never offer a bill as distant as $\bar{t}$. There necessarily would be a chance the president would veto the bill a second time.

Finally, suppose the configuration is that shown in Figure 5.7. In this divided government scenario, the president is so far from Congress that the legislature begins by offering a bill tailored for an override attempt. It will be vetoed, but the veto may fail. If so, the override model predicts repassage of the same bill, and another veto.

In the first scenario, acceptance is possible or even assured. In the second, acceptance is possible but never assured. In the third, acceptance is impossible. The first scenario could occur under divided government but is far more likely under unified government. The second and third scenarios occasionally may occur under unified government but are

144

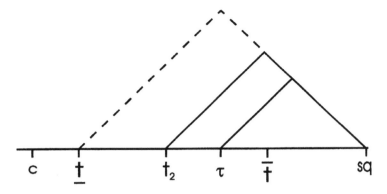

The first veto excludes types between t̲ and t₂.
The second offer will fall between t₂ and τ.

Figure 5.6. Second Offers during Divided Government: Sequential Veto Bargaining

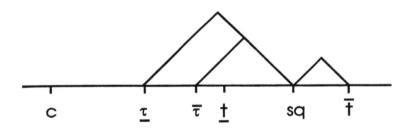

The first bill is geared toward an override:
If vetoed, no types are excluded
and the same bill is repassed.

Figure 5.7. Second Offers during Divided Government: The Override Case

much more likely during divided government (especially the third scenario). The prevalence of the first scenario under unified government, and that of the second and third scenarios under divided government, provide an explanation for the greater frequency of revetoes during divided government.

Why Reveto Rates Were Higher after a Failed Override (6b). Pattern 6b, the higher rate of revetoes after failed override attempts, might seem puzzling absent the override model. After all, one might suppose a president would be more circumspect about revetoing a bill after Congress has already shown sufficient gumption to attempt an override. The override model shows why this reasoning is fallacious. The president vetoed the initial bill knowing there was a chance the bill would be overridden, and Congress attempted to do so because there was a reasonable chance of success. Given this, Congress is unlikely to reposition the second bill; it will just try to pass the bill via an override again. The president will reveto that bill for the same reason he vetoed it the first time. Pattern 6b is a strong prediction of the override model.

Why Reveto Rates Were Higher with the First Repassage but Not the Second (6c). Pattern 6c indicates that second bills – bills that were passed, vetoed, and passed again – were more likely to be revetoed than were third bills, those bills vetoed twice and passed a third time. Why this should be true is not at all obvious from the models. Indeed, it initially seems to conflict with pattern 4c. Pattern 4c indicated that override rates rose with second offers. The models suggested pattern 4c was a consequence of a round-2 concession: as Congress made concessions, overrides became possible and were often more attractive than trying to write a bill the president would sign. But if this was true, why weren't third offers also geared for override attempts? It is worth taking a closer look at the data to see what is going on.

Between 1945 and 1992, only twelve veto chains lasted through three rounds of bargaining (the veto bargaining over welfare in the 104th Congress would increase this total by one). Table 5.7 displays relevant data for these twelve chains. Included is a brief description of the bills and other relevant information about veto bargaining.[16]

The first chain, Truman's vetoes of Republican tax cut bills in the 80th Congress, seems to follow the script of the override model. There was a close override vote in the House; Congress repassed virtually the same bill; the override was successful in the House but failed in the Senate. Congress made concessions in the third bill, but this may be explained by an unexpectedly poor showing in the Senate's override attempt. (I discuss this chain in detail in Chapter 8.)

Four of the remaining chains appear to be classic examples of sequential veto bargaining. In these chains – numbers 3 (flood control projects in 1956–58), 5 (insurance for federal employees in 1966–68), 11 (authorization of the Corporation for Public Broadcasting in 1984), and 12 (D.C. appropriations/abortions) – Congress made concessions

[16] I coded concessions based on the legislative histories in *Congressional Quarterly Almanac.*

146

Table 5.7. *Lengthy veto chains*

Description	Significance[a]	Bill 1		Bill 2		Bill 3		
		Override attempt	Concession	Override attempt	Concession	Concession	Result	Model
1. Income tax cuts 1954	A	268–137 (2 short)	No	299–108, 57–36 (5 short)	No	Yes	Overridden	Override
2. Postal pay raise 1954–55	C	Pocket veto	No	54–39 (8 short)	No	Yes	Signed	SVB (but no concession for bill 2)
3. Flood control 1956–58	C	Pocket veto	Yes	No	Yes	Yes	Signed	SVB
4. Housing act of 1959	A	55–40 (8 short)	Yes	58–36 (4 short)	Yes	Yes	Signed	SVB
5. Insurance for federal employees 1966–68	B	No attempt	Yes	No	Yes	Yes	Signed	SVB
6. Rehabilitation act of 1973	C	Pocket veto	Yes	60–36 (4 short)	Yes	Yes	Signed	SVB
7. Continuing resolution: Turkey aid 1974	D	223–135 (16 short)	No?	161–83 (2 short)	Yes?	Yes?	Signed	SVB (perhaps no concession at bill 2)
8. Oil pricing 1975	D	No attempt	Yes	61–39 (6 short)	Yes	Yes	Signed	SVB
9. Supplemental appropriation 1982	C	253–151 (17 short)	Yes	242–169 (32 short)	Yes	Yes	Signed	SVB
10. Labor HEW appropriation 1972	C	203–171 (47 short)	Yes	Pocket veto	Yes	Yes	Signed	SVB
11. Public TV 1984	C	No attempt	Yes	Pocket veto	Yes	Yes	Signed	SVB
12. DC appropriation/abortion	C	No attempt	Yes	No attempt	Yes	Yes	Signed	SVB

[a]For levels of significance, see Chapter 2.

bill to bill and no override attempt was made. Once Congress made sufficient concessions, the president finally signed the bills.

The remaining eight chains (numbers 2, 4, 5, 6, 7, 8, 9, and 10) display an anomaly. In these chains, Congress made concessions bill to bill, as predicted by the sequential bargaining model. But Congress also attempted to override the vetoes during the course of the bargaining. Given the concessions, the SVB model suggests the override attempts at rounds 1 and 2 should not have occurred. Conversely, the override model suggests that, given relatively close override attempts (as occurred at round 2 in chains 2, 4, 6, 7, and 8), Congress should not have made concessions in the third bill. But it did.

These eight anomalous cases appear to be counterexamples to the models. Can they be turned into solved problems? In my presentation of the models in Chapter 4, I allowed only one source of incomplete information in each model. Thus, in the override model I assumed Congress knew the location of the president's reserve policy but was somewhat uncertain about the location of the override player's reserve policy. In my presentation of the SVB model, I assumed Congress was somewhat uncertain about the location of the president's reservation policy but knew with certainty the location of the override player's reservation policy. This was appropriate since the purpose of each model was to explore the implications of one type of incomplete information. But suppose *both* types exist simultaneously. What happens? Imagine Congress proceeds according to the SVB model, but is somewhat uncertain about the location of the override player's reservation policy. Congress might make a concession, trying to win the president's acquiescence. But as it did so, it might enter the region where an override was possible though perhaps not very probable, that is, the left-hand portion of $[\underline{\tau}, \overline{\tau}]$. If the cost of an override attempt were not too high, Congress might well essay an override attempt if the president vetoed the bill.

Dual uncertainty would explain the eight anomalous cases. Given dual uncertainty, in the early phases of bargaining Congress would make concessions, as indicated by the SVB model. But as offers entered $[\underline{\tau}, \overline{\tau}]$, the region in which overrides are possible, Congress might try some "long-shot" override attempts. If this were true, then if Congress attempted to override the veto of bill one, it would also attempt to override the veto of bill two. In other words, if the override was worth a try for bill one, it was worth another try for bill two, where the probability of success should have been greater given a concession. This pattern actually characterizes the data, as shown in Table 5.7. Also, the margins in the override votes get closer to the two-thirds mark in the second attempt. Because they did not quite reach it, and because the president's preferences were relatively distant from Congress's, the chains became lengthy.

Why Reveto Rates Increased with Legislative Significance (6d). Pattern 6d indicates that, given a veto and repassage, reveto rates were higher for more significant legislation. This is a major prediction by the SVB model: a lower breakdown rate allows for tougher bargaining.

CONCLUSION

In this chapter I reviewed veto probabilities for initially passed bills, the frequency and length of veto chains, repassage and breakdown rates, the frequency of override attempts and their likelihood of success and failure, and the probability of revetoes following repassage. The sequential veto bargaining and override models provide compelling explanations for pattern after pattern. The explanatory success of the models is not due to an excess plasticity that allows them to rationalize any imaginable pattern. If the probability of a veto increased with a move to unified government, or decreased with legislative significance during divided government, or if the probability of a reveto typically fell after a failed override attempt, the models would be bound for the junk heap. But they do not.

Working scientists' criteria for good models require them to do more than explain a phenomenon's natural history. As I noted at the end of Chapter 3, really convincing models make predictions that go beyond natural history, predictions that are both novel and distinctive. And the model's predictions are borne out. Can the veto bargaining models stand up to this test? I turn to this question in the following chapter.

Appendix to Chapter 5

In this appendix, I provide the calculations for examples employed in the discussion of pattern 1b. Recall from Chapter 4 the equations governing offers and the indifferent type (equations 4.4–4.6):

$$x_2 = \frac{1 + 4q - q^2}{2(1 + 3q)} x_0 + \frac{(1 + q)^2}{2(1 + 3q)} t \qquad \text{(first offer)}$$

$$x_1 = \frac{1 + 5q}{2(1 + 3q)} x_0 + \frac{(1 + q)}{2(1 + 3q)} t \qquad \text{(second offer)}$$

$$t_2 = \frac{2q}{1 + 3q} x_0 + \frac{1 + q}{1 + 3q} t. \qquad \text{(indifferent type)}$$

In both examples, $q = \frac{1}{2}$ and $x_0 = 1$.

In the first example, involving moderate policy divergence, $T = [-\frac{2}{3}, \frac{1}{3}]$. If we use the equation for a second offer above, $x_2 = \frac{1}{2}$. But Congress would never make such an offer as it exceeds the top of the type space. So this is an example of a "constrained" offer – if Congress makes a second offer it will be $\frac{1}{3}$. Cameron and Elmes (1995) show that in games with n rounds, if the last offer is constrained, then the first $n - 1$ offers are those generated in an unconstrained game with the same parameters but with $n - 1$ rounds. So in this case, the first offer is the same that would be made in a one-shot game. The best one-shot offer is given by $x = \frac{x_0 + t}{2} = \frac{1}{6}$. Hence the two offers are $\frac{1}{6}$ and $\frac{1}{3}$.

For the type indifferent between these two offers,

$$V(\tfrac{1}{6}; t_2) = \tfrac{1}{2} V(\tfrac{1}{3}; t_2) + \tfrac{1}{2} V(1; t_2).$$

Because of the normalization of the president's utility function, $V(1; t_2) = 0$. Recall from Chapter 4 that

150

$$v(x;x_0,t) = \frac{|x_0 - t| - |t + x_0 - 2x|}{2}.$$

Substitution into the preceding equation and solution for t_2 then yields $t_2 = 0$ (the same result may be derived directly from the preceding equation for the indifferent type). Since types are initially uniform on T, the probability of an initial veto is just $1 - \dfrac{t_2 - \underline{t}}{\bar{t} - \underline{t}} = \dfrac{1}{3}$.

In the second example, extreme policy divergence, $T = [\frac{1}{3}, 1\frac{1}{3}]$. Substitution into the first equation above yields $x_1 = .8$, which is less than the top of the type space. The offer is not constrained. Simple substitution then yields $x_1 = .725$ and $t_2 = .6$.

6

Testing the Models

In the previous chapter I asked the models to explain many patterns they were not designed to explain. These repeated confrontations with data provided tough tests of the models. However, the patterns analyzed in Chapter 5 were all drawn from the statistical portrait of vetoes in Chapter 2. In this chapter I reverse the procedure: I use the models to generate predictions that lie outside the initial data. Then I test the predictions using new data. The predictions deal with three distinctively different phenomena: concessions, deadlines, and the legislative productivity of Congress.

In Chapter 2, I reported information gleaned from a content analysis of legislative histories. The legislative histories often reveal concessions in successors to vetoed bills, though sometimes the record is ambiguous and hard to interpret. The prevalence of concessions supplied the starting place for the model of sequential veto bargaining. Is there additional support for the fundamental "stylized fact" targeted by the model? Beyond this, do patterns in concessions conform to the predictions of the models? In this chapter I combine data on roll call votes on initial and successor bills with estimates of legislators' preferences, derived from all roll call votes, to derive estimates of the direction and magnitude of policy concessions between successive bills in veto chains. These new data on concessions confirm the importance of concessions in veto bargaining and provide several tests of the game theoretic models.

A strong test for a model comes from predictions about a hitherto unstudied phenomenon. The bargaining models make several striking predictions about a phenomenon that political scientists have not previously studied: changes in the probability of vetoes immediately before presidential elections, a "deadline effect." Both the sequential veto bargaining model and the override model predict, first, that the probability of vetoes of important legislation should decrease immediately before a presidential election under divided government. Second, they predict that this deadline effect should be smaller for less important legislation. Finally, the sequential veto bargaining model predicts that immediately before a presidential election the probability of a veto for very important and less important bills should be the same. I present new data on deadline effects that corroborate the predictions for important and routine legislation.

Another tough test for a model is using it to gain leverage on a problem far from the model's domain of initial success. In the third section of the chapter I examine a phenomenon, the legislative productivity of Congress, that has received increased attention in the wake of David Mayhew's innovative study *Divided We Govern* (1991). At first glance vetoes seem likely to exert only a modest effect on the legislative productivity of Congress, since vetoes kill so few pieces of landmark legislation. Although full-blown models of legislative productivity lie outside the scope of this book,[1] the models of interbranch bargaining in Chapter 4 imply that *anticipation* of vetoes, the "second face of power," should depress production of important bills during divided government, relative to unified government. The data on the legislative significance of bills used in the earlier chapters allow a test of this prediction.

CONCESSIONS DURING SEQUENTIAL VETO BARGAINING

Given precise information about key variables such as the location of the status quo policy, the ideal policy of the relevant congressional actor (e.g., the median voter), and the range of possible presidential types, the game theoretic models of Chapter 4 yield precise predictions about the placement of bills during sequential veto bargaining.[2] Many of these predictions are both interesting and subtle. For example, the sequential veto bargaining model predicts smaller concessions for more important bills than less important ones, ceteris paribus. Unfortunately, an observer who is not totally immersed in the presidential-congressional bargaining cannot know the location of the status quo and the range of possible presidential types with sufficient precision to allow the critical phrase "ceteris paribus" to have any bite. And it is not true (for example) that concessions in *any* sequence of important bills will be smaller than concessions in *any* sequence of unimportant ones – it depends on the values of the unobservables, such as the status quo. In short, the inability

---

[1] Krehbiel 1998 set a very fast pace for building such models.

[2] This section is based on joint work with Yuen Kwok and Charles Riemann (1995).

to measure the location of the bills, the status quo, and other important variables would seem to blast any hope of rigorously testing the models with data on policy concessions.

Fortunately, this conclusion is unduly pessimistic. It is possible to test the model with data on concessions, but the prediction tested must be quite special. It must be *robust* in the sense that it does not depend delicately upon the exact values of unobserved parameters. Instead, the prediction must hold across a wide range of plausible parameter ranges.[3] Robust predictions about concessions tend to be obvious rather than subtle and lack a certain drama. Nonetheless, they provide a valuable test simply because they are robust. At least in principle, data on concessions can decisively reject the models.

The Prediction

I examine three robust predictions. First, in general, the observed *direction* of concessions should reverse depending on whether the president is a Republican or a Democrat. The two configurations constitute distinctly different "regimes," in the parlance of statistics. The second prediction, derived from the override model, constitutes an exception to the first prediction: when successive bills in a chain are both clearly geared for an override attempt, observed concessions should be very small. Putting the two predictions together yields a third prediction: concessions should be larger when the bills in a chain are clearly not geared for an override attempt, than when they are.

Method and Data

The Cut-Point Method for Measuring Concessions. The principal empirical difficulty in testing these predictions is finding a convincing measure of the policy content of the bills. In some cases – bills raising the minimum wage, authorizing funds for a specific activity, or setting a red-letter date such as a deadline – a seemingly natural metric presents itself. Yet caution is required even in cases with a seemingly natural metric. For example, in 1976 Congress passed a military construction bill (H.R. 12384 in the 94th Congress), authorizing $3.3 billion in military construction. Economy-minded President Ford vetoed the bill. Congress repassed the bill with an identical authorization, apparently indicating the failure of the veto to win any concessions. In fact, however,

---

[3] The solution suggested in this paragraph mirrors that employed in cross-industry tests of game theoretical models of industry competition. In particular see Sutton 1991.

the authorization level was never in dispute. Instead, the controversy concerned a provision in the original bill requiring advance notification of base closings. Congress favored a lengthy notification; the administration opposed the provision. The initial bill required a one-year advance notice but following the president's veto, Congress reduced the length of notification to sixty days, a modest but clear-cut concession. Ford signed the repassed bill. The lesson: apparently natural metrics can be misleading absent close attention to legislative history.[4]

A further problem remains even if a natural metric is clear. The problem concerns comparability across veto chains. How can one compare concessions in base-closing notification periods with concessions in raising the minimum wage? Was the concession over closing notification larger than the concessions over, say, the minimum wage in the Bush administration or income taxes in the 80th Congress? Natural metrics allow statements about concessions only within a chain, but the predictions to be tested require data from across chains. Such testing requires a common metric. But no such metric is obvious simply from reading a bill.

Fortunately, common metrics emerge from multidimensional scaling of congressional roll call votes. Such scalings use roll call votes to place congressmen in hypothesized policy spaces. Poole and Rosenthal (1997), for example, find that most roll call voting is compatible with fixed positions on a single issue dimension; the dimension roughly corresponds to liberalism-conservatism (occasionally a second dimension, related to race, appears to be at play). This empirical finding suggests a way to study policy concessions during veto bargaining.[5]

To see the logic of the method, consider Figure 6.1. The figure indicates the location of seven congressmen in an issue space, like Poole and Rosenthal's hypothetical policy space. Shown for purposes of illustration are a status quo and bill, represented by points on the line. If each congressman makes a decision to vote for the bill or against it according to the indicated utility functions then there will be a cut point p in the policy space located between the bill and the status quo: all congressmen to one side of the cut point will vote in favor of the bill and all those on the other side will vote in favor of the status quo. The cleanness of separation between yeas and nays provides a test of the hypothesized

[4] This veto chain contains roll call votes in the Senate that yield cut points, as discussed later. The initial vote was close to unanimous (80–3) so the cut point measurement is censored; the override attempt failed by a wide margin, 51–42; the second bill passed with a near unanimous margin (82–2), so the second cut point observation is also censored. The double censoring prevents the detection of the concession even with the cut point method.

[5] A somewhat similar method for studying bill placement is deployed in Mouw and MacKuen 1992.

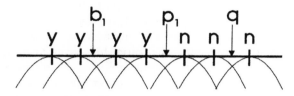

Figure 6.1. A Cut Point in the Policy Space

scaling. Actual roll call votes in W-NOMINATE space strongly resemble the one pictured in the figure, though of course separation between yeas and nays is rarely so perfect.

Now suppose the president vetoes the bill in Figure 6.1 and Congress passes a subsequent bill so the two bills form a veto chain. In practice one cannot locate either bill or the status quo in the hypothesized policy space on the basis of bill content. The status quo, however, will have remained fixed between the two bills since no legislation has passed (if one assumes that no exogenous changes occur to the status quo). Hence, *the location of the second cut point relative to the first provides a measure of the direction and magnitude of the change in content between the two bills.* This process is illustrated in Figure 6.2. Somewhat surprisingly, one need not place bills or status quos in the policy space in order to study the direction and approximate magnitude of concessions. Instead, one can measure concessions by matching roll call votes with ideology scores and locating cut points.

Data. The unit of analysis is pairs of bills in veto chains. To calculate the dependent variable, the shift in cut points, roll call votes are needed for adjacent bills in a veto chain. Moreover, I require the roll call votes to be votes on final passage, that is, votes on conference reports or final floor votes absent a conference. This is important since the estimated cut points need to reflect the content of the bill actually presented to the president. In a few cases I use the final floor vote before the vote on the conference report, but only if no roll call vote on the conference report took place and the legislative history of the bill recorded in *Congressional Quarterly Almanac* makes it clear that only minor changes occurred in conference.

As I discussed in Chapter 2, during the period 1945 to 1992 there were 145 veto chains consisting of 160 pairs of bills in chains (see Tables 2.5 and 2.8). Of course, many of these bills did not receive roll call votes at the time of final passage. However, Yuen Kwok, Charles Riemann, and I were able to match ideology scores and roll calls on final passage

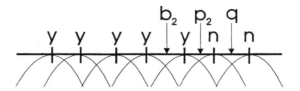

Figure 6.2. Measuring Concessions.

for adjacent bills in veto chains for 62 of the pairs of bills (39% of total pairs), comprising 56 different veto chains (38% of all chains). Not surprisingly, this group of bills is drawn disproportionately from the higher levels of legislative significance. Some 20%, 18%, 50%, and 13% of the represented chains are classified as significance levels A, B, C, and D, respectively. In the universe of veto chains, the equivalent percentages are 10%, 11%, 42%, and 37%, respectively.

The roll call data were matched with ideological scores for each House and Senate member, depending on the chamber in which the votes took place. For this purpose we employed Poole and Rosenthal's "common space" NOMINATE scores.[6] Poole and Rosenthal (1985) initially derived the scores by scaling all roll call votes from 1789 through the mid-1980s; the scores have been periodically updated since then. Initially the scores for House and Senate members were derived separately from one another, since the members of the different chambers never vote together. However, many House members have "graduated" to the Senate. This interchamber migration provides measurements of the same individual on both House and Senate scales. Exploiting this fact, Keith Poole (personal communication) has recently recalibrated the scales to put them on a common footing. It is these recalibrated scores that we employ. In the postwar Congresses that we study, the common space scores range from about −.7 for an ultraliberal member to about +.7 for an ultraconservative one.

To derive the cut points, we devised a computer program that sorts the yeas and nays in a roll call vote in ascending order of ideology scores. The program then locates the cut point or cut points that minimize the number of misclassified votes (e.g., if we assume all votes to the left of the hypothesized cut point are yeas and all to the right are nays).[7] Min-

---

[6] The NOMINATE scores yield locations in a two-dimensional space. However, in most cases the main dimension, a liberal-conservative dimension, is far more important in roll call voting than the minor dimension, generally a racial politics dimension. We employ the scores on the major dimension. For additional discussion, see Poole and Rosenthal 1997.

[7] We minimize the total number of wrong votes rather than the sum of squared distances of errors in order to avoid the distorting effect of extreme outliers. For

imizing the number of misclassified votes does not always yield a uniquely best cut point; several may be equivalent. However, multiple cut points usually lie close to one another. We used the average of multiple cut points, unless the legislative history argued strongly for or against a particular cut point.

Results

Figure 6.3 presents the cut point measures of concessions. In each panel, the horizontal axis indicates the location of the initial cut point. The vertical axis shows the movement in the cut point – that is, it is the value of the second cut point minus the value of the first cut point. Thus, points that lie *above* the zero line indicate a pair of bills in a veto chain with movement in the *conservative* direction between the successive bills. Points below the zero line indicate a pair of bills in a veto chain with movement in the *liberal* direction between the successive bills. The diagonal lines show a censoring line – that is, given the initial cut point and the maximum or minimum possible value in the policy space, the line shows the largest possible movement in the subsequent cut point that could possibly be observed. Points on or abutting the diagonal line show pairs of bills in which maximal movement occurred (in other words, the vote on the second bill was unanimous). Triangles indicate pairs of bills in which not only the first but the second bill was vetoed.

The figure shows quite dramatically the regime switching predicted by the model. That is, all the veto chains that occurred during Democratic administrations lie at or below the zero line, indicating concessions in the liberal direction.[8] Almost all the veto chains that occurred during Republican administrations lie at or above the zero line, indicating concessions in the conservative direction (all these observations come from periods of divided government). The censoring that patently affects many of the data points in the Republican regime and a few points in the Democratic regime tends to reduce the apparent size of concessions. Nonetheless, the mean concession in the Republican regime is .20 while that in the Democratic regime is $-.17$, a difference in means that is very highly statistically significant ($p = 0$).

The three points in the Republican regime that lie discernibly below

unanimous votes, the cut point is assigned to the extreme member in the ideological direction of the president (for a unanimous yea vote). This implies a degree of censoring in the data – the "true" cut point may lie further to the left or right in a unanimous vote but is unobservable.

[8] The three triangles in the left-hand figure occurred during divided government – Truman and the 80th Congress. They are the Republicans' tax cut bills (H.R. 3950 and H.R. 4790 [P.L. 80–471], following H.R. 1) and the Taft-Hartley Act (H.R. 3020 [P.L. 80–101], which followed the Case Bill H.R. 4908 of the 79th Congress).

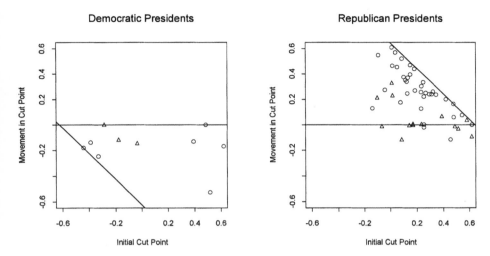

Figure 6.3. Concessions during Veto Bargaining

the zero line may simply involve noisy data but they also hint at the possibility of "blame game vetoes." The three cases are the ban on military aid to Turkey during the Ford administration, conflict over renewing the Clean Water Act during the latter part of the Reagan administration, and a dispute over federal funding of abortions in the District of Columbia during the Bush administration.[9] Twelve points lie on or abut the zero line. Presumably these bills were geared for an override vote, and indeed nine of the twelve or 75% involve bargaining episodes in which the second bill in the pair of bills was vetoed.

Figure 6.4 addresses the second and third predictions. The figure provides box plots of concessions measured with the cut point method. The bills are those in the right-hand panel of Figure 6.3, that is, the pairs of bills vetoed during Republican administrations. Is it true that concessions are small between successive bills, when both are geared for passage via an override attempt? The leftmost box plot in Figure 6.4 presents data on pairs of bills with two override attempts ($n = 6$). That is, Congress passed a bill; the president vetoed it; Congress repassed the bill; the president revetoed; and Congress attempted yet again to override the veto. As shown, concessions in such bills were very small. The second box plot shows data for similar pairs of bills, but for these bills Congress attempted to override only the second of the two vetoes ($n = 4$). All but

[9] Respectively, the chain H.J. Resolution 1131/H.J. Resolution 1163 in the 93rd Congress, the chain S. 1128 in the 99th and H.R. 1 in the 100th Congress, and the chain H.R. 3026/H.R. 3610 in the 101st Congress.

159

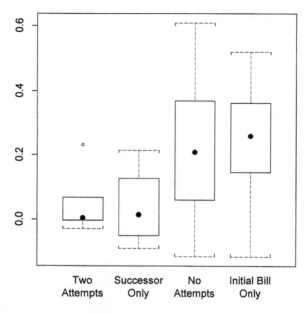

Figure 6.4. Concessions and Override Attempts

one of these pairs involve bills that were initially pocket-vetoed. Again, the measured concessions are very small. Since the first category is surely composed of bills geared for override attempts, and the second probably so, the data strongly confirm the second prediction.

The third and fourth box plots address the final prediction. The third box plot indicates concessions in pairs of bills, neither of which involved an override attempt ($n = 14$). The median concession among such bills was about .2 on the Poole-Rosenthal scale. The mean concession in this group was statistically significantly different from that of the first two groups ($p = .02$ and $p = .06$, respectively). The fourth box plot examines pairs of bills in which Congress attempted to override only the first of the two bills ($n = 28$). Only two of the successor bills in these pairs were vetoed, and those two were pocket-vetoed. Hence, these bills do not seem to have been geared for an override attempt upon repassage (in some cases the initial override attempt failed by a wide margin). Again, the median concession is substantial and statistically significantly different from the two categories most likely to contain bills geared for override attempts ($p = .003$ and $p = .04$ respectively).

Discussion

The evidence mustered in this section goes well beyond the "stylized fact" of concessions built into the sequential veto bargaining model. The patterns in the concessions data clearly corroborate the models. It is important to acknowledge, though, the predictions I tested were quite general because the difficulty of measuring key variables (like the spatial location of the bill and the status quo) precluded tests more closely tied to the fine structure of the models. Indeed, any sensible alternative model of veto bargaining should be able to generate the predictions about concessions that I tested. Consequently, the tests in this section can be seen less as support for the specific model of veto bargaining used throughout this book than for the broad, bargaining orientation embedded in those particular models.

DEADLINES AND THE PROBABILITY OF VETOES

Predictions about phenomena that have never been studied afford a particularly attractive venue for testing a model. Fortunately, the veto bargaining models of Chapter 4 make predictions about a hitherto unstudied phenomenon, for which it is possible to gather the needed data. The prediction concerns a deadline effect: for important legislation, the probability of a veto should decrease in the "last period," that is, at the end of a Congress immediately preceding a presidential election. This prediction emerges directly from the SVB model and indirectly from the override model.

The Predictions

Why does the model predict a deadline effect? The prediction is easier to understand in the override model. It would be senseless to schedule a bill geared for an override in the final days of a Congress since the president can simply pocket-veto the bill. Such a bill must be scheduled earlier in the session; if it cannot be, the content of the bill must be altered to make presidential acceptance more likely. Since congressmen will shift such veto-prone bills from the final days of the session into the earlier period, veto rates in the later period should be lower than in the earlier period.

The sequential veto bargaining model also predicts a drop in the probability of a veto, but the mechanism is more subtle. In the SVB model, bargaining takes place in the shadow of an electoral deadline. In the last period, strategic turndowns no longer make sense for the president – there is no more value in building a reputation for the future because "the future is now." This factor makes the president more inclined to accept Congress's offers. There are two countervailing forces, however. First, Congress will anticipate the president's greater receptivity and toughen its offers, thereby increasing the probability of veto. Second, Congress can now make a real take-it-or-leave-it offer to the president, since it is the last period. This offer will be tougher than it would be absent the deadline, and may also provoke a veto. Given the presence of contending effects – greater willingness to accept offers but a greater propensity to make tougher offers – one can imagine the probability of vetoes falling, rising, or remaining the same. Securing a definite prediction requires actually solving the equations governing offers and acceptances. When one does, one finds that the model predicts tougher offers but not ones so tough they completely offset the president's greater propensity to accept bills. In other words, the probability of vetoes should *fall* in the last period.

Figure 6.5 illustrates the predicted deadline effect, using explicit solutions to the equations governing offers and acceptances.[10] The figure is based on a five-period game, given a status quo of 1 and a type space of [0, 1]. Each line in the figure shows that expected rates of presidential acceptance – settlement rates, that is, one minus the veto probability – at each period in the game at a given level of q, the probability of a bargaining breakdown (recall that low q corresponds to important bills). As shown, settlement rates in the five-period game are generally flat over the early periods of bargaining, fall in the penultimate round if the probability of a breakdown is low (i.e., if the legislation is important), and then increase in the last period. This increase in the settlement rate is the deadline effect – the probability of a veto should *fall* in the last period. If the bill is important, so that q is low, the predicted deadline effect can be dramatic.

The figure actually indicates three hypotheses about the deadline effect:

1. The deadline effect should be larger for more important bills; it may be small or nonexistent for less important bills.
2. Within a significance class, the probability of a veto should be no higher in the last period (the deadline effect) than earlier.
3. In the last period, the probability of a veto should not vary across significance classes.

The last prediction arises from the fact that in the last period the probability of a breakdown in bargaining ceases to have any meaning:

[10] The figure requires solutions to the SVG game for any finite length, an extension of the analysis in the appendix of Chapter 4. These solutions can be found in Cameron and Elmes 1995.

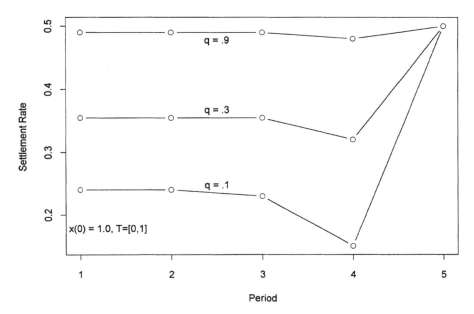

Figure 6.5. Settlement Rates in a Five-Period Game

there is no longer the possibility of making another offer anyway, at least before the election delivering the players' payoffs.

This analysis assumes substantial policy differences between president and Congress. It is a divided government scenario. During unified government, the probability of vetoes is so low that it can hardly decrease any more, so attempts to detect a deadline effect would be pointless. For practical purposes, the hypotheses concern divided government.

Data

The data consist of all bills presented to the president in the congressional sessions terminating in a year of a presidential election, during divided government in the postwar period. That is, they consist of all bills presented to the president in the sessions of 1948, 1956, 1960, 1972, 1976, 1984, 1988, and 1992. During these years, Congress enacted 3,558 public laws and presidents vetoed 128 public bills. However, 15 of the vetoes were overridden. Hence, the number of bills presented to the president was $3,558 + 128 - 15 = 3671$ with an overall veto rate of $128/3671 = 3.5\%$.

I operationalize the "final period" as the final two weeks of the sessions in question. Determining which bills were presented to the pres-

Table 6.1. *Bills presented, vetoes, and veto rates early versus late in congressional sessions*

	Early in session			Late in session			
Significance	Bills presented	Vetoes	Veto rate	Bills presented	Vetoes	Veto rate	Deadline effect
A or B	52	14	27%	33	3	9%	18
C	163	22	13%	127	14	11%	2
D	1,875	21	1%	1,417	54	4%	−3
Total	2,090	57	3%	1,577	71	5%	−2

Note: Data for congressional sessions with divided government and a presidential election (1948, 1956, 1960, 1972, 1976, 1984, 1988, and 1992). "Late" indicates last two weeks of congressional session; "early" is the remainder of the session. For levels of significance, see Chapter 2.

ident in the last two weeks of these sessions (presented, not signed into law during that period) turns out to be surprisingly difficult.[11] My best estimate is that 2,090 bills or 57% were presented to the president "early" in those sessions (before the last two weeks) and 1,577 bills or 43% were presented "late" in the sessions (during the last two weeks). These figures testify to the frenetic pace of law making at the close of congressional sessions.

Results

Table 6.1 indicates the number of bills presented to the president, vetoes, and veto rates in years with divided government and presidential elections. In Table 6.1 I combine significance categories A and B in order to achieve enough observations for reliable results. Figure 6.6 portrays the data. There, the actual data are shown with the letters *e* for early rates and *l* for later rates. The logit model in Table 6.2 (discussed later) summarizes the structure in the data. The lines in the figure show the fit from the statistical model.

Overall, as shown in Table 6.1, the veto rate early in the congressional

[11] In some years, the dates are easily found in the summary listing of public laws in *CQ Almanac*, while the dates of vetoes are readily available. However, in many years the *CQ Almanac* did not include this information in its summary listings. For those years I matched each bill signed during the last two weeks of the session, or after its close (as indicated in the summary listings in the *Daily Digest* portion of the *Congressional Record*), with the legislative histories in *Congressional Index*. All such bills were then cross-matched with the significance data.

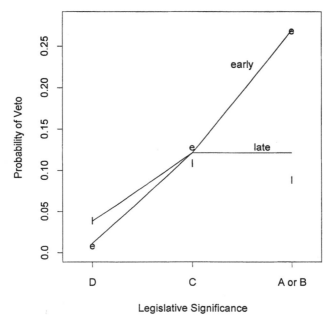

Figure 6.6. The Deadline Effect

sessions in question was about 3% while that in the last two weeks of the session rose somewhat, to 5% – the opposite of the supposed deadline effect. In point of fact, though, the models' predictions concern deadline effects *within* and *across* significance classes. The data in the table need a closer look.

The first prediction is that, *for important legislation,* the probability of a veto should fall in the last period. For the most important legislation, levels A and B, the veto rate during the bulk of the session was 27%. During the last two weeks it fell to 9%, a decrease of 18 percentage points or two-thirds.[12] A simple proportions test indicates little chance that the rate late in the session is not smaller than that early in the session ($p = .04$).[13]

The model also predicts that the deadline effect – the decrease in veto

[12] In categories A and B considered separately, the veto rate fell from 31% to 14% and 22% to 5%, respectively. Thus, the deadline effect was 17 percentage points in both cases. However, the number of observations is so small, especially for B-level legislation, that these numbers cannot be taken very seriously.

[13] Given the hypothesis that the rate at the end of the session should be lower than that earlier, the indicated probability is from a one-tailed test. The equivalent p value from a two tailed test is $p = .08$.

rates – should be larger for more important legislation than less important legislation. As indicated, the actual deadline effect for level C (routine) bills and level D (minor) bills was 2 percentage points and −3 percentage points, respectively. In other words, the deadline effect for important legislation (18 percentage points) appears much larger than that for routine and minor legislation. Simple difference of means tests (not shown) indicate only tiny chances that the deadline effect for major legislation was not larger than that for routine legislation and the deadline effect for routine legislation was not larger than the deadline effect for minor legislation.

The second prediction is that *within* a significance class, the probability of a veto should be no higher in the last period than earlier. The proportions test for important legislation, discussed earlier, strongly supports this prediction for important legislation. For routine legislation, the level C bills, the veto rate early in the session was 13% while that later in the session was 11%. This deadline effect has the correct sign but it is very small. Neither one-sided nor two-sided tests reject the hypothesis that the two rates are the same.[14] In short, the prediction is borne out for important and routine legislation.

The case is quite different for minor legislation. Among the D level bills, the veto rate early in the session was only 1%. The rate late in the session actually rose, to about 3%. This difference is quite small, but proportions tests indicate the difference is statistically significant ($p = 0$), hardly a surprise given the large sample sizes.

The third set of predictions concerns veto rates across significance levels for bills late in the session: the rates should be equal. A proportions test indicates that the rates for important and routine legislation (9% and 11%, respectively) do not differ statistically significantly ($p = .99$). However, it is quite clear that the veto rate for minor legislation, 4%, is indeed different from that of routine and important bills ($p = .0002$).[15]

The logit model in Table 6.2 neatly summarizes the patterns in the data; fitted values from the model are shown via lines in Figure 6.6. The small residual deviance relative to the null deviance shows that the model fits the data extremely well. The interaction between A or B legislation and the condition "early" is the most noteworthy deadline effect in the

[14] Let the null hypothesis be that the rates are the same. If the alternative is that the late rate is greater, $p = .67$; if the alternative is that the two rates are different, $p = .65$.

[15] The reported probability is a two-tailed test of the Ds versus the As, Bs, and Cs pooled together. A test for the Ds versus the Cs yields the same result ($p = .04$). The test fails to find a statistically significant difference between the D rate and the A or B rate ($p = .28$) but this is clearly a result of the small n in the A or B legislation.

Table 6.2. *Logit model of deadline effects*

Independent variables	
Minor legislation	−1.24**
	(.22)
Minor: Early	−1.25**
	(.26)
Major: Early	0.99**
	(.36)
Intercept	−1.99**
	(.17)
Null deviance (df = 5)	123.3
Residual deviance (df = 2)	0.74

Note: Standard errors in parenthesis.
** $p < .05$.

data. The model estimates the magnitude of the effect as about 15 percentage points. Forcing equality between early and late rates for routine legislation introduces little lack of fit into the model. Finally, the striking difference between minor (D level) legislation and the other levels is indicated by the variable D and its interaction with the condition "early."

Discussion

The theoretical models make novel, nonobvious predictions about deadline effects within and across categories of legislation. Both within and across *important* and *routine* legislation, observed deadline effects look exactly like those predicted by the models. At the same time, the models fail badly in their predictions about minor legislation. Why? One possibility is that the models are simply wrong, despite their success with more consequential legislation. Another possibility, though, is that the models omit something important about the politics of minor legislation.

To see what might be missing, consider *how* minor legislation deviates from what we would expect on the basis of the models and the rest of the data. First, *the veto rate in the last period is too low*. The models predict constant rates across significance classes in the last period, and indeed we observe a rate of about 12% in both routine and important legislation. We would therefore expect the same rate in minor legislation, about three times the actual rate (4%). There is an obvious reason for this discrepancy, however. The models implicitly assume the president cares about the legislation in question. If he doesn't, there is no chance of a veto. Presidents surely care about important legislation; they probably care about most routine bills; but only rarely will they have preferences about minor legislation. Most minor bills will never be in danger of a veto, hence the surprisingly low veto rate. This argument applies not only to minor bills offered early in the session but also to those offered late, and indeed veto rates for such bills are also very low.

Second, the *veto rate rises rather than falls in the last period*. What missing element could explain why this is true *only* for minor bills? One answer involves the logic of bill scheduling. First, recall that Congress enacts a vastly disproportionate number of bills in the last few days of a session. The sequential veto bargaining model explains why this happens: if there is a chance the president will veto a bill, Congress is better off making a single take-it-or-leave-it offer rather than engaging in sequential veto bargaining. This surprising fact is illustrated in Figure 6.7, which graphs the expected utility of Congress for bargaining sequences of different lengths (again the figure is based on explicit solutions to the SVB model). As shown, the expected utility of a single offer is greater for Congress than the expected utility of multiple offers. The reason is simple: the president has a stronger incentive to accept a one-shot offer, ceteris paribus, and so Congress can write a tougher bill. With a longer bargaining horizon, the president can behave strategically and extract concessions.

The attractiveness of one-shot offers – a surprising consequence of sequential bargaining – explains why so much of Congress's business takes place in its final hours. Of course, there is a limit to how many bills can be processed at the end of a session. Moreover, a filibuster becomes a potent threat when the agenda is crowded and the end of the session looms large. Hence, congressmen will schedule some important legislation earlier in the session. But absent the threat of a filibuster and excessive congestion costs, congressmen have a strong incentive to schedule a bill late in the session if they anticipate presidential opposition to the measure.

Now consider two minor bills, one facing at least some chance of a veto and the other facing no chance at all. The sponsor of the first bill has an incentive to delay its consideration until the end of the session; the sponsor of the second bill does not. Indeed, congestion costs and competition for agenda space may compel early consideration of the uncontested bill, the bill with no chance of a veto. Suppose there are many uncontested bills, as is surely true for minor legislation. If the logic of scheduling plays out repeatedly, the uncontested minor bills will be concentrated in the earlier periods while contested minor bills will be slotted disproportionately into the later period. Consequently, the veto

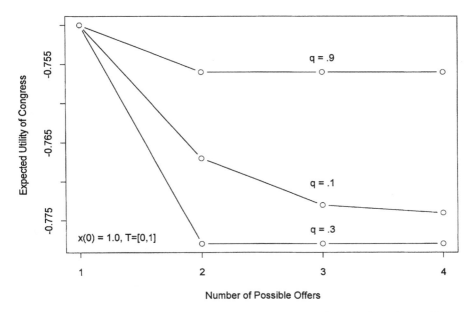

Figure 6.7. Expected Utility (EU) of Congress and the Number of Possible Offers

rate for minor legislation should actually rise in the final period. This mechanism will not apply to important or even routine bills, where uncontested bills are rarities.

The argument in the preceding paragraphs sketches a theory of bill scheduling in Congress. In this theory the peculiar behavior of minor legislation emerges not despite the logic of veto bargaining but because of it. Whether this theory has merit and hence turns an apparent counterexample into a solved problem requires much more elaboration and empirical investigation than I can muster here. Nonetheless, it provides some grounds for "bracketing" the peculiar behavior of minor bills, at least temporarily. At the higher levels of significance, the models' predictions about deadline effects find strong, consistent, and unambiguous support.

DIVIDED GOVERNMENT AND LEGISLATIVE PRODUCTIVITY

The criticism most frequently leveled at the separation-of-powers system is that it is terribly susceptible to gridlock.[16] Despite the need for new

[16] Parts of this section are drawn from Cameron et al. 1997.

policy initiatives and new legislation, the criticism goes, the separation-of-powers system locks into immobility if policy differences between the branches are at all severe. If government is to act vigorously (in this view) the separated institutions need to be reunited through the extra-constitutional mechanism of a strong political party, in effect mimicking a parliamentary system (Sundquist 1988). Or better yet, the separation-of-powers system should be junked in favor of a parliamentary system. Among political scientists, criticism of this sort is often advanced by advocates of parliamentarism.[17] But it has a long history among specialists in American politics as well.

It was long believed that the historical experience supported this view. Certainly some notable cases can be mustered to support the view that unified government brings surges in legislative productivity and divided government slumps. For example, the Great Society Congress, the 89th, was a unified party Congress. So were the New Freedom and New Deal Congresses earlier in the century. Some of the apparently unproductive Congresses of the 1950s, under Eisenhower, were divided party Congresses. The 102nd Congress, under Bush, was widely perceived as a gridlock Congress and it was, of course, a divided party Congress.

The conventional wisdom received a severe check with the publication of David Mayhew's ingenious *Divided We Govern: Party Control, Lawmaking, and Investigations, 1946–1990* (1991). Mayhew took the unprecedented step of counting the number of landmark enactments, using a defensible scheme for scoring legislative significance. (The data on legislative significance described in Chapter 2 are lineal descendants of Mayhew's data.) Simple statistical tests revealed at best small differences in the legislative productivity of unified versus divided party Congresses, at least for landmark enactments.

Mayhew's finding is somewhat disturbing from the perspective of the class of models used in Chapter 4. Those models seem to imply a degree of "gridlock" in American government when the policy preferences of the executive and legislative branches are systematically at loggerheads, as often happens during divided government. The mechanism is not the direct murder of bills through the veto. Instead, the mechanism is indirect, the *anticipation* of vetoes. In this account, anticipation of vetoes – the second face of power – ought to lead Congress to avoid some enactments that it otherwise would offer, if the president were more accommodating.

The data on significant legislation used throughout this book offer the chance to revisit the debate on divided government and legislative pro-

---

[17] See, for example, Linz 1994. Comparativists advance other criticisms as well, many quite thought-provoking in the American context. These are ably reviewed, and partially rebutted, in Shugart and Carey 1992: chap. 3.

ductivity. Using these data, one can estimate the size of the "anticipation effect" during divided government. The results should be taken with a grain of salt, since models of legislative productivity are in their infancy. Even so, the results provide another test of the models and allow an evaluation of the gridlock critique of American government.

The Prediction

The relationship between the separation-of-powers models of Chapter 4 and legislative productivity is more complex than one might initially suppose. So it is worth taking some pains to lay out the prediction.

At first glance, the sequential veto bargaining model and the data in Chapter 2 may suggest that the veto ought not to depress counts of important legislation. The reason is, vetoes are not fatal bullets but bargaining ploys, at least for important legislation. Using the data on veto chains from 1945 to 1992, one can count the number of level A (landmark) bills actually killed by presidential vetoes – that is, bills that were vetoed, not overridden, and not ultimately enacted in a successor bill in the president's administration. The number of such bills is five, hardly enough to seriously depress overall counts of congressional production of very important legislation, even with individual Congresses.[18]

Unfortunately, this argument is quite incomplete because it neglects the second face of power discussed in Chapter 4. To see the impact of the second face of power in this context, return to Figure 4.5 with its illustration of accommodating, compromising, and recalcitrant presidents. First consider the top figure, illustrating an accommodating president. Assume for the moment that the president has an absolute veto, and focus on the simple case of complete and perfect information. Given the ideal points for president and Congress shown in the figure, what set of status quos is Congress willing and able to move? The answer is, only those status quos that lie outside of the interval between the ideal points of the two players. For example, if the status quo lies to the left of c, Congress's ideal point, Congress can move the policy to its ideal point without fear of a veto. If the status quo lies to the right of the president's ideal point, Congress can move the policy to a point within the interval between the two ideal points (perhaps even to its own ideal point). But points between the two ideal points cannot be moved closer to Congress, because the president will veto such moves. Now consider the lower

[18] The bills are: H.R. 7935 in the 93rd Congress (raised the minimum wage for nonfarm workers), S. 425 (strip mining regulation) also in the 93rd Congress, H.R. 5900 in the 94th Congress (common site picketing), H.R. 1487 in the 101st Congress (State Department authorization), and H.R. 11 in the 102nd Congress (urban tax bill).

panel of Figure 4.5, illustrating a recalcitrant president. Again the same logic applies. What is important to note is that the set of immovable points has grown much larger, because the president's ideal is located much farther from that of Congress. Understanding this fact, Congress will not even attempt to move many status quo policies that it could easily move were the alignment like that in the top panel.

The top panel, in which the ideal points of president and Congress are relatively close, can be taken as representative of unified government. The bottom panel, where the ideal points are more distal, can be taken as representative of divided government. In either case, there are many status quo policies that cannot possibly be moved. But in the divided government scenario, the "immovable region" is far, far wider. If the legislative productivity of Congress is inversely proportional to the size of the immovable region, then legislative productivity should be lower under divided government than unified government.

Many objections surely suggest themselves. Political scientist Keith Krehbiel has explored some of these in a sophisticated and ambitious analysis of gridlock (1998: chaps. 2–3). Krehbiel's analysis uses simple spatial models of the kind employed in Chapter 4. He refers to the region containing immovable policies as the "gridlock region," and his more carefully considered calculation of the region takes into account veto overrides and filibusters in the Senate. He also discusses "quasi-dynamic" extensions to the analysis. For example, he notes that if a configuration of ideal points persists for an extended time, legislative productivity might decline as the supply of movable policies is exhausted. (In the longer run, though, social change will continually add to the stock of new issues.) He also considers a kind of "winnowing down" in the stock of movable policies that might occur as one configuration of ideal points succeeds another. I alluded to this intriguing argument in Chapter 5, when I discussed the success of the Bush administration in beating override attempts. Using the winnowing notion and particular placements of filibuster players, Krehbiel is able to generate examples in which general gridlock prevails even during unified government. Nonetheless, even within Krehbiel's much more elaborated model, it is usually true that, ceteris paribus, a switch from a president with preferences distal to Congress (i.e., the median voter in Congress) to one with proximal preferences decreases the size of the gridlock set, and vice versa.

In short, then, the prediction is that the number of highly significant laws produced during periods of divided government should be smaller on average than that produced during unified government, ceteris paribus. However, the direct death of bills through the veto should contribute only modestly to the decline in important bills. Instead, the reduction should be attributable to a decline in the number of very important laws passed by Congress.

Data

In Chapter 2, I briefly described the data on legislative significance that William Howell, Scott Adler, Charles Riemann, and I have collected, so I will not repeat the description here. In the analysis that follows, I focus on just the level A bills, the bills identified by contemporary observers as legislative landmarks.

Figure 6.8 presents the data, showing the production of landmark enactments by Congress from 1945 to 1994 (the data include only public laws). The dotted line in the panel is the fit from a highly flexible, locally weighted regression, as an aid in visualizing the data. As noted by Mayhew, landmark enactments steadily rise through the late 1950s, peak in the Congresses of the late 1960s and early 1970s, and decline thereafter. At the time I write, the cause for this bulge in enactments remains a mystery. Because it extends over unified and divided governments, rising and falling during both, it seems hard to account for in a simple way based on this distinction.

The time trend represented by the bulge creates problems for a statistical analysis. For example, a simple t-test for the difference in means between periods of unified versus divided government will largely reflect the distribution of periods of divided government relative to the "bulge" of enactments, rather than the true effect of divided government.

Moreover, data of this kind – called "nonstationary" in time series analysis – violate the assumptions underlying standard regression techniques. Fortunately, it can be shown that these data are "trend stationary" (Cameron et al. 1997). In other words, if one controls for the bulge, standard regression techniques can be appropriately applied to the data (Enders 1995).[19] The analysis searches for an effect of divided government on legislative productivity *controlling* for the bulge in enactments, which itself remains unexplained. If unified government were somehow responsible for the upswing in the bulge, and divided government somehow responsible for its downswing, then the divided government effect reported here would be an underestimate.

Results

The first column in Table 6.3 reports the results of regressing a constant, time, time-squared, and a dummy variable, "unified," on the level A

[19] The critical point is the residuals from the regression are stationary, which is the case here (Cameron et al 1997).

173

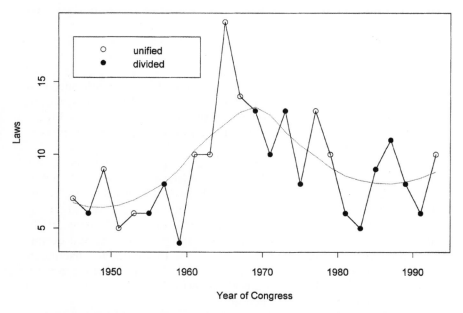

Figure 6.8. Surges and Slumps in the Production of Landmark Legislation

enactments. The constant, time, and time-squared control for the bulge, while the critical effect is captured by "unified." The model indicates that during periods of divided government, Congress produces about three fewer landmark bills per session than during periods of unified government. The effect is statistically significant at $p = .02$.[20]

Krehbiel argues that a better test uses *changes* in productivity and putative *changes* in the gridlock region (1998). The second column in Table 6.3 pursues this suggestion. The dependent variable in this regression is differences in the detrended level A enactments. I first detrended the level A enactments by regressing a constant, time, and time-squared on the level A enactments. The residuals from this regression are detrended level A enactments. The change in this variable serves as the dependent variable. The independent variables are a constant and *change in party status*, the first difference of "unified." The latter is of course the proxy for change in the size of the gridlock region. This variable takes a value of "one" if government switches from divided to unified,

[20] Poisson regressions can be more appropriate than OLS regressions for count data (McCullagh and Nelder 1989). We report Poisson regressions in Cameron et al. 1997. The Poisson regressions fit the data slightly better but the statistical and substantive results are virtually identical. I report the OLS estimates here, since they are somewhat easier to interpret.

Table 6.3. *Divided government and legislative productivity,*
1945–1994

Variables	Group A	Change in detrended group A
Unified	3.05**	—
	(2.1)	
Change in control	—	5.25***
		(1.8)
Time	1.07***	—
	(0.3)	
Time-squared	−0.04***	—
	(0.01)	
Constant	1.62	0.83
	(2.1)	(0.7)
n	25	24
df	21	22
D-W	1.5	2.4
R^2	.34	.24

Note: Standard errors in parenthesis.
** Significant at .05 level; *** significant at .01 level. Results estimated with OLS.

"zero" if party control does not change, and "minus one" if party control switches from unified to divided. As shown, change in party status is highly statistically significant. The coefficient suggests that a switch from divided to unified party government increases the production of landmark enactments by about five bills, relative to the production in the previous divided party configuration.

The results in Table 6.3 should be taken with a grain of salt. Theories about the legislative productivity of Congress are in their infancy. The time series are short, better measures of the gridlock interval are needed, and the dynamic structure of the data demands a closer look. We can anticipate many changes in our understanding of legislative productivity in the years ahead. Nonetheless, *the results seem to show the second face of power in operation, exactly as predicted in the models of Chapter 4 and in Krehbiel's theory of gridlock.*

How large is the effect? In Cameron et al. 1997, we use slightly more sophisticated methods that adjust for the fact that the data are counts and cannot go below zero. We investigate the properties of a model similar to the first reported here. In that model, the predicted magnitude of the divided government effect ranges from a low of 1.6 laws in the 79th Congress (1945–46), to a maximum of 3.7 laws in the 93rd Congress (1973–74). In that model, the percentage effect of divided government is constant. We find a 28% reduction in output by the move from unified to divided government and, conversely, a 39% increase in output by the move from divided to unified. Over the period 1945–94, Congress actually enacted 226 level A laws (which is, of course, the cumulative sum predicted by the model). A simple simulation shows that the cumulative production predicted by the model is 270, if we assume unified government throughout that period. The difference is 44 landmark enactments. The historical record shows that vetoes directly killed only 5 such laws. The remainder – 39 enactments – provides one estimate of the cumulative magnitude of the second face of power.

Discussion

My statistical analysis of divided government and legislative productivity is at some variance with the "no effect" finding reported in David Mayhew's *Divided We Govern* (1991). But does the analysis undermine Mayhew's basic conclusion, "divided we govern"? Not really. Mayhew's conclusion acted as a needed corrective to those who argue that the separation-of-powers system is plagued by paralytic gridlock. The data show quite clearly that even during periods of divided government, Congress and the president still enact landmark legislation, in considerable though somewhat reduced numbers. In addition, Congress and the president enact more routine legislation like clockwork. If "gridlock" means "paralysis" and "inability to legislate," then it is indeed the case that "divided we govern."

Nonetheless, an important proviso is needed: "divided we govern" but *in a different way than "united we govern."* The data on concessions and the data on legislative productivity taken in combination suggest the following picture, at least for very important bills. During divided government, a few items are taken off the legislative table that would have found a place under unified government. However, many others remain. Importantly, the *content* of the remaining items may differ from what would have been under unified government. And haggling between the branches, in the form of veto bargaining, shapes some items even further. Occasionally, when bargaining breaks down, the haggling kills an item. But breakdowns are rare for very important bills. In most cases Congress and the president find their way to an agreement that reflects the preferences of both parties.

Testing the Models

In Chapter 5, I began with data and then used the models to explain empirical patterns. In this chapter, I reversed this process. I began with the models and then searched for or created new data to see if predicted patterns, some quite subtle, actually exist. I used three very different data sets from three very different areas: deadline effects in vetoes, concessions during veto bargaining, and legislative productivity. Across all three data sets and across very different types of predictions, the predictions hold up. The cumulative effect of both investigations is to suggest that the models capture a systematic, important component of interbranch bargaining. In the following chapter I extend the analysis to include not just vetoes but veto threats.

7

Veto Threats

With John Lapinski and Charles Riemann

Let them be forewarned, no matter how well intentioned they might be, no matter what their illusions may be, I have my veto pen drawn and ready for any tax increase that Congress might think of sending up. And I have only one thing to say to the tax increasers: Go ahead and make my day.

President Ronald Reagan (Berman 1990:12)

Repeatedly I have said there are right ways and wrong ways to cut the deficit. This legislation [H.R. 15161, FY 96 Foreign Aid and State Department Authorization] is the wrong way. We did not win the Cold War to walk away and blow the opportunities of the peace on shortsighted, scattershotted budget cuts and attempts to micro-manage the United States foreign policy. If this bill passes in its present form I will veto it.

President Bill Clinton (*CQ Weekly Report*, May 27, 1995:1514)

Veto threats pose a puzzle. The political struggles between the president and Congress are not the verbal sparring matches of college debating societies. They involve real stakes: redistributing wealth, creating rights, making war. But a veto threat is just words. How can the president's verbal posturing, mere words, make much difference in high-stakes bargaining? The problem is a general one in political science. "Actions speak louder than words" is a profound principle of politics, and one that is easy to understand. But why should words, the sheerest "cheap talk," speak at all? Yet they seem to. Rhetoric often has a profound influence on the course of bargaining.[1] But when and when not? And why?

[1] The literature on negotiations provides many examples; see, for instance, Raiffa 1982. More generally, formal theorists have detailed causal mechanisms at work in a variety of settings that involve political rhetoric. The principal innovator in this literature has recently offered an excellent survey (Austen-Smith 1992).

Veto Threats

Veto threats offer an attractive venue for studying political rhetoric. First, veto threats occur regularly during legislative bargaining between the president and Congress. The threats and their effects are well documented in multiple sources. So it is possible, though laborious, to compile systematic data on when threats are used and with what consequence. Second, the type of models developed in Chapter 4 can be modified to incorporate threats. So we can match data about rhetoric during an important form of political bargaining with a model laying out an explicit causal mechanism explaining why rhetoric might be consequential. The resulting lessons are revealing about presidential power, but their implications extend well beyond, to politics in general.

In the following section, we present a brief case study illustrating veto threats in action. The case involves the Surface Transportation Efficiency Act of 1991, an important law whose legislative history shows how threats can shape a bill into a form the president is willing to sign. (The case study on welfare reform, in Chapter 1, illustrates threats leading to a veto.) Following the case study, we describe an ingenious model of veto threats developed by economist Steven Matthews (1989). The model offers a way to understand the events in the case study. But can it also serve as a broadly applicable model of veto threats? To answer that question, we need systematic data. Accordingly, the next two sections describe systematic data on veto threats and assemble them into a statistical portrait of veto threats. These data are among the first ever gathered on veto threats.[2] Can Matthews's model explain the patterns? To a surprising extent it can, though there are some cases at variance with the model. We then briefly consider an alternative to Matthews's model. The alternative fails as a general model of veto threats but hints at interesting possibilities for presidential rhetoric.

VETO THREATS IN ACTION: A CASE STUDY

The Surface Transportation Efficiency Act of 1991 (P.L. 102–240) was one of the major legislative enactments of the 102nd Congress. The sweeping $151 billion bill authorized highway and mass transit programs for the next six years, and made important changes in federal highway policy. Veto threats enabled the Bush administration to shape important parts of the bill.[3]

When highway programs had come up for authorization in 1982 and 1987, Democratic Congresses had largely ignored the wishes of Republican administrations. This is often the fate of an administration's legis-

---

[2] Spitzer 1988:100–3, reports data on veto threats mentioned in the *New York Times Annual Index, 1961–1986.* He found fifty-one veto threats during this period.
[3] This account is drawn from *CQ Almanac* 1991:137–51.

lative initiatives during divided government. This time, however, the Bush administration and its Transportation Secretary, Samuel Skinner, were determined to put some mark on the bill (transportation programs were due to expire on September 30). On February 13, 1991, President Bush announced his transportation proposal. It featured a new national highway system that would link the interstate highway system with local feeder routes, by building a new 155,000-mile system of roads. But in the Senate, Senator Daniel Patrick Moynihan, chair of the Environmental and Public Works Subcommittee on Water Resources, Transportation, and Infrastructure, had his own plans for a bill. Largely ignoring the administration's proposal, his committee crafted a much more radical plan, one that turned policy largely over to the states and envisioned no new system of roads.

Because of the desirability of enacting a "jobs bill" the Democratic leadership put the Moynihan bill on a fast track. In late May, the Senate Environmental and Public Works Committee marked up the bill – and the administration issued its first veto threat. In a letter delivered to the committee chair on the day of the markup, Skinner indicated that failure to include the new National Highway System would probably draw a presidential veto. The committee sent Moynihan's bill to the floor. But there, in "hopes of dodging a White House veto threat," the Senate overwhelmingly agreed to endorse Bush's proposal for a new National Highway System.[4] Skinner called the modification "a step forward" but continued to voice reservations about the bill.

The bill also faced a stormy passage in the House. The Public Works and Transportation Committee wrote a pork-barrel bill, one that raised gas taxes by five cents per gallon (gas taxes had been due to drop by that much) and larded the bill with many special projects. Two days before the committee sent its bill to the floor, Skinner intimated that these provisions might provoke a veto. Rank-and-file Democrats began to worry that the bill's "pork would give Bush a golden opportunity to veto the bill and sock them once again as inveterate tax-and-spenders."[5] When it became clear the new tax would not raise as much money as initially estimated, the tax proposal came unglued. The committee went behind closed doors and rewrote the bill, dropping the tax and trimming the pork. It then reported a new bill. But again Skinner communicated a veto threat, this time concerning the low rate at which states had to match construction costs. Nonetheless, the bill passed the House 343–83.

The bill now went to conference. It had passed both chambers with enough votes to override a veto. But the president is often able to convert

[4] Ibid., 141.
[5] Ibid., 143.

votes in an override fight. Accordingly, the administration kept up a "backdrop" of veto threats so that it could maintain some leverage in the conference committee. Ultimately, the conference report continued to endorse the National Highway System. The increase in the gas tax stayed out. Pork was reduced somewhat. The final bill did not increase the state matching rate but did grant states somewhat more flexibility, as favored by the administration. When the bill finally emerged from conference, the administration dropped its veto threats. It sailed through Congress, 79–8 in the Senate and 372–47 in the House, and was signed by the president. The administration did not get everything it wanted; but its veto threats clearly altered the content of the bill in major respects.

A MODEL OF VETO THREATS

The case study illustrates veto threats at work. But to understand the causal mechanism driving the events, we need a model. In fact, rational choice analysts have developed two different theories of political rhetoric.[6] In both models rhetoric alters the course of political bargaining. But the two models employ very different causal mechanisms to explain why words matter, and the two models have distinctly different implications. For the moment, I focus on the first and more powerful of these models. I briefly examine the second near the end of the chapter.

The first model, the *coordination model*, is illustrated by President Bill Clinton's words at the head of the chapter. In this model, rhetoric helps the two sides avoid a bad outcome and reach a mutually advantageous agreement. But the rhetoric is hardly neutral in its effects. Speakers may use it strategically, to bend agreements in their favor.

The Coordination Model

The coordination model is closely related to Chapter 4's models of veto bargaining. In fact, the override and sequential veto bargaining models are dynamic versions of the coordination model, minus the veto threat. Thus, like those models, the coordination model incorporates an explicit representation of the president's policy reputation, as perceived by Congress. The president enters the model with a policy reputation in Congress, reflected in Congress's beliefs about the president's type t.

The following point is fundamental: if the president's veto threat is to have any effect on the legislature, Congress must be somewhat unsure

[6] The first model is that of Matthews 1989; the second is provided in Ingberman and Yao 1991. I discuss Ingberman and Yao's model later.

181

about what policies the president will accept. His type cannot be known with certainty. If it were, the threat could not possibly work since Congress would know what the president will do. The coordination model therefore incorporates incomplete information.

The coordination model modifies the sequence of play in the basic model of Chapter 4 to allow the president to send a message to Congress before it enacts a particular bill. The model places no a priori restrictions on the exact form of the message. However, the message is assumed to be "costless" in the technical sense that it is "payoff irrelevant" for both players. In other words, it costs no money directly and consumes no valuable time either to send or receive. It is just words. But though the message is "cheap talk," it may still have an effect on Congress *if the words alter the president's policy reputation.* The thrust of the analysis is to show how this happens, under what conditions, and with what consequences.

The model's author, economist Steven Matthews, proves that only two types of equilibria are possible in the model. In the first type ("size 1" equilibria) veto threats do not work. All messages elicit the same bill from Congress. For example, suppose the exact value of t were unknown but Congress was certain the president was an accommodator. Some accommodators might prefer for Congress to pass a bill $x > 0$ (recall that Congress's most preferred policy is normalized to zero), though they would be willing to accept $x = 0$. (I provide an example momentarily). Even if these presidents and only these presidents send a veto threat, Congress would not alter from $x = 0$, for it knows that when push comes to shove the president will accept $x = 0$. Size 1 equilibria always exist for any configuration of types and possible beliefs.[7]

In the second type ("size 2" equilibria) threats do work, in that two distinctly different bills are elicited depending on the message received. The first bill is $x = 0$, elicited by a message whose equilibrium meaning is "Congress, I will accept your most preferred policy." The second bill is a bill $x > 0$, elicited by a message whose equilibrium meaning is "Congress, I may not accept your most preferred bill." In addition, Matthews proves that, at most, two bills are elicitable.

An Example

The following example illustrates Matthews's coordination model. The example is slightly contrived but only to simplify the presentation. The

---

[7] For example, so-called babbling equilibria always exist. In such an equilibrium, the president issues veto threats randomly. Knowing they are random, Congress ignores them; and because Congress ignores them, the president is free to issue random threats. I address problems created by such equilibria later.

Veto Threats

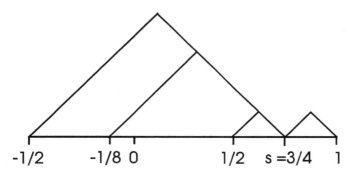

Figure 7.1. An Example of the Coordination Game

policy space is a line running from $-\frac{1}{2}$ to 1 inclusive (see Figure 7.1). There are four possible types for the president: type 1, for whom $t = -\frac{1}{2}$; type 2 for whom $t = -\frac{1}{8}$; type 3 for whom $t = \frac{1}{2}$; and type 4 for whom $t = 1$. The status quo is $\frac{3}{4}$ and Congress's ideal point is normalized to 0. Thus, types 1 and 2 are accommodators, type 3 is a compromiser, and type 4 is recalcitrant. The president's initial policy reputation is captured via a common knowledge prior probability distribution on the four types. Let p_i indicate the probability the president is actually type i ($i = 1,4$). In the appendix to this chapter, I show that Congress offers its ideal point if there is sufficient probability the president is an accommodator. Otherwise, it offers the most favorable policy a compromiser will accept.

In the example, assume Congress begins with $p_1 = \frac{1}{8}$, $p_2 = \frac{1}{8}$, $p_3 = \frac{3}{8}$, and $p_4 = \frac{3}{8}$. If no threat were possible then, using the analysis in the appendix, Congress would offer $x = 0$.[8] But in the threat game the following is an equilibrium: If the president is type 1, he sends a "green light" message. If he is types 2–4, he sends the "veto threat." If Congress receives the "green light" message, it offers its ideal point, which is accepted by types 1 and 2 but vetoed by types 3 and 4. If Congress hears the veto threat, it offers $\frac{1}{2}$. This offer is accepted by types 1, 2, and 3 but vetoed by type 4. In the appendix I provide a proof.

There are thus three paths of play. In the first, the president sends the

[8] Because, using the "offer lemma" in the appendix, $p_1 + p_2 = \frac{1}{4} < \frac{1}{2} p_3 = 3/16$. This result may seem counterintuitive since Congress is so pessimistic about the president accepting $x = 0$. But note that, if the president is recalcitrant, he will veto anything Congress would find more attractive than the status quo. So the recalcitrant types have no influence on a choice between $x = 0$ and $x = \frac{1}{2}$. And even though Congress expects the president to reject $x = 0$ it is still a worthwhile gamble given the attractiveness of $x = 0$ and the relatively small gain from $x = \frac{1}{2}$ relative to $s = \frac{3}{4}$. The specified behavior is indeed rational.

183

"green light" message, Congress responds with $x = 0$, which the president accepts. In the second, the president sends the veto threat, Congress responds with the compromise offer $x = \frac{1}{2}$, which the president accepts. In the third, the president sends the veto threat, Congress responds with the compromise offer $x = \frac{1}{2}$, which the president vetoes.

The behavior of the type 2 president is particularly interesting. This type issues the veto threat but in fact is bluffing: he would accept $x = 0$ if it were offered. But he prefers $x = \frac{1}{2}$ and so issues the threat. The bluff works because the type 3 president also sends the threat, sincerely, trying to avoid a veto that would maintain the status quo.[9]

The example also indicates an important fact about the model: the presence of accommodators is a necessary condition for size 2 equilibria, for without them the "green light" message cannot work (Matthews, 1989:358, remark 2). For example, suppose Congress was sure all types were compromisers but was unsure about the exact location of t. Based upon its beliefs, Congress would prepare a compromising offer. If the president then sent a "green light" message indicating certain acceptance of the compromise, Congress would update its beliefs about the president *and submit a tougher offer*. But then the president, anticipating this, would not send the "green light" message. In other words, only a size 1 equilibrium would be possible. If veto threats are to work, Congress must be uncertain about the president's policy preferences, and uncertain in the right way.

Interpreting the Case Study

The coordination model offers a way to understand the veto threats used in the bargaining over the Surface Transportation Efficiency Act. Just as it had in 1982 and 1987, Congress moved to write its own bill, ignoring the desires of the president. Bush then flashed a veto signal over the issue of the National Highway System. Perhaps Bush was bluffing, but if not, Congress would have a vetoed bill on its hands. Compromise was not too difficult and, as predicted by the model, Congress yielded ground on the issue. The president then sent another veto signal, this time over the gas tax and excessive pork. Again, he may have been bluffing but his reputation lent his message credibility. Again Congress compromised. By this point, the bill looked like it was veto proof and the compromises

[9] In the example, the type 3 president is actually indifferent between the status quo and the offer. This is an uninteresting consequence of the type space in the example. If the type space were continuous, then in a size 2 equilibrium there would be a range of compromisers who sincerely threaten and thereby benefit; the problem could also be avoided by allowing several types of compromisers in the example.

came to an end. But the president's threats, taken in conjunction with his policy reputation, allowed him to shape the bill in important ways.

SYSTEMATIC DATA ON VETO THREATS

Veto threats are neither tracked nor cataloged. Data on them must be assembled from scratch. Political scientists John Lapinski, Charles Riemann, and I have collected data on veto threats from a random sample of bills. The following sections report findings from our research with these data.

Sampling Strategy

We defined the relevant universe of bills as all initially passed nonminor bills presented to the president from the 79th to 102nd Congress (1945–92), the Truman to Bush administrations. This universe consists of 2,284 bills. We did not study veto threats directed at bills that were never passed, for three reasons: the model does not address nonpassed bills, defining a valid sampling strategy for nonpassed bills is problematic, and collecting data on some of the relevant covariates is impossible. Veto threats may decrease the probability of a bill's passage but we cannot measure this effect with our data. By "nonminor," we mean level A, B, and C legislation as defined in Chapter 2. We excluded minor bills – level D bills – from the study because they aren't particularly interesting, presidents rarely direct threats at them, and data for them are often sketchy and unreliable. We also excluded bills that were repassed in modified form after an earlier veto by the same president, in other words, successor bills in veto chains. The reason is a previous veto may well affect the credibility of a threat directed at the repassed bill. The coordination model, however, does allow for this effect. Rather than muddy the waters by including repassed bills, we excluded them.

We partitioned the universe of initially passed nonminor bills presented to the president into bills signed by the president and bills vetoed by the president. To provide observations on the former, we drew a random sample of nonminor signed bills stratified by legislative significance. The sample consisted of 281 signed bills in three categories of legislative significance. To provide sufficient observations on vetoed bills, which are rare events, we oversampled vetoes of nonminor bills. In fact we employed all such cases, a total of 162 bills distributed across the three categories of legislative significance. In all, the number of bills in the study totals 443. The random sample of initially presented signed bills consists of 91 level A bills, 94 level B bills, and 96 level C bills. The initially presented, vetoed bills consist of 26 level A bills, 26 level B bills, and 110 level C bills.

Because we oversampled vetoed bills, this research design is an example of *choice-based sampling*. Researchers frequently use such samples in biomedical research, evaluations of training or treatment schemes, studies of transportation or participation choices, and other cases where a particular outcome is a rare event.[10] Choice-based samples provide an attractive method for economizing on sample sizes. However, standard maximum likelihood techniques applied to such samples yield biased estimates of probabilities. Fortunately, a simple weighing scheme allows estimation of unbiased estimates. The appendix provides more details for those interested.

Variables

For each bill in the study, we compiled an event history detailing whether there was a veto threat, whether there was an apparent concession by Congress following the veto threat, the relationship between the concession and what the president had objected to, whether the president signed or vetoed the bill, whether there was an override attempt, and whether the veto was overridden. To gather this information, first we searched legislative histories for each bill in the annual editions of the *Congressional Quarterly Almanac*. Then, for each bill, we searched the relevant volumes of the *Public Papers of the Presidency* to find additional threats not mentioned in the *Congressional Quarterly* legislative histories. In all cases two of us coded the information independently; the third broke any disputes. Finally, we conducted a search of Nexus for all articles in the *New York Times* and *Washington Post* mentioning veto threats (1977–92). The search of Nexus uncovered no threats not contained in the two other sources.

Veto Threats. We defined a veto threat as any statement made by the president himself or in some cases certain officials that explicitly indicates the president's intention to veto the legislation or implicitly suggests an impending veto. For example, statements by administration officials stating clearly that the president will veto the bill and statements by a congressman indicating certain knowledge based on communications with the president that he will veto the bill were coded as legitimate veto threats. We also coded as veto threats statements in which the president expresses severe reservations about a piece of legislation and implies that he will use his veto power, but does not use direct language

---

[10] Imbens 1992 provides citations to relevant examples.

(e.g., "I will not sign," I will have to veto," etc.). We did not code as threats more ambiguous negative mentions of bills. Nor did we code as threats speculation about vetoes or the opinions of congressmen or other officials. The random sample of initially presented bills contains 106 threatened bills: 30 level A bills, 29 level B bills, and 47 level C bills.

Concessions. For each threatened bill in the sample, we determined whether Congress made concessions on the legislation. *Following* a veto threat by the president, did Congress make changes in the final version of the bill? If so, were these changes in the direction indicated by the president? Did they meet all objections of the president or only some of the objections? To answer these questions we first identified the particular aspects of the bill (i.e., specific provisions, language, and/or general topic) mentioned by the president in the threat. We then examined legislative histories in the *Congressional Quarterly Almanac* and bill signing and veto messages in the *Presidential Papers* to determine how changes in the bill finally presented to the president were connected to the president's objections, taking care to check the timing of threats and concessions. Of the 106 threatened bills in our sample of initially presented bills, Congress made no concessions on 33, "some" concessions on 63, and "capitulated" on 10 bills.

A Check on the Data

In Chapter 2, I calculated the probability of vetoes by significance level under unified and divided government, using the entire universe of legislation presented to the president (see Figure 2.2). It is straightforward to estimate similar rates using the random sample of level A, B, and C legislation, as a check on the soundness of the sampling strategy. Using the entire universe, the veto rates under unified government for level C, B, and A bills were 3%, 4%, and 3%, respectively. Under divided government, the rates for level C, B, and A bills were 9%, 12%, and 20%, respectively. In both cases, the estimated rates in the random sample are the same: 3%, 4%, and 3% under unified government and 9%, 12%, and 20% for divided government.

A STATISTICAL PORTRAIT OF VETO THREATS

Systematic data allow answers to some basic questions about veto threats. What is the probability of a veto threat? What gets threatened? How likely are concessions, given a presidential veto threat? How likely are large versus small concessions? Do threats lead to or head off vetoes?

What effect do concessions have on the probability of a veto? We tackle each of these questions in turn.

Threats

Of the 443 bills in the data base of initially presented nonminor bills, 106 were threatened by the president. If we take into account the sample design, the estimated rate of threats is 14%. However, the rates between unified and divided government show a pronounced difference: less than 4% for unified government and 23% for divided government. During unified government, the observed threat rate was low across all three significance categories. But during divided government, the rate rose dramatically with legislative significance, from 20% for level C to 27% for level B to 34% for level A. Thus, during divided government, presidents threatened to veto more than one-third of the most important bills passed by Congress. This statistic underscores the importance of the veto threat as a legislative tool for presidents during periods of divided government.

Model 1 in Table 7.1 reports a logit model of the probability of veto threats. The fit from this model along with the observed frequencies are displayed in Figure 7.2. Letters show actual frequencies during unified (u) and divided (d) government, respectively. The lines show the fitted values. As shown, the model fits the data reasonably well. Two points stand out. First, there is a very pronounced effect on the probability of a threat due to the switch from unified to divided government. Second, during divided government, there is a distinct difference in the probability of threats between level A or B legislation and level C legislation.

Concessions Following Threats

In the 106 threatened bills in our sample, concessions occurred after the veto threat in all but 33. Appropriately weighing observations in accordance with the sampling scheme, concessions occurred 90% of the time. Some 63 threatened bills showed "some concessions," a rate of 64%. Another 10 showed congressional capitulation, that is, total acquiescence to the demanded changes, an effective rate of 26%.

Threats are so rare during unified government that little can be said about the impact of this variable on the probability of concessions. Model 2 in Table 7.1, a multinomial logit model, investigates the impact of legislative significance on concessions. As shown in Table 7.1, legisla-

Table 7.1. *Logit models of veto threats*

Independent variables	Model 1: Probability of a veto threat	Model 2: Probability of a concession after a threat		Model 3: Probability of a veto	Model 4: Probability of overrides
		Some	Capitulation		
Divided government	1.97***	—	—	.94**	—
	(.43)			(.51)	
Divided government*	.50*	—	—	—	—
	(.34)				
Significance A or B	—	—	—	—	—
Threat	—	—	—	1.04***	.26
				(.51)	(.42)
Significance A* threat	—	—	—	1.34*	—
				(.82)	
Significance B* threat	—	—	—	.75	—
				(.81)	
Significance A or B		.56	−.36	—	—
		(.75)	(−.41)		
		1.67***	1.01***		
Constant	−3.33***	(.38)	(.41)	−3.57***	—
	(.39)			(.42)	
Log-likelihood	−161.46	−90.59		−101.82	−72.96
N	443	106		443	162

Note: Models 1–3 corrected for choice-based sampling; correction unnecessary for Model 4. Standard errors in parentheses. Dependent variables are:

Model 1: 0 for no threat and 1 for threat.

Model 2: 0 for no concessions, 1 for some concessions, and 2 for capitulation.

Model 3: 0 for no veto and 1 for veto.

Model 4: 0 for not override attempt + unsuccessful override attempt and 1 for successful override.

$* p < .15$; $** p < .10$; $*** p < .05$.

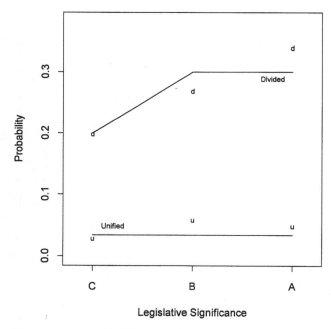

Figure 7.2. Probability of a Veto Threat

tive significance does not exert a statistically significant effect on the probability of "no concession," "some concessions," or "capitulating."[11]

Threats and Vetoes

For the bills in the sample, the overall probability of a veto was 7%, appropriately weighing observations from the sampling scheme. However, as shown in model 3 in Table 7.1, there were pronounced differences in the probability of a veto between threatened and nonthreatened bills, unified and divided government, and bills of different significance levels.

Figure 7.3 shows actual frequencies of vetoes and fitted values from model 3. Again, fitted values are shown as a line while the actual values are shown by tokens numbered 1–4 (1 for nonthreatened bills under unified government, 2 for nonthreatened bills under divided government, 3 for threatened bills under unified government, and 4 for threatened bills under divided government). As shown, the model fits the data quite

[11] A variety of alternative specifications failed to uncover statistically significant covariates.

190

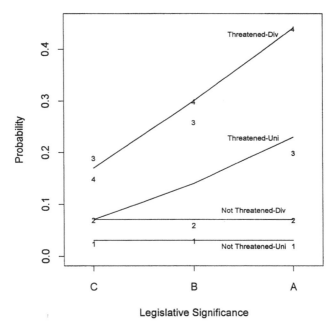

Figure 7.3. Threats and the Probability of a Veto

well except for the threatened bills during unified government. The paucity of observations for this case means that inferences for this category should be drawn with care.

As shown in model 3 and Figure 7.3, if a bill was *not* threatened, the estimated probability of a veto was low across all significance levels. Since these bills were not threatened before they were vetoed, they can be called "shock vetoes." The probability of a shock veto was low. But the probability of a shock veto was about twice as high under divided as unified government, 3% versus 7%.

If a bill *was* threatened, the probability of a veto was much higher than if it were not threatened. For threatened bills, the statistical model indicates that the probability of a veto was again about twice as high under divided as unified government, though this conclusion should be treated with care because of the rarity of veto threats under unified government. The model indicates that for threatened bills the probability of a veto increased dramatically at the higher significance levels. During divided government, where observations are frequent enough to warrant confidence, the estimated frequency of vetoes for threatened bills rose from 17% for level C bills to 30% for level B bills, to 44% for threat-

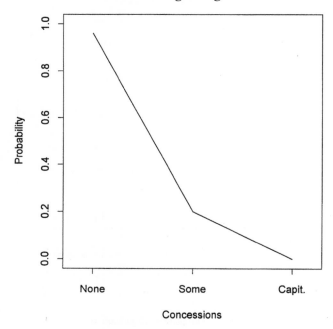

Figure 7.4. Concessions and the Probability of a Veto

ened level A bills. Given the overall rarity of vetoes, the latter is a remarkable number.

Vetoes and Concessions

The magnitude of congressional policy concessions following a threat has a dramatic effect on the probability of a veto. Figure 7.4 displays actual frequencies of vetoes by concession categories.[12] If Congress failed to make a concession in a bill following a veto threat, the president almost invariably vetoed the bill. In contrast, presidents vetoed only 20 percent of bills in which Congress made "some" concessions.[13] If Congress capitulated to the president's demands in a veto threat, the president invariably accepted the bill. There is an obvious puzzle in this data: why would Congress fail to make concessions if such bills are invariably

[12] The lack of variation in the "no concessions" and "capitulation" categories precludes estimating a logit model for this data.

[13] The actual frequency of vetoes for bills in this category was only 4% during unified government but such cases were extremely rare; a t-test fails to uncover a statistically significant difference in veto rates between bills under unified and divided government.

vetoed? We return to this question shortly, when we examine ineffectual veto threats more carefully.

Summary

In sum, an analysis of systematic evidence on veto threats from the postwar period reveals the following patterns:

1. During unified government veto threats rarely occur regardless of the significance of the legislation.
2. During divided government veto threats are frequent and increase in frequency with legislative significance.
3. If a bill is not threatened, a veto is unlikely though not impossible.
4. If a bill is threatened, the probability of a veto increases dramatically, especially during divided government and at the higher levels of legislative significance. But vetoes are not certain even after a threat.
5. Veto threats usually bring concessions.
6. Concessions deter vetoes. The bigger the concession the less likely a threatened bill is to be vetoed.

UNDERSTANDING (MOST) VETO THREATS

How does the model fare at explaining the patterns in the statistical portrait? What can it explain, and where does it seem to fail? Is the picture of threats conveyed by the model at all plausible?

Explaining the Patterns

The model neatly explains why veto threats are rare during unified government but relatively frequent during divided government. During unified government the policy preferences of president and Congress are close. If Congress is close to the president, he is likely to be an accommodator and hence a threat will not be credible. Therefore, we should not see threats. Conversely, during divided government the preferences of Congress and the president are likely to be more distant. But, they are not necessarily at loggerheads. Accordingly, threats can be credible.

The rarity of "shock vetoes" – vetoes without threats – is one of the major implications of the coordination model. Why, however, do shock vetoes occur at all? Some of the cases we record may simply reflect measurement error. Veto threats may have been communicated but not reported in the *Congressional Quarterly*, the *Public Papers*, or the newspapers. In other cases, the president may have been so clearly recalcitrant that a threat was superfluous (only a size one equilibrium was possible).

In these cases, if Congress were serious about enacting a law, the bill should have been geared for an override and therefore should either have passed in an override vote or narrowly failed in such a vote. Of the ninety-three shock vetoes we record, only fourteen were overridden. So it appears that more than anticipated recalcitrance was at work. Legislative histories indicate that once in a while presidents simply change their minds about a bill after it has been presented to them, vetoing it without a threat. An example is President Clinton's veto of a bill limiting shareholder lawsuits, his only veto to be overridden in his first term. The veto seemed to reflect a last-minute shift by Clinton and was genuinely unexpected by observers (*CQ Weekly Report* 1995: December 2: 3641–3643, December 9: 3729, December 23: 3879–80). This kind of randomness could be incorporated into the model but with little illumination of the dynamics of veto threats. In sum, the model's broad prediction about shock vetoes is correct but there are cases in which more is at work than the model allows.

The fact that vetoes are much more likely after a threat, but are by no means certain, is another of the principal predictions of the model. Of course, this pattern accords well with our everyday intuitions about threats and concessions. But the model explains *why* our intuitions work. In the model, Congress, hearing the veto threat, makes a concession in order to reduce the chance of a veto. But the threat is somewhat ambiguous since it cannot convey exactly what the president's preferences are. (A compromiser president would never be willing to state exactly what his reservation policy is since Congress would simply use the information against him.) As a result of this ambiguity, Congress sometimes fails to make a large enough concession, triggering the veto. This line of reasoning also explains why credible threats bring concessions, why concessions deter vetoes, and why larger concessions are more likely to deter vetoes. These patterns emerge directly from the model.

"Significance" is not a component of the coordination model, so it cannot explain why the frequency of veto threats during divided government increases with the significance of the legislation, or why the probability of a veto for a threatened bill increases with legislative significance during divided government. But by now this type of pattern should be familiar from data in earlier chapters. If the coordination model were modified so that revetoes and repassage were possible, with random breakdowns following vetoes, this pattern would probably emerge.

Overall, then, the statistical portrait of veto threats looks very much like what we would expect if the model captures the essential dynamic of most veto threats. The notable exception is ineffectual threats, which are worth examining more closely.

Veto Threats

Ineffectual Threats

Thirty-three observations in the data involve ineffectual threats, that is, no concession followed the threat. Taking into account the sampling scheme, only about 10% of threatened bills show this pattern, so the sequence is rather rare. Ineffectual threats are technically possible in the coordination model, for example, if it were understood that the president's threats were meaningless noise and (conversely) Congress never paid attention to them. But this is hardly a satisfactory explanation for the observations since the presidents involved vetoed every one of these bills. Their threats were manifestly not meaningless noise. What was going on?

Most of these cases involved override attempts that narrowly succeeded (six cases) or narrowly failed (twelve of the observations failed an override vote by ten or fewer votes). If the bills were shaped anticipating a veto and override attempt, concessions following a threat may simply have been too small to warrant notice in the legislative histories. But perhaps no concession was made, and the purpose of the presidential veto threat lay outside either model – for example, position taking for the benefit of the public.

Five of the cases with failed override attempts occurred in presidential election years and failed the override attempt by a wide margin.[14] Such bills clearly fit the profile of Groseclose and McCarty's "blame-game vetoes," bills deliberately constructed to draw a politically damaging veto (Groseclose and McCarty 1996). The remaining ten cases do not display such a clear-cut blame-game profile, either because no override was attempted (three were pocket vetoes) or because the veto occurred in an off-election year (seven cases).[15] It is not clear why Congress passed these bills when they seemed doomed to fail, but such cases amount to less than 3% of threatened bills.

Can The Model Possibly Be Right?

Although close scrutiny reveals some aberrant cases, the broad patterns in the data provide substantial support for the coordination model. But, putting aside the empirical evidence, does the model's portrayal of veto threats make sense? The model portrays veto threats in an almost sunny way: threats work because they help both sides avoid a veto and strike a mutually satisfactory bargain. Needless to say, Senator Moynihan might not have seen President Bush's threats in such a rosy light, for the

[14] These cases are: S. 323 (1992), H.R. 2507 (1992), S. 3 (1992), H.R. 8617 (1976), H.R. 15714 (1972).
[15] The latter might still be blame-game vetoes, of course.

president was blasting legislative hopes the senior senator from New York had nurtured for more than thirty years.[16] Yet the view of threats in the coordination model is essentially beneficent. Most of us, in contrast, associate "threats" with the intimidation of a schoolyard bully, the cry of a holdup man, or the depredations of a Hitler or Saddam. Can the sunny view of threats in the coordination model possibly be correct?

A perspective from the literature on bargaining and negotiations is helpful. Most bargaining situations do not resemble a stickup in a dark alley. They are more akin to buying and selling a house. Here, the trick is "getting to yes" (Fisher and Ury 1981; Raiffa 1982; Young 1991). Abundant evidence from case studies and laboratory experiments, as well as analytical models, indicates that "cheap talk" can help bargainers identify opportunities for mutual gain and avoid bad outcomes. For example, a verbal expression of favorable interest at the beginning of negotiations, though nonbinding and thus a form of cheap talk, can help the partners realize there are mutual gains to be had (Farrell and Gibbons 1989). An indication that a particular provision or demand is a "deal breaker" can keep negotiations on track. The insight of the coordination model is that veto threats – at least much of the time – are a bargaining tactic essentially like those seen in other types of bargaining. The empirical evidence backs up the insight.

AN ALTERNATIVE MODEL: THE COMMITMENT MODEL

There is another way to think about veto threats, however. This perspective is based upon the idea of commitment. The intuition is well conveyed by President Ronald Reagan's words at the head of the chapter. Here, the effect of political rhetoric is to constrain the speaker so he can't retreat from his position without paying a steep price. The speaker's commitment then alters the behavior of opponents. This concept will resonate with anyone familiar with the work of game theorist Thomas Shelling (1960; Crawford 1991). Shelling's work illustrates the power of irrevocable commitments. As he shows, being able to make such a commitment is often equivalent to winning a negotiation. This idea is formalized in the context of veto threats by the commitment model (Ingberman and Yao 1991).

There are striking cases in which presidents apparently make commitment threats. For example, President Bill Clinton leveled a dramatic threat during the State of the Union Address in which he announced his

[16] Moynihan had written an essay in 1960 that contained many of the proposals he wrote into his bill (*CQ Almanac* 1991:139).

health care proposal. "If you send me legislation that does not guarantee every American private health insurance that can never be taken away, you will force me to take this pen and veto the legislation," Clinton declared, waving a pen for emphasis (Johnson and Broder 1996:267). Representative Pete Stark subsequently cited Clinton's threat to ward off attempts to weaken his own, rather liberal proposal for health insurance.

Commitment threats are clearly a two-edged sword. Bush's celebrated threat about tax increases, "read my lips," boomeranged badly when he signed a bill increasing taxes. Clinton came to regret his dramatic threat. He later explained the rationale for making it: "We thought if we did this, we could energize our own supporters, increase the chance that the Republicans would submit a good bill, and that we could then engage in a real serious dialogue." But, in fact, the threat boxed the administration into a position that could not prevail and deterred necessary compromises until too late. Reflecting on the failure of the proposal, the president later concluded, "I shouldn't have issued the veto threat as it turns out" (Johnson and Broder 1996:269–70, 612).

Does the commitment perspective provide a useful alternative to the coordination model as a general framework for understanding most veto threats? Unfortunately, the formal model leads to some strikingly counterfactual predictions. For example, the model predicts that all vetoes of threatened bills should be overridden. Among the 162 initially presented, nonminor bills that were vetoed, 43% were threatened and 57% were not. Among the nonthreatened vetoed bills, the override rate was 15%. Among the threatened vetoed bills, the override rate was 19%, quite far from the predicted 100%. The 95% confidence interval for this proportion is [.11, .30]. Model 4 in Table 7.1 examines the effect of a threat on the probability of a successful veto override, conditional on a veto. As shown, the presence of a veto threat does not increase the probability of a successful veto override.[17] The model's prediction seems quite far from the mark.

The model also predicts that a president vetoes threatened bills unless Congress capitulates to the president's demands. The data on veto threats indicate that 53% of threatened bills violate this prediction. That is, the president threatens the bill, Congress makes a concession but does not capitulate, yet the president signs the bill. Of course, this pattern is exactly what the coordination model would lead one to expect.

The difficulty with the current model of commitment threats is that, while offering insights on the *consequences* of a successful commitment, it is silent on the special circumstances in which the president will have the incentive and ability to *make* a commitment threat. Whether it will

---

[17] Controlling for unified versus divided government does not change the result.

be possible to refine models of commitment threats to identify better those circumstances is a question for future research.

CONCLUSION

Presidential scholars have long suspected that veto threats are a powerful tool for presidents. Standard textbooks, for example, often make this assertion. The data presented in this chapter provide some of the first systematic evidence on the frequency and potency of veto threats. The evidence confirms what had been suspected. What is surprising, however, is just how frequently presidents threaten important legislation during divided government, and how effective threats seem to be in wresting concessions from Congress.

We posed a question at the beginning of the chapter: how can cheap talk be important in high-stakes bargaining? The coordination model supplies an answer. Bargaining outcomes reflect presidential power – but power, as I have argued throughout this book, rests on reputation and beliefs. Under the right circumstances words, mere words, can affect the president's policy reputation and thus the outcome of interbranch bargaining.

Appendix to Chapter 7

This appendix provides proofs for the examples and some technical results needed for the empirical analysis.

Offer Lemma for the Coordination Model Example

Lemma: Congress offers $x = 0$ iff $p_1 + p_2 \geq$ ½ p_3 and $x =$ ½ otherwise.

Proof: Types 1 and 2 will accept $x = 0$ while Types 3 and 4 will veto it. So the expected utility of such an offer is

$$(p_1 + p_2)0 + (1 - p_1 - p_2)(-\tfrac{3}{4}) = (p_3 + p_4)(-\tfrac{3}{4}).$$

Types 1, 2, and 3 will accept $x =$ ½ but type 4 will veto it so the expected utility of $x =$ ½ is

$$(p_1 + p_2 + p_3)(-\tfrac{1}{2}) + (p_4)(-\tfrac{3}{4}).$$

Thus the expected utility of $x = 0$ is greater than or equal to the expected utility of $x =$ ½ iff

$$(p_3 + p_4)(-\tfrac{3}{4}) \geq (p_1 + p_2 + p_3)(-\tfrac{1}{2}) + (p_4)(-\tfrac{3}{4}).$$

$$\Rightarrow p_1 + p_2 \geq \tfrac{1}{2} p_3.$$

Congress has no incentive to make any offer other than $x = 0$ or $x =$ ½ as such offers can only offer less expected utility than one of these two offers. Q.E.D.

Proof for the Coordination Model Example

Claim: the strategies specified in the text constitute a perfect Bayesian equilibrium.

Proof: First, consider a type 1 president. Not only is he accommodating, he actually prefers $x = 0$ to $x = \frac{1}{2}$. So he has no incentive to elicit other than $x = 0$, which he accepts (and he would also accept). Type 2 is also accommodating but prefers to $x = \frac{1}{2}$ to $x = 0$ (his ideal point $z(t) = \dfrac{t + s}{2} = \dfrac{5}{16}$, which is much closer to $\frac{1}{2}$ than 0). So he elicits $x = \frac{1}{2}$ and has no incentive to elicit $x = 0$, though he would accept it. Type 3 will veto $x = 0$ but prefers $x = \frac{1}{2}$ to the status quo. So he elicits $x = \frac{1}{2}$ and has no incentive to deviate. Type 4 will veto both offers (in fact, any offer Congress prefers to the status quo), thus assuring the status quo. So he is indifferent between sending either of the messages and has no incentive to deviate.[18] Now consider Congress's beliefs after it receives a message. Suppose the president sends the "green light" message. Given the specified strategies, after receiving the "green light" Congress must believe $p_1 = 1$ and $p_2 = p_3 = p_4 = 0$, since a type 1 president sends the message. Given these beliefs, using the offer lemma $x_1 = 0$. Conversely, suppose the president sends the other message, the veto threat. Then $p_1 = 0$ since type 1 presidents never send this message in a size 2 equilibrium. But types 2–4 all would send this message. Using Bayes's rule, $p_2 = 1/7$ and $p_3 = p_4 = 3/7$. From the lemma, $x_2 = \frac{1}{2}$ (since $1/7 < 3/14$). Q.E.D.

Weights for the Empirical Analysis

This section derives the weights used in the empirical analysis. The weights allow recovery of unbiased estimates of probabilities from a choice-based, stratified random sample.

The universe of initially presented nonminor bills by significance level was 223 As, 288 Bs, and 1773 Cs. The number of these that were signed were 197 As, 262 Bs, and 1663 Cs. The number that were vetoed were 26 As, 26 Bs, and 110 Cs. The corresponding figures for the sample were: 91 As, 94 Bs, and 96 Cs initially presented and signed; 26 As, 26 Bs, and 110 Cs vetoed. Thus we know the percentage of signed bills and the percentage of vetoed bills in the original universe and in our sample. This allows the calculation of Manski-Lerman weights by stratum,

---

[18] Matthews 1989: 354, condition E2, imposes an equilibrium refinement that requires a president to elicit the most favorable elicitable proposal. According to this refinement, type 4 must elicit $x = \frac{1}{2}$, even though he plans to veto it.

Table 7.2. *Weights to adjust for choice-based stratified random sample*

	Sample		Universe		Conversion factor		Stratification weights	Final weights	
Significance	Signed no. (rate)	Vetoed no. (rate)	Signed no. (rate)	Vetoed no. (rate)	Signed	Vetoed		Signed	Vetoed
A	91 (.778)	26 (.222)	197 (.883)	26 (.117)	1.135	.527	.3674	.417	.194
B	94 (.783)	26 (.217)	262 (.910)	26 (.09)	1.162	.415	.4797	.557	.199
C	96 (.466)	206 (.534)	1663 (.938)	110 (.062)	2.013	.116	1.6688	3.359	.194

as shown in columns labeled "conversion factor" in Table 7.2 (Manski and Lerman 1977).

The per stratum conversion factors need to be adjusted to account for the stratification of the sample. We calculated the proportion of each category of bills in the sample and in the universe. The "stratification weights" adjust the former to bring them in accord with the latter. Multiplying the per stratum conversion factors by the indicated "stratification weights" appropriately adjusts each observation. The final set of weights is shown in Table 7.2 (Manski and McFadden 1981).

8

Interpreting History

Historians often note that Truman moved left in 1947–48. Somehow, they say, the joy of combat with the "do-nothing" 80th Congress liberated him to "become himself." Historians also comment on the surprising way Eisenhower moved right in 1959–60. Contemporaries noted how Reagan lost his "flawless touch" for the deft legislative compromise after 1986, seemed to become more rigid, and lost more battles with Congress (*New York Times*, November 7, 1987:33; quoted in Nathan 1990). Finally, after the Republicans seized control of Congress in 1994, political commentators observed that President Bill Clinton emerged from a period of drift. But unlike Truman in 1947, Clinton seemed to move right rather than left. Are these incidents unrelated accidents of history? Or do they show the same causal mechanism at work?

Using a Model as an Interpretive Framework

Interpreting history is central to political science. In presidential studies, historical interpretation often takes the form of a narrative illustrating how presidents use power, manage the transition between administrations, handle crises, make appointments, and so on. When the narratives work as political science – and some work brilliantly – the selection of facts and their presentation flow almost inexorably from an underlying causal mechanism. An implicit model supplies the framework for interpreting history. It must be so, else the narrative remains only a chronology. But even though it is the model that scripts the drama, directs the actors, and moves the scenery, it rarely appears on stage. It remains behind the scenes, usually unexpressed and invariably informal.

Concealing the model carries a cost. At moments of tension, the interpreter may fudge her story without realizing it – change premises in mainstream, employ contradictory or inconsistent mechanisms at different places, or invoke so many mechanisms that the story becomes mud-

203

dled. She may overlook interesting implications of her own understanding of the story. In addition, she may have a tough time with "counterfactuals." Much of the action in a political narrative depends on what *would have happened* if people had made different choices or found themselves in a slightly different situation. For example, in the second face of power game in Chapter 4, the action actually taken by Congress depends on its *anticipation* of an undelivered veto. But since the narrator's counterfactual speculations are unconstrained by what *did* happen, her arguments may seem ad hoc or improbable.[1]

There is an alternative: model-driven history. Here, the model is a leading player in the drama. In fact, the curtain's rise reveals the model as the central protagonist. This kind of history has become the norm in some parts of the social sciences, particularly economics, where it is exemplified in the work of Nobel Laureates Douglass North and Robert Fogel (North 1981; Fogel 1989). With the development of formal political theory, it is now possible to write the same kind of political history, as an increasing number of examples illustrate.[2]

Model-driven history has three strengths, all connected to the way the model forces a consistent perspective on the interpreter. First, there can be a satisfying "ah-ha" effect. Puzzling, random, or seemingly anomalous events, apparently requiring a succession of ad hoc explanations, suddenly snap into place as part of an intelligible pattern. Second, inconsistencies in explaining events stand out more clearly than they do in model-free narratives. The interpreter can more easily detect fudging, and eliminate it. Finally, the model supplies structure for counterfactuals. In the absence of discipline from the historical record, the model supplies a constraint.

If the models in this book actually capture important elements of veto bargaining, they should supply an interpretive framework for recent history. My task in this chapter, then, is to use the models to structure a succession of case studies. The case studies are not *tests* of the model, in the way the material in Chapter 6 was. Nor are the case studies the inspiration for the models.[3] Instead, the case studies are a *payoff* from the earlier efforts at theory building and systematic theory testing.

---

[1] For a discussion of this problem and the value of explicit models in circumventing it, see Belkin and Tetlock 1996, especially the essays by Weingast, Bueno de Mesquita, and Kiser and Levi.

[2] An example of model-driven political history is Stewart and Weingast 1992.

[3] This difference separates the approach taken in this book from that in the "analytic narratives" research program (Bates et al. 1998). Otherwise the spirit of this chapter is quite similar to that of analytic narratives.

Selecting the Cases

Which vetoes deserve interpretation? I have argued throughout this book that veto bargaining is important because it affects important legislation. I see little point in tracing the profound impact of veto bargaining on public policy for rabbit meat inspection. So I focus on vetoes involving the most important legislation of the postwar period. I try to place each veto within the *strategic context* confronting the president – divided versus unified government, the relative location of the president and veto override player, and so forth – in other words, the factors identified by the models as important for bargaining. The strategic context will often determine which of the various models is most useful for interpreting the events in a particular case. Finally, I focus on the important vetoes of the Truman, Eisenhower, Ford, and Reagan presidencies. Space precludes examining every important veto while these presidencies encompass a variety of interesting strategic situations. I consider the Clinton presidency in the following chapter.

Notable Vetoes

Table 8.1 lists the thirty-three vetoes of landmark legislation that occurred between 1945 and 1992. As I discussed in Chapter 2, knowledgeable contemporaries judged such legislation the most important of the period.[4] The table provides a capsule summary of the veto bargaining connected with each veto. I also indicate a model that works well for interpreting the bargaining. For example, the sequential veto bargaining (SVB) model explains the dynamics on view in the bargaining over agricultural price supports in 1958. In addition, the president's veto threats and Congress's response follow the script of the veto threat model. Bargaining over strip mining in 1974–75 looks like SVB, with the second bill tailored for an override attempt. The bargaining over cable television reregulation tracks the predictions of the override model. About half the cases display the dynamics of sequential veto bargaining; the other half follow the pattern of the override model. As I discuss later, the strategic situation – for example, the location of the president relative to the veto override player – helps determine which model applies.

The case studies uncover some anomalies, the cases of the "missing vetoes," also noted in Table 8.1. In these cases the models suggest the president should have vetoed a successor to a vetoed bill, but the presi-

---

[4] Because the list of landmarks is constructed to mirror the lists of landmark enactments in Mayhew's *Divided We Govern* (1991), it excludes appropriations bills.

Table 8.1. *Notable vetoes, 1945–1992*

Congress/Year	Vetoed bill	Bargaining history	Interpretive framework
Truman administration			
79 1946	Case Bill	Predecessor to Taft-Hartley; override sustained in House by 5 votes	SVB
80 1947	Taft-Hartley	Overridden easily in House, by 6 votes in Senate	Override
80 1947	Income Tax 1	Override sustained in House by 2 votes; no concessions in successor (next veto)	Override
80 1947	Income Tax 2	Overridden in House, sustained in Senate by 5 votes; concessions in successor (next veto)	Override
80 1948	Income Tax 3	Overridden easily in both chambers	Override
81 1950	Internal Security Act	Overridden easily in both chambers	Override
82 1952	Immigration Act	Overridden by 2 votes in Senate	Override
Eisenhower administration			
84 1956	Agricultural Price Supports 1956	Easily sustained in House; concessions in successor and president signs	SVB
85 1958	Agricultural Price Supports 1958	No attempt to override; concessions in successor and president signs	SVB, threat
86 1959	Housing 1	Easily sustained in Senate; limited concessions in successor (next veto)	SVB, threat
86 1959	Housing 2	Sustained by 5 votes in Senate; concessions in successor and president signs	SVB
Nixon administration			
91 1970	Political Broadcasting	Sustained by 4 votes in Senate; concessions in successor and president signs	SVB, threat

91	1970	Public Service Employment	Sustained by 8 votes in Senate; concessions in successor and president signs	SVB, threat
92	1972	Clean Water Act 1972	Overridden easily	Override, threat
93	1973	Minimum Wage	Override failed in House by 23 votes, died	SVB, threat
93	1973	War Powers Act	Overridden easily in Senate, by 4 votes in House	Override, threat
Ford administration				
93	1974	Freedom of Information Act Amendments	Overridden easily in House, by 3 votes in Senate	Override, threat
93	1974	Strip Mining 1	Pocket-vetoed, but would have been sustained easily; concessions in successor (next veto)	SVB
94	1975	Strip Mining 2	Sustained in House by 3 votes; died	SVB (override)
94	1975	Oil Import Fees	No attempt to override (would have failed in House); no concessions in successor and president agrees; a missing veto	SVB, threat
94	1975	Common Site Picketing	No attempt to override; died	SVB, threat
Reagan administration				
97	1982	Anti-Crime	Pocket-vetoed; concessions in successor and president signs	Split Congress SVB
99	1986	Anti-Apartheid Act	Overridden easily in House, by 12 votes in Senate	Split Congress Override
99	1986	Clean Water 1	Pocket-vetoed (would have been overridden); no concessions in successor (next veto)	Split Congress SVB
100	1987	Clean Water 2	Easily overridden in both chambers	Override
100	1987	Highway Reauthorization	Overridden easily in House, by 1 vote in Senate	Override, threat
100	1988	Trade/Plant Closing	Sustained by 5 votes in Senate; small concession on trade in successor, none on plant closing in separate successor, president signs both. Missing veto on plant closing	Override, threat

Table 8.1. *(cont.)*

Congress/Year	Vetoed bill	Bargaining history	Interpretive framework
100 1988	Civil Rights Restoration	Overridden easily in House, by 8 votes in Senate	Override
Bush administration			
101 1989	Minimum Wage	Easily sustained in House; concessions in successor and president signs	SVB, threat
101 1989	Iran/Contra Amendment	No attempt to override; concessions in successor and president signs	SVB, threat
101 1990	Civil Rights	Sustained by 1 vote in Senate; no or few concessions in successor and president signs; a missing veto	Threat, override
102 1992	Cable TV Reregulation	Overridden easily in House; by 9 votes in Senate	Override
102 1992	Urban Tax Bill	This bill was a successor to a level B veto sustained in House by wide margin; pocket-vetoed despite concessions (would have been sustained in House)	SVB

dent actually signed the successor bill. I examine these cases in the penultimate section.

TRUMAN

In 1945 Truman found himself in a complex strategic situation. Problems that Franklin Roosevelt and the wartime Congress had postponed until the war's end suddenly fell to him to solve. Managing the transition from total wartime to a peacetime economy, building a new international economic order, forging an alliance against communism, guiding the United States to unprecedented levels of wealth and economic power – these amounted to nothing less than inventing a new America for a new world.

How Congress and the nation would respond to the foreign-policy crisis soon became clear. First, in the face of imminent war with a truculent Soviet Union, the Democratic Party shed its pro-Communist Popular Front left, which followed Henry Wallace into the irrelevancy of third-party politics. In turn, the Republicans suppressed their isolationist, protectionist fringe, which then turned its frustrated energies to hunting "reds."[5] Within the broad middle ground that resulted, elites within both parties could work together to build a foreign policy based on anticommunism.

Domestic politics was a different story. Wildly different initiatives were compatible with the anti-Communist consensus, ranging from pre–New Deal laissez-faire to the anti-Communist liberalism of the Americans for Democratic Action. Truman's instincts almost always led him to the liberal option. But Congress was rarely inclined to follow. Not surprisingly, the veto was an important part of the political strategy Truman crafted.

The difficulties of Truman's political situation can be seen in Figure 8.1. The two panels contrast the distribution of senators by ideology score in the 79th and 80th Congresses. The ideology scores on display are Poole's W-NOMINATE scores, based on a scaling of all roll call votes.[6] Low scores (those to the left) denote liberalism, higher scores (those to the right) conservatism. The undulating line superimposed on the histogram is a nonparametric density smoother, fit to the ideology scores. It provides a good approximation of the actual distribution of

---

[5] Useful background is offered in Reichley 1981, especially chap. 2.

[6] The first dimension from a multidimensional scaling similar to the more familiar D-NOMINATE scores. Such scores correlate very highly with interest group ratings and other putative measures of ideology. We thank Keith Poole for making these data available to us.

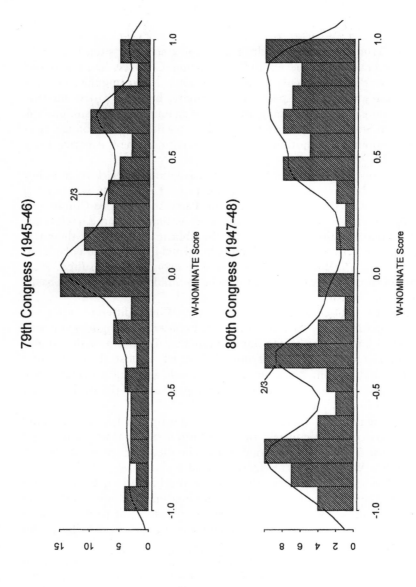

Figure 8.1. The Makeup of the Senate: 79th versus 80th Congress

the data.[7] The point marked "2/3" indicates the location of the member one-third from the end of the distribution in the direction away from the bulk of the members in the dominant party.

The moderate-conservative coalition that characterized the 79th Congress is readily seen in the top figure. This was a Congress dominated by the center, and it was here that its leadership resided. The heart of the 79th was the famous coalition of Southern Democrats and Republicans, which lay almost dead-center in the W-NOMINATE space. From this center the distribution declined almost monotonically in the liberal and conservative directions. Given these contours, the 79th was not a Congress that would support additional New Deal–style legislation, but neither was it a Congress inclined to overturn the core New Deal programs. Truman himself was relatively far to the left, though this was hardly apparent in 1945–46. In this configuration, Truman would usually be an accommodator.

The distribution in the lower panel of Figure 8.1 is dramatically different. The elections of 1946 devastated the congressional center. As a result, the new Senate was extraordinarily polarized. Three distinct camps occupied the ideological terrain. On the far right was a huge block of extreme conservatives who now controlled the Senate, at least nominally. On the far left was a resurgent block of extremely liberal New Deal Democrats. About one-third of the way between the two warring camps was a group of moderate liberals. In this group resided the veto override player. Given this configuration, the basic strategies of the Senate conservatives, led by Robert Taft, and the president were almost foreordained. The Republicans would try to govern from the right to the center, picking up enough votes in the devastated middle to pass legislation rolling back the New Deal (though never as far as the conservatives wished). In turn, the president would use the veto aggressively, never compromising but instead forcing the Republicans to place their bills far enough to the left to gain the support of the veto override player. The New Deal Democrats supplied the base for the president's vetoes, but the critical factor determining the content of controversial bills would be the willingness of moderate liberals to sustain the president's vetoes.

Much of this strategy was laid out for Truman in the famous Rowe Memorandum (Rowe 1946). Political operative James H. Rowe Jr., a former Roosevelt aide and associate of power broker Tommy "the Cork" Corcoran, devised a strategy for the president in December 1946.[8]

---

[7] The estimation employed S-Plus's kernel-density smoother density, with bandwith = .3. For details see Venables and Ripley 1994, sec. 5.5, and Everitt 1994: chap. 11.

[8] At the time, Rowe was working for Budget Director James Webb. For more details on this fascinating story, see Hamby 1973:180–81 and Gosnell 1980:320–21.

Truman's later actions tracked the suggestions in the memo to a remarkable degree – Truman reportedly kept the memorandum in his desk and periodically referred to it. First, Truman began in a conciliatory vein. He made only vague legislative requests and offered every gesture of bipartisanship. After all, the public had just slammed the Democratic Party and seemingly endorsed the Republican's push for a new direction. Gradually, though, as the extremity of the Republican program began to dawn on labor, farmers, urbanites, and the less affluent, the president took calculated steps to map out a new policy reputation: protector of the New Deal and champion of the little man. As the Rowe Memorandum had envisioned, the veto was central to this strategy, especially for high visibility items involving important political principles.[9] By the time of the Democratic Convention, the new "Give-'em-Hell Harry" Truman was in full blossom, and totally credible. Liberals had never warmed to Truman, who seemed to them a crass interloper after the death of their paladin Roosevelt. But Richard Strout, author of the famous TRB column in *The New Republic*, anticipated the spirit of the campaign when he wrote of Truman's pugnacious acceptance speech at the Democratic Convention, "It was fun to see the scrappy little cuss come out of his corner fighting. . . . Unaccountably, we found ourselves on top of a pine bench cheering" (quoted in Hamby 1973:244).

Richard Neustadt's epitaph for the Fair Deal captures well the role of veto politics in the domestic presidency of Harry Truman:

As a consolidator, as a builder on foundations, Truman left an impressive legislative record; the greater part achieved, of course, in less than two years time, and by a single Congress [the 81st]. Moreover as protector, as defender, wielder of the veto against encroachments on the liberal preserve, Truman left a record of considerable success – an aspect of the Fair Deal not to be discounted. He could not always hold his ground, sustained some major losses, but in the process managed to inflict much punishment on his opponents. (1973:40)

The 80th Congress

The Income Tax Vetoes.   Prominent among the Republican's campaign pledges in 1946 was a cut in income taxes. Delivering on this pledge was perhaps the highest priority for the incoming Republicans of the 80th Congress. In their view, lower taxes were good in themselves. But another purpose of a tax cut, as the new chairman of the Ways and

---

[9] Other actions played a part in the strategy, as well. For example, Truman recalled the "Do-Nothing" Congress for a special session to deal with inflation, which Truman blamed on their termination of price controls. He then denounced their legislative efforts as feeble.

Means Committee, Harold Knutson, explained, was to "cut off much of the government's income by reducing taxes and compelling the government to retrench, live within its income" (Witte 1985:132). Knutson proposed a straight 20% reduction in income taxes across all brackets, a proposal that conferred much larger benefits on the wealthy. This bill became H. R. 1, the Republican's flagship legislation of the 80th Congress.

In his January budget message Truman announced his opposition to any tax cut in 1947. Truman's veto threat was unmistakable. As a result, the Republican House Steering Committee met soon thereafter to discuss veto-proofing the bill. The party leaders decided to increase benefits for the poorest income tax payers and for everyone over the age of sixty-five. Knutson's Ways and Means Committee made these changes and sent the bill to the floor. The House passed the modified bill handily, though the roll call votes suggested that the bill still did not have enough support to beat a veto. The Senate Finance Committee then took up the bill, scaling back the cut in the highest brackets and delaying the bill's effective date. The revised bill passed the Senate 52–34, again suggesting an override would be a difficult though perhaps not impossible task: the bill might need to pick up more than 10 votes to beat a veto. The Senate's changes largely prevailed in conference (*CQ Almanac* 1947:101–3; Witte 1985:132–33).

The Republican response to the president's veto threat clearly followed the basic script of the coordination model in Chapter 7: they scaled back the offending provisions and calibrated the bills for a possible override attempt. In 1947, Truman gave every sign of being recalcitrant on tax cuts – the right impression to convey if he wanted to extract maximum concessions from Congress.

Not surprisingly, Truman vetoed the bill. It "represents the wrong kind of tax reduction at the wrong time," he thundered, a phrase that leapt from his veto message to the front pages of newspapers around the country. Within forty-eight hours, House members cast their votes in the override attempt. By a vote of 268–137, a scant two votes short, the override failed. Knutson and the leadership had calculated finely but missed the bull's-eye. Within a week, Knutson introduced a new tax bill.

The override model predicts the Republicans would simply repass the same bill, hoping for a slightly better outcome on the override. And indeed Knutson's new bill was virtually identical to the previous one, except for a delay in the effective date of the tax cuts.

Action on the new bill came very quickly. Again the bill passed both chambers handily; again Truman vetoed the bill. This time, however, the House voted to override in a vote of 299–108, thus sustaining Republican hopes by the exceedingly narrow margin of two votes. Those hopes came to naught in the Senate, however, where the veto was sustained 57–36, a 5-vote margin. Time had run out on the first session of the 80th Congress. On the last day of the session, Knutson introduced his bill for the third time. But action on it would have to wait for the second session.

How should the Republicans calibrate their third try at tax reduction? By 1948 an unexpectedly robust economy had filled the government's coffers, increasing the attractiveness of a tax cut. In fact, in his 1948 State of the Union Address Truman moved away from an adamant rejection of tax reduction. However, his proposal, a forty-dollar cost-of-living credit for every taxpayer and dependent coupled with an increase in corporate income taxes, had zero appeal to the Republicans. Nonetheless, the offer revealed the president as a compromiser rather than a recalcitrant. A sufficiently large concession, but probably still far from what he had proposed, might well gain his signature. On the other hand, the two failed override attempts showed the Republicans they had almost the right formula for success. The override model would predict repassage of the 1947 bill. Yet, the vote in the Senate may have suggested to the leadership that they were overreaching if only slightly. For his third try, Knutson recalibrated his bill, vowing to make it "as vetoproof" as he could. The key was broadening the tax cut outside the highest income brackets, to pick up additional support among Democrats. Thus, the new bill included some provisions the Democrats had tried but failed to insert in the two previous bills, such as further benefits for the aged and blind and an increase in personal and dependent's exemptions.[10]

The recalibrated bill was brought to the floor for two days of debate. Again it passed handily, but failed to secure a two-to-one majority. Clearly, the Senate would need to reduce the cut even further, which it did, substantially (the Finance Committee estimated that the House bill would reduce revenue by $6.9 billion, while its bill would reduce it only $5.1 billion). After three days of debate, the Senate passed the bill 78–11.

Truman vetoed the bill yet again, though he must have recognized that an override was now very likely. Both houses easily overrode the veto: 311–88 in the House and 77–10 in the Senate.

Though the Republicans had done the best they could to redeem their campaign pledge, they ended up far from a 20% across-the-board slash in income taxes. The final bill reduced rates in the highest bracket only 5%. Truman's stubborn vetoes had wrested enormous concessions from the initially jubilant Republicans.

---

[10] The material in these paragraphs draws on *CQ Almanac* 1948:344–50.

The Labor Vetoes. Although tax reform may have been the Republican's number-one priority, perhaps the single most notable veto of the 80th Congress lay in the area of labor policy. In fact, Truman's veto of the Taft-Hartley Act looms large in the entire cohort of postwar vetoes. The president's willingness to veto Taft's bill forced major changes in what became the fundamental American labor law. Moreover, the veto galvanized union members, who ultimately supplied Truman with his margin of victory in the 1948 election. If Truman had instead signaled a willingness to sign the Taft-Hartley bill, its content would have been far more anti-union. And without the enthusiastic support of labor he probably would have lost in 1948.

Veto bargaining over labor legislation actually began in the 79th Congress as labor-management relations emerged from the deep freeze of World War II. Strikes rocked the country. John L. Lewis's coal miners forced brownouts. The crowning blow came with a paralyzing railroad strike in May 1946. On May 17 Truman seized the railroads. On May 24 he addressed the nation over radio. Then, on May 25 the president went before a special joint session of Congress to ask for temporary emergency legislation, allowing the government to draft workers who struck government-seized industries. During the president's address, the secretary of the Senate rushed into the chamber to announce the capitulation of the striking rail unions. Nonetheless, within two hours the House voted the president the emergency legislation he had requested.[11]

The Senate's immediate response was the passage of the so-called Case bill, the Federal Mediation Act. Earlier the bill had passed the House but was amended extensively in the Senate during two weeks of stormy debate that often kept the Senate in session until after midnight. To cut off an apparent filibuster by diehard New Dealers, supporters of the bill had begun to circulate a cloture petition, but Truman's address effectively ended the debate and the Senate finally voted on the bill, passing it 49–29. Though mild compared with the Taft-Hartley Act, it toughened labor laws, outlawed certain types of labor racketeering, instituted a cooling-off period, and formed a Federal Mediation Board to take over duties performed by the secretary of labor (then Henry Wallace, a doyen of the Democratic left). In contrast to the president's temporary emergency legislation, however, the bill was permanent and applied to all types of labor disputes, not just those involving government-seized industries.

Following the Senate's action, the House Rules Committee issued a privileged rule for the amended Case bill, allowing it to move directly

---

[11] Taft blocked it in the Senate. On the background to the Taft-Hartley Act, see Lee 1966: chaps. 1 and 2.

to the floor absent a conference committee. The special rule required a two-thirds vote, which it easily achieved; the resolution approving the Senate's work passed 230–106.

Labor leaders, who had reacted to Truman's dramatic antistrike moves with howls of outrage and declarations of electoral war, now turned to him with pleas for a veto. On June 11 Truman vetoed the Case bill, calling it (perhaps somewhat disingenuously) "utterly different" from his proposed emergency legislation. Immediately upon receipt of the veto message the House sustained the veto 255–135, a margin of 5 votes.

The close margin on the override vote may suggest that Congress geared the bill for such a vote, as the override model would suggest. On the other hand, the bill's ability to command about a two-thirds majority may have reflected the apparent need to achieve cloture (a two-thirds vote to end a filibuster) in the Senate and then gain the special rule in the House. (The latter was essential since a conference committee seemed likely to end in deadlock.)[12] Truman seems to have been unsure until the last moment whether he should veto the bill; his administration was thoroughly split on the question (Lee 1966:39–43). His failure to issue a veto threat probably reflected this ambivalence, as well as the speed of the action and the need to press his own antistrike plan without sending confusing signals. Within weeks he signed the Hobbs Anti-Racketeering Act, which had been a clause in the Case bill.[13] In short, despite the narrowness of the override vote, the bargaining over labor legislation in the 79th Congress seems to follow the sequential veto bargaining script.

The situation was quite different in the 80th Congress. The Republican's campaign slogan of 1946 was "Had Enough?" – a reference to the strikes and labor unrest of 1946. In 1947, as they entered the Congress they now controlled, the Republicans were determined to pass the toughest anti-union bill in American history, much tougher than the Case bill. From the very beginning the Republican's principal strategist, Senator Robert Taft, anticipated a veto. Every element of his tactics seem calculated to achieve as tough a bill as he could yet still beat the veto (Lee 1966:69; *CQ Almanac* 1947:285–86).

The House Education and Labor Committee under Chairman Fred Hartley made the first move. Hartley's bill was based on provisions of the Case bill, but then added many new ones suggested by the National Association of Manufacturers. The bill was intended to be particularly

[12] See the comments by Halleck, quoted in *CQ Almanac* 1946:297.

[13] This sequence is not counted as a veto chain in the data presented in Chapter 2; there the chain is scored as Case bill – Taft-Hartley.

tough, so that later concessions would appear more dramatic. After three days of heated debate, a coalition of Republicans and southern and southwestern Democrats passed the bill, 308–107.

In the Senate, Taft touted his bill as less drastic than Hartley's, though its opponents saw few real differences. The bill passed the Senate 68–24, supported by the same coalition that had manifested itself in the House. Almost all Republicans supported the bill; the Democrats split 50–50, with southern and southwestern Democrats supporting and northeastern Democrats opposing it. The bill then went to conference. As Hartley later recalled, he knew they "had to write a final bill that would be enacted over a veto," and this was the major task of the conferees (Lee 1966:72). The margin in the Senate may have suggested to Taft there was room to toughen the bill. In final form, it included some of the tougher House provisions.

Not surprisingly, the House resoundingly adopted the conference report on the somewhat milder bill, 320–79, amid speculation about a veto. The real question was how well Taft had counted noses in the Senate. There, the vote was 54–17, an ambiguous result though one boding ill for the administration. The count exceeded the 2:1 ratio needed for an override but 22 senators had failed to vote. The veto might be sustained but only if the administration could pick up the bulk of the missing votes.

The passage of the bill kicked off a huge, nationwide campaign by labor and business, aimed partly at Truman and partly at the wavering senators. Postcards and telegrams flooded the White House and Capitol Hill; advertisements appeared in the mass media; mass rallies were held; lobbying was frenetic. Truman understood perfectly well that his decision would play a central role in the 1948 presidential election. *Business Week*, reflecting the common wisdom, suggested his veto message would be "one of 1948's hottest campaign documents." To the surprise of few, on June 20 (the last day possible) Truman vetoed the bill.

Within the hour, the House overrode the veto, 331–83. Events in the Senate were even more dramatic. The president had scheduled a nationwide address later that evening to explain his veto. Liberal senators proposed postponing the vote over the weekend to allow the country to absorb the president's message. They undertook a thirty-one-hour filibuster to delay the vote, the "long debate."

Counts of support in the Senate had varied during the runup to the final vote, but most indicated the administration could rely on about thirty votes, especially if the tally were close. Plans were made to bring Senator Robert Wagner, desperately ill, from his sickbed in New York; Wagner declared his willingness to cast a tie-breaking vote even if it killed him. Senator Elbert Thomas offered to fly back from Switzerland to vote against the bill. But the administration lacked the final margin for victory. The Senate overrode the veto 68–25.

The story of the Taft-Hartley veto is filled with color and dramatic details. But how are we to understand it? Many accounts seem to imply that the veto was a failure because Congress enacted the bill in the teeth of Truman's opposition. The override model suggests a different view. Given the strategic configuration in Congress, passage of some form of the law was almost assured. The real issue was the bill's content. Absent the threat of Truman's veto, Taft and the Republicans would have enacted a far more severe bill. If the initial override attempt had failed rather than succeeded, the Republicans would have proceeded exactly as they did with the income tax cut: pass a very similar version, which probably would have beaten the veto (or so the model suggests). In fact, the upper limit on Republican concessions was not really determined by Truman at all, once he committed to the veto. The limiting factor was the support for anti-union legislation among moderate liberals in the Democratic Party. It was this group that contained the veto override player.

Other Important Vetoes.   Truman vetoed other notable pieces of legislation in the 80th Congress. Among these were the Bulwinkle bill, which would have exempted railroads from important antitrust provisions, and the Gearhardt resolution, which removed newsboys and others from Social Security. The fate of the New Deal–like U.S. Employment Service was also decided through an extended piece of sequential veto bargaining. In each of these cases, Truman used the veto to project and reinforce a policy reputation calculated to wrest concessions from Congress.

Unified Government

As remarkable as Truman's divided government vetoes were, his unified government vetoes were even more unusual. No other postwar president vetoed even a single landmark bill during unified government; Truman vetoed *three*. In fact, Kennedy, Johnson, Carter, and the unified-government Eisenhower *together* vetoed only four important (level B) bills, legislation of much less significance. Few indicators reveal so graphically Truman's antipathy to the conservatives who came to dominate even his own party. Illustrative of the unified party vetoes was the veto of the McCarran-Walter Immigration Act of 1952.[14]

[14] The first of Truman's landmark unified-government vetoes was the Federal Mediation Act, which I discussed with the Taft-Hartley veto. The second was the McCarran Internal Security Act of 1950.

McCarran-Walter Immigration Act of 1952. The McCarran-Walter immigration bill was the most important piece of legislation in the field of immigration policy since 1924.[15] The legislation codified and locked in place informal restrictions on immigration that had grown over the years, made national-origin quotas somewhat more rigid, and tightened restrictions on subversives and other undesirables. Although the bill stepped back from earlier, overtly racist restrictions on Asians, it can be seen as a step in a conservative direction. Liberals, including Emmanuel Celler and Jacob Javits in the House and Herbert Lehman and Hubert Humphrey in the Senate, vigorously opposed it. They were joined by the president.

The liberals were far too weak to move immigration policy in their favored direction. Instead, under the cover of the president's threatened veto, they offered various compromises to deflect the bill's conservative thrust (LeMay 1987:106). During seven days of vigorous debate in the Senate, most of these compromises were rejected as the bill's sponsors crafted it with an eye to an override.

The bill was presented to the president June 11, 1952. He vetoed it on June 25, declaring some of its provisions "worse than the infamous Alien Act of 1798." The House overrode the veto on June 26 by the vote of 278–113, a margin of 18 votes. The real test came in the Senate, however. On June 27, by a vote of 57–26, that chamber also overrode the veto. A switch of only 2 votes would have sustained the veto.[16]

What is the lesson of the immigration veto? On its face, this episode of veto bargaining appears to be a nearly pure case of the override model.[17] What is remarkable, though, is that the bargaining occurred during unified party government. The immigration veto thus demonstrates that unified party government is not an automatic antidote to vetoes of important legislation. If the president's policy preferences are sufficiently estranged from those of his copartisans in Congress, vetoes can occur. Of course, such deep estrangement is rare. Few presidents are

[15] See LeMay 1987: 74–109; *CQ Almanac* 1952: 154–60.
[16] During the 1952 election, Truman tried to use the immigration veto as he had Taft-Hartley in 1948. In a statement sent to the national conference of the Jewish Welfare Board, he labeled those who had voted to override the immigration veto (like Eisenhower's running mate Richard Nixon) as anti-Semitic and anti-Catholic. The bill's supporters were even somewhat akin to the Nazis, Truman suggested. This wild accusation sent Eisenhower into a rage and only served to give Truman, and by extension the Democratic nominee Adlai Stevenson, a black eye (Donovan 1982: 400–1).
[17] Truman's veto of the McCarran Internal Security Act is rather similar. Reagan's veto of the Anti-Apartheid Act also bears some resemblance to the McCarran-Walter veto, at least structurally. Of course Truman and Reagan could hardly be more different ideologically.

preference outliers with respect to their own party in Congress. But when they are, veto bargaining can occur.

EISENHOWER

For the first three Congresses of the Eisenhower administration, partisan control of the legislature hung by a thread. In the first Congress, the 83rd of 1953–54, the Republicans had a single-vote majority in the Senate. Their majority in the House consisted of less than a dozen. The Republicans lost control of both houses in the next election, but the Democrat's majority in the 84th was almost as thin as the Republicans' in the 83rd. Again, a single vote gave the majority party nominal control of the Senate. In the House the Democrats enjoyed a thirty-vote margin, more comfortable than in the Senate but nonetheless thin. The 85th Congress, of 1957–58, had a more Democratic complexion but the shift was largely at the margin.

The top panel in Figure 8.2 displays the ideological distribution of senators in the 83rd Congress. A large block of conservatives on the right faces another large block in the middle. There is little strength on the left. In short, it is a centrist Congress.

Given this makeup, neither party could hope to accomplish much without the support of at least the center-leaning part of the other. In fact, with a single exception, all the landmark enactments in this era passed with either a bipartisan majority or with a two-thirds majority in one or both houses.[18] Southern Democrats, moderate Democrats, and liberal-progressive Republicans could often find a working majority to support the creation of national infrastructure, the development of national resources, and anticommunism abroad and at home.

This was political terrain in which Eisenhower, one the great proponents of progressive or "modern" Republicanism, moved easily. On occasion, conflict could be sharp in the first three Eisenhower Congresses. During the midterm election of 1954 Eisenhower invoked the prospect of a "cold war" between president and Congress if the Republicans lost control of Congress. But when it actually happened, a domestic cold war never really materialized, except perhaps in the immediate runup to the election of 1958. Instead, between 1953 and 1958, Congress worked with the administration to produce landmark legislation initiating the national highway system (perhaps its outstanding domestic policy achievement), the St. Lawrence Seaway, and the upper Colorado River project; granted statehood to Alaska; established civilian control

[18] See Mayhew 1991: tables 5.2–5.5. The single exception was the legislation creating the St. Lawrence Seaway.

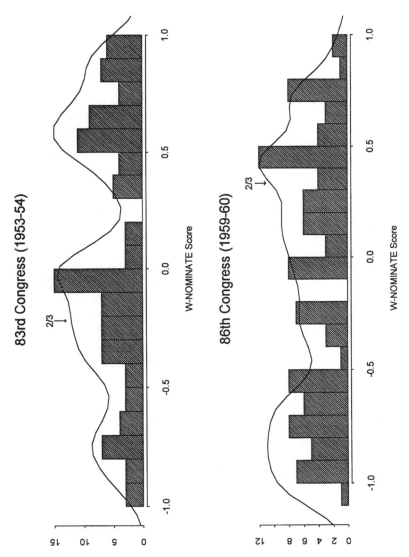

Figure 8.2. The Makeup of the Senate: 83rd versus 86th Congress

of atomic energy in the Atomic Energy Act; moved the tax code in a more probusiness direction; created NASA; and expanded federal support for higher education. In 1957 Congress passed a civil rights bill, modest compared with the scope of the problem, but the first progressive race legislation since Reconstruction. All these measures could be enacted within the broad middle ground of American politics.

In these three Congresses, historian Stephen Ambrose notes, "Eisenhower had so effectively staked out the middle of the road as his territory, Democrats hardly knew whether to attack him from the left or the right" (1984:300). There was one prominent exception to Eisenhower's centrism: farm policy. Only there did veto politics find much scope. Otherwise, Eisenhower's tactics between 1953 and 1958 provide a lesson in how a coalition president governs from the center.[19] Vetoes do not play much part in such tactics.

All this came to an end with the election of 1958. When voters responded to the slumping economy, the Democrats pulled off their biggest congressional sweep since the New Deal. Democratic holdings in the House jumped by forty-six seats, and those in the Senate by thirteen. All in all, the Democrats enjoyed nearly a 2–1 advantage in both chambers. The liberal wing of the party was reborn.

The bottom panel of Figure 8.2 shows the resulting alignment in the Senate. The resurgent New Deal wing of the Democratic Party is clearly visible as the large block on the left. This group would press for "progressive" policies, much the way the block of conservatives in the 80th Congress had pushed for rolling back the New Deal. But despite the Democrats' gains, the far right was hardly devastated. The right-hand sides of the smoothed distributions for the 83rd and 86th Congresses are actually quite similar. Consequently, the critical override player remained rather far to the right.

Eisenhower's strategic situation was transformed, and he knew it. Gone was the possibility for consensual, coalition government from the center. He was in a fight with the "big spenders." And, as he informed the Republican leaders, "When I'm in a fight, I want every rock, pebble, club, gun or whatever I can get" (Ambrose 1984:497). Given the strategic configuration, the veto would prove a formidable piece of artillery in the hands of the architect of D-Day.

The First Three Congresses: The Agriculture Vetoes

Ambrose notes that farm policy was an area in which Eisenhower had "deep and unchangeable convictions." He goes on to suggest that "farm

[19] See Ambrose 1984:624, and Greenstein 1982. Of course, there were blunders, especially in 1957–58, as discussed in Neustadt 1960:49–60.

policy was the only area in which Eisenhower called for a repudiation of the basic New Deal economic structure" (Ambrose 1984:160). There can be little doubt of Eisenhower's convictions about farm policy. But the important role of vetoes in shaping farm policy reflected much more than the president's personal convictions. It reflected the almost unique opportunities his administration had in this area, and how the veto furthered those opportunities.

Two factors were critical. First was the tension between farmers and the other members of the Democratic coalition. Farmers had rallied to the Democrat's standard in 1948, responding to the Republican's efforts in the 80th Congress to reduce farm supports. But farmers fit poorly in a coalition of urban liberals, union members, immigrants, and southern segregationists. They remained Republicans at heart. In turn, urban liberals increasingly (and accurately) saw price supports as nothing more than taxes on milk, bread, and cheese.[20] Finally, the farmers themselves had trouble coming together effectively, for their own interests varied widely depending on which crop they raised.[21] Thus, careful play by the Eisenhower administration could splinter the coalition backing increased price supports.

A second critical element in veto bargaining over agriculture was the location of the status quo. When the Republicans controlled both chambers during the 83rd Congress of 1953–54, they passed the Agricultural Act of 1954, a bill that created increasingly flexible price supports. The 1954 act granted the president authority to set the supports anywhere between 82.5% and 90% of parity in 1955, with a further decline to 75% of parity to be permitted in 1956. Though Congress switched party control in 1955, the declining parity path remained locked in place, a critical fact in what was to come (Pach and Richardson 1991:55; *CQ Almanac* 1956:378).

The shaky footing of the farmers' coalition and the favorable ground created by the 1954 act allowed Eisenhower and his secretary of agriculture, Ezra Taft Benson, to use the veto as political jiujitsu on the Democratic Congress.

Agricultural Act of 1956. The veto of the Agricultural Act of 1956 provides an interesting variant on sequential veto bargaining, with Congress "bundling" two different proposals together, and the president using the veto to "unbundle" the two proposals. The story began in January 1956, when Eisenhower announced a new initiative in agricultural policy, the "soil bank." The idea was to take land out of production

[20] Hamby 1973:303–10, is very helpful on this point.
[21] On this historic problem for farmers, see Hansen 1991.

while continuing to support farmers' incomes ("paying them not to produce" in Benson's somewhat outraged phrase) rather than channel all the supports through artificially inflated prices. The latter not only created huge surpluses of commodities that were expensive to store but kept in production marginal land that might better be used for conservation.

The Democrats saw an obvious opportunity: give Ike his soil bank – which the Democrats were inclined to support anyway – in exchange for a return to rigid 90% parity. In other words, they would bundle together two proposals, one supported by the president and one opposed by him. Ike immediately grasped the essential feature of the plan. As he explained to his aides, "The Democrats are going to do a simple thing, write a bill that has something for everybody and if I then veto it, a lot of people will be mad" (Ambrose 1984:300). The vehicle for the Democrat's maneuver was H.R. 12, a bill establishing 90% parity. The bill had been passed by the House in 1955 but languished in the Senate in the face of a presidential veto threat. Now the Senate Agriculture and Forestry Committee took up the bill, added the soil bank, and sent it to the floor in mid February.[22] Amendments softened some sections, with Vice-President Nixon casting a key tie-breaking vote, but the core of the bill remained high price supports coupled with the soil bank. The bill passed the Senate 93–2. Eisenhower expressed his unhappiness with the bill but his failure to issue an explicit veto threat may have encouraged the bill's sponsors. In any event, the Conference Committee actually restored the rigid supports removed in the Senate. The House adopted the conference report 237–181, the Senate 50–35.

Clearly, the bill was far from veto-proof. The question was, Would Ike buy the whole package to get the part he wanted? Or would he use the veto to unbundle the proposals, at the risk of killing the part he favored? The answer was, veto. In his veto statement, the president labeled the rigid 90% parity unacceptable, and singled out several other provisions for criticism. The House scheduled an override vote, but it failed miserably, 202–211 – the bill's sponsors could not even deliver a majority, much less a two-thirds vote.

Within two weeks, the House Agriculture Committee reported a new bill. The new bill, H.R. 10875, retained most of the noncontroversial portions of H.R. 12 and simply dropped the rest. Gone was rigid 90% parity. The floor rapidly passed the bill, 314–78. The Senate Agriculture and Forestry Committee followed suit. The report that accompanied the bill stated, "H.R. 10875 contains most of the provisions of H.R. 12. . . . the provisions objected to by the President having been either elim-

---

[22] The committee's bill was S. 3183; on the floor, the Senate took up H.R. 12 and substituted the language of S. 3183 into H.R. 12.

inated or modified." The Senate passed the bill by a voice vote. The Conference Committee made relatively few changes, the Senate adopted the report by a voice vote, and the House did so by a vote of 305–59. On May 28, Eisenhower signed the bill. He had his soil bank without rigid price supports.

The bundling of the two proposals and their subsequent unbundling unquestionably strains the one-dimensional sequential veto bargaining model. Nonetheless, the patterns predicted by that model repeat themselves here: a "tough" initial offer, a veto, concessions (in this case, virtual capitulation) in the second offer. A similar pattern also occurs in appropriations politics. There, Congress sometimes bundles appropriations with nonappropriation "riders" altering policy. Presidents have often used the veto to strip the riders from the appropriations bills. In the case of agriculture policy in 1956, the shrinking path of price supports set in place in 1954 strongly favored the president. He had little incentive to accept that change, while the Democrats were desperate to bring home something to the farmers, if only the soil bank. Under those circumstances, the veto was a formidable weapon.

Agricultural Act of 1958. In 1958, the Democratic Congress resolved to try again. Hard times in the farm belt spurred the hope that Eisenhower would bend on price supports in order to shore up the Republicans' sagging prospects in the upcoming election. Indeed, in his January 16 farm message, Eisenhower signaled his willingness to make some changes in farm policy. He recommended increasing or removing acreage allotments. He continued pressing for lower price supports for some commodities but indicated flexibility in the timing of the reductions (he later supported a temporary, one-year freeze). This opening encouraged the Democratic leaders. Lyndon Johnson in particular saw a great opportunity in the 1958 election. Given the nationwide slump in the economy, Johnson saw the chance to woo voters by casting the president in the "Do Nothing" role and Congress as the protector of the little man. Pushing farm legislation fit perfectly with his strategy (Pach and Richardson 1991:176–77).

Emerging from the Senate Agriculture Committee in March 1958, S.J. Res. 162 would have indefinitely frozen price supports and acreage allotments for any commodity except tobacco (the subject of separate legislation), not allowing the supports to decline from the 1957 levels. The bill drew an immediate veto threat, so dairy-state senators, many of them Republicans, introduced a second bill that protected only dairy supports. Though this bill went nowhere – the other agricultural interests had no intention of letting dairy-state Republicans cut a separate deal with the

225

president – the action was symptomatic of the difficulty of holding the price freeze coalition together. S.J. Res. 162 passed the Senate 50–43 on March 20.

In the face of the presidential veto threat and weak support in the Senate, the House Agriculture Committee moved to temper the bill. Only if they could find something the president would sign could they hope for success. Therefore, the House Committee amended S.J. Res. 162 to freeze price supports for only one year, rather than indefinitely. The House passed the amended bill by a vote of 211–172, also far from a 2–1 margin. The Senate acceded to the House amendment by a vote of 48–32. Despite the concession brought by the veto threat, Eisenhower still vetoed the bill, demanding Congress enact exactly what he had recommended in his farm message. Given the hopeless prospect for an override, the bill's supporters in the House never brought it to a vote.

In an effort to build a veto-proof coalition, the House Agriculture Committee assembled an omnibus bill that included something for every commodity group. This effort died quickly when urban Democrats joined Republicans in opposition.

Hoping that a third try would prove a charm, farm-belt congressmen, now desperate to bring something home to their constituents, cobbled together another bill. Late in June the Senate Agriculture Committee reported S. 4071. The bill still set a permanent limit on price reductions, rather than a temporary one, but tied the supports to market prices and maintained a fig-leaf parity level of 60%, exactly the level the president had requested. In this form, it passed the Senate 62–11. Given this margin, the House leadership may have scented the possibility of an override. In any event, the House Agriculture Committee backed away from the almost total capitulation of the Senate bill. Instead, it abandoned the link to market prices and boosted the minimum parity percentages and support prices. The administration again sounded a tough note on these changes. Speaker Rayburn then attempted to bring the amended bill to the floor under a suspension of the rules. This would require a two-thirds majority, indicating a reasonable chance for an override. But House Republicans scuttled the attempt, which failed on a 210–186 vote. Rayburn gruffly declared the bill dead, and it appeared for a time that bargaining had indeed broken down. But pressure from commodity interests kept Congress focused on the issue.

Given the lessons of the previous attempts, the House leadership could clearly do little else than cut a deal with the administration. In negotiations with the administration, the House leaders agreed to drop minimum price supports entirely; the administration agreed to an increase in the parity floor. The administration's acceptance of the modified bill propelled it through Congress, with voice votes in both chambers. *Congressional Quarterly* scored the legislation as a "significant victory for the Administration."

The process that created the Agricultural Act of 1958 is readily understandable using the ideas in the previous chapters. The president's farm message signaled to Congress that he was not recalcitrant, that he would be willing to accept some legislation in this area – but what? Congress responded with a rather tough bill. The president's veto threat extracted important concessions. But the president was willing to veto the modified bill to demonstrate his policy convictions, gambling that the bargaining would not break down. Congress needed some experimentation to convince itself that a more attractive yet veto-proof bill was an impossible goal. Once convinced, Congress presented to the president a bill incorporating substantial concessions.

The 86th Congress: The Housing Vetoes

The housing vetoes exemplify the "new" Eisenhower of 1959–60, the fighting president who scored stunning coups against the overwhelmingly Democratic Congress. The background to the vetoes was straightforward. By 1959 the country had emerged from its recession. The federal government was running a deficit of some $12 billion, generating fears of inflation among the president's economic advisers. Eisenhower therefore resolved to hold the line against the "big spenders." Accordingly, the president used his budget message of January 1959 to suggest that federal participation in urban renewal be curtailed – an idea that stirred controversy – and that money for public housing remain constant (Keith 1973:131; *CQ Almanac* 1959:247). The president was by no means opposed to the housing program, but was adamant about holding the line on huge new expenditures.

This resolve put Eisenhower on a collision course with Congress. In 1958, even before the influx of the new Democrats, an expansionary housing bill had passed the Senate and nearly passed the House, only to die in the closing hours of the 85th Congress. The graveyard for the bill was the Rules Committee, whose chairman, the infamous "Judge" Smith, entombed it before it could reach the floor. During that episode, an effort to suspend the rules and bring the bill to the floor, which required a two-thirds vote, had failed by only half a dozen votes. Democratic leaders were confident their newly swollen ranks foretold a different outcome for 1959.

In early February 1959 the Senate Banking and Currency Committee reported S. 57. The bill contained over a billion dollars more in loans and grants than the administration had suggested. The Senate rapidly passed the bill 60–28. The House Banking and Currency Committee also moved rapidly, reporting a bill the Republican members labeled "budget busting." A challenge awaited the House bill in the Rules Committee, where again the formidable Smith tried to pigeonhole it. Speaker Rayburn personally intervened and the bill went to the floor in late May.[23] Despite repeated challenges from Republicans and Southern Democrats, the House's version of S. 57 passed largely intact, 261–160.

Aware that the two bills constituted little more than veto bait, the Conference Committee moved to cut them. They reduced the levels of the conference bill far below those in either of the two bills. The cuts were described as "a 'block that veto' attempt" (*CQ Almanac 1959*: 252). Johnson publicly expressed the hope that the cuts would satisfy "officials downtown." The Senate adopted the conference report 56–31, the House 241–177, margins suggesting the futility of an override attempt. But the cuts had been in vain: Eisenhower vetoed the bill, labeling it "extravagant" and "unnecessary." After delaying a month the Senate attempted an override, which failed by 9 votes, 55–40. Senators speculated that the other chamber would also have sustained the veto.

In mid-August, the Senate Banking and Currency Committee reported a new bill, S. 2539. The bill contained concessions, albeit fairly modest ones. The chairman of the Housing Subcommittee, John Sparkman, described the bill "as an effort to accommodate further the view of the President." The Senate passed the new bill 71–24. Moving quickly, the House Committee released the bill without amendments. Debate centered on whether the Senate had moved sufficiently to forestall another veto. The bill passed the House unchanged 283–106. It thus went directly to the president. Ending the uncertainty in the House, he vetoed it a week later. In his veto message he declared it little better than the previous bill, and outlined specific changes needed for him to accept such a bill. The bill returned to the Senate, which sustained the veto by a vote of 58–36, a margin of 5 votes.

In less than a week, with adjournment drawing near, the Senate committee reported its third try, S. 2654. According to the *Congressional Quarterly*, this bill was designed to meet Eisenhower's objections. It incorporated major changes from the second bill. Moreover, reported Senate Banking and Currency Committee chairman A. Willis Robertson, he had Eisenhower's "positive assurance" that we would sign the new bill. It rapidly passed the Senate 86–7. Then, in an effort to expedite the bill, the House suspended its rules and passed the Senate's handiwork unchanged, by voice vote. The bill went to the president September 9.

Since Congress adjourned September 15, Eisenhower could now

---

[23] The Rules Committee would not play a role in the remaining veto bargaining, though it did block a large omnibus housing bill in 1960.

pocket-veto the bill and completely avoid the danger of an override. But the third bill was a far cry from the dramatic new expansions originally envisioned by Congress. All in all, it represented an incremental expansion of the housing program. On September 23, following the departure of Congress, the president signed the bill.

The housing vetoes clearly follow the script of the sequential bargaining model. In fact, Eisenhower's willingness to sign the third bill raises the possibility that his second veto was a strategic turndown – he may have been willing to accept it, but vetoed it to extract more concessions.

The housing vetoes were but one move in the game played between Eisenhower and the 86th Congress. Besides the two housing bills, he vetoed two public works bills, three farm bills, and a pay raise for federal workers. His budget proposals reinforced his penurious image, as did his news conferences and public speeches (Ambrose 1984:497). The result was, in Neustadt's judgment, a transformation in Eisenhower's policy reputation (Neustadt 1960:61–62). And, as the housing vetoes illustrate, this reputation enabled him to extract concessions from Congress. Pach and Richardson's evaluation seems representative of later judgments: "By the time it adjourned, Congress had hardly increased spending, and the budget ran a surplus – the third and last of the Eisenhower presidency – of $1.3 billion. All in all, Eisenhower's ability in holding down spending was a resounding victory, all the more so because it was so unlikely" (1991:212). His victory may have seemed unlikely because Ike was a lame duck facing a hugely Democratic Congress. But given the dynamics of veto bargaining, his success does not seem so strange after all.

FORD

The central task of the Ford administration was to restore, if only partially, the trust in government squandered by Richard Nixon. On this point the public and the president were in accord, and historians continue to agree. But the Ford presidency was more than "a time to heal," as Ford titled his autobiography. Like the Nixon administration, the Ford administration faced the difficult job of managing relations with the USSR. At the same time, the oil shock of 1973 wreaked havoc on the domestic economy. In dealing with these challenges, President Ford faced contentious issues from his administration's inception.

What approach would the new president take? Although the scholarly literature on Ford and his administration is thin, the most astute portraits reveal a president whose values and temperament fitted the Eisenhower mold. Historian John Robert Greene offers this assessment: "Although Ford never articulated it, the administration apparently had an

229

agenda – a continuation of the policies that had been followed by the moderate wing of the Republican party since World War II – a conservative approach to economic and social policy and a cautiously internationalist approach to foreign policy" (1995:192). Governing from the center with a bipartisan coalition would have suited the new president, a team player and consensus builder throughout his career. It was a strategy that would have worked well to expunge the memory of the combative, confrontational Nixon. But presidents do not get to pick the strategic configuration in which they find themselves. Instead, the strategic configuration shapes the nature of each presidency.

The public revulsion with the Nixon administration, coupled with an economy reeling from the oil shock, swept into Congress the famous class of 1974, the "Watergate babies." In the 94th Congress the Democrats had majorities of 23 in the Senate and 147 in the House. At least nominally, House Democrats had a two-thirds-plus-one margin. Nor was the sheer size of the Democrats the only factor at work. Both parties were becoming more homogeneous and more polarized. This allowed the emergence of caucus-driven politics, somewhat more disciplined and certainly more adversarial (Rhode 1992; Cox and McCubbins 1993; Aldrich 1995; Rae 1989). Not surprisingly, then, the 94th Congress opened in mid-January 1975 on a triumphalist note. Congressional Democrats announced a new era of "congressional government." Speaker of the House Carl Albert, in a kind of inverted State of the Union Message, presented the Democrat's own "national agenda for economic action," to be implemented by Congress (*CQ Almanac* 1975: 3). By implication, the president was simply to step out of the way. Congress would do the rest.

What could the president do, in the face of an overwhelmingly hostile Congress and severe national problems? In A. James Reichley's estimation, Ford "understood the internal politics of Congress better than any postwar president except Lyndon Johnson" (1981:318). Certainly he knew his strategic situation was a more extreme version of Eisenhower's in 1959–60, not 1953–58. Legislative tactics had been Ford's bread and butter for more than two decades. He fully grasped the logic of sequential veto bargaining. For example, in July 1975 the master legislative tactician offered participants in a conference on domestic and economic affairs a small lesson in "the positive side of the veto." The president explained, "The veto is not a negative, dead-end device. In most cases, it is a positive means of achieving legislative compromise and improvement – better legislation, in other words."[24] Ford also understood the value of

---

[24] *Public Papers of the Presidents* 1975:1:915, quoted in Hoff 1993:293–308. In addition see Ford's comments in *Virginia Papers on the Presidency* (1980:34–45).

a policy reputation in dealing with Congress. As he explained to Greene, "When they in the Congress knew I meant business, and they certainly did after awhile, they respected me, and they soon learned that they couldn't get away with these various things that they were trying to ram through" (1992:208).

The result was the famous "veto strategy."

The Veto Strategy

A highly placed aide explained later to political scientist Paul Light, "By March 1975 we knew that we were going to be using the veto frequently. We never deliberately sat down and made the decision that we would veto sixty bills in two years. Each one came in separately and was reviewed separately. We knew that the veto was the best option" (1982: 112).

The Ford veto strategy was indeed distinctive. Seeing just how distinctive it was requires parsing the Ford vetoes by legislative significance. In the 94th Congress, Ford vetoed three landmark bills, after vetoing two in the 93rd. By way of contrast, Truman vetoed four landmark bills in the 80th Congress, as did Reagan in the 100th Congress. The veto rates for landmark bills in the 80th, 94th, and 100th Congresses were 50%, 27%, and 36%, respectively. Eisenhower's two vetoes of landmark legislation in the 86th Congress (1959–60) yield a veto rate of 33% for landmark bills (the 86th Congress produced relatively few landmark bills). Thus, at the highest level of legislative significance Ford's veto activity doesn't appear all that unusual, certainly in light of the extremity of his strategic situation.

The situation is very different, however, at the next level down, as shown in Figure 8.3. Ford vetoed *ten* level B bills, important but not landmark bills, all in the 94th Congress. Reagan vetoed only one such bill in the 100th Congress, and Truman vetoed none at all in the 80th. Reagan vetoed two such bills in the 99th Congress (this yields a 25% rate for level B legislation but only because the 99th Congress was a very poor producer of level B legislation). The only veto record that at all resembles Ford's was that of President Bush in the 102nd Congress. Bush vetoed four level B bills in the 102nd Congress, for a veto rate of 20%. Ford, however, vetoed two and one-half times as many level B bills, establishing a veto rate of 38% of all level B legislation passed by the 94th Congress. For level B legislation, Ford's veto record was unprecedented and unmatched in the postwar period.

What explains Ford's extraordinary catalog of vetoes of level B legislation? Answering this question requires not just a model of vetoes but a model of congressional legislative activity. But some clues are offered by

231

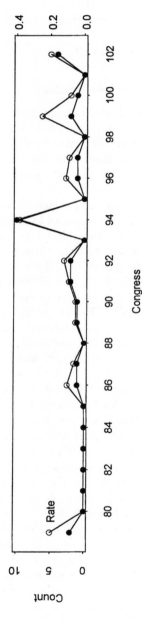

Figure 8.3. Number and Rate of Level B Vetoes, 1945–1992

comparing the legislative records of the 93rd and 94th Congresses. The 93rd Congress enacted fifteen pieces of level B legislation, none of them via an override. In fact, there were no vetoes of level B legislation in the 93rd Congress. The 94th Congress attempted to override every one of Ford's ten level B vetoes and succeeded in five cases. The 94th Congress enacted twenty-one pieces of level B legislation, six more than the previous Congress.

This pattern is what one would expect if the Democratic surge in 1974 shifted the veto override player. In that case, as suggested by Krehbiel's gridlock model, a number of previously blocked level B proposals would be potentially enactable through overrides (Krehbiel 1998). If this explanation is correct, though, the override lead surge probably should extend to level A enactments. It clearly did not: there were thirteen level A enactments in the 93rd Congress but only eight in the 94th. But perhaps the paucity of new level A legislation reflects the critical role played by the slumping economy. Congress seems to have passed every economic recovery bill it could, whether at the A or B level; most of the enactments at both levels dealt with jobs, taxes, and government expenditures.[25] So some of the energy that might have yielded more level A enactments was funneled into a surge of level B laws dealing with economic recovery.

The Veto Strategy at Work

At the highest levels of significance, the veto strategy is well illustrated by Ford's vetoes of two landmark bills regulating strip mining.

The Strip Mining Vetoes. The "preeminent environmental legislation" in the 93rd Congress was S. 425, a bill that would have forced coal mining companies to reclaim and restore strip-mined land. The bill would also have put unreclaimable land off limits to strip mining, thereby halting the destruction of millions of acres. But these undoubtedly laudable goals necessarily would reduce coal production during an energy crises and cost mining companies vast sums. Evaluating the bill's political trade-offs was no easy matter. The Nixon administration made the legislation one of its top priorities in 1973. The fledging Ford administration was deeply split. For example, Ford's secretaries of interior and environment favored the bill; the treasury secretary and the president's new energy czar opposed it. Until close to the end, the president himself did not announce a position.

[25] For a overview of the 94th Congress that supports this view, see *CQ Almanac* 1976:3–5.

The Senate passed S. 424 in the fall of 1973 by an 82–8 vote, despite bitter debates and intense lobbying by the coal industry. Interior Secretary Rogers Morton described the bill as one the Nixon administration could "live with" (*CQ Almanac* 1973:13). In late May 1974, the House Interior and Insular Affairs Committee finally reported its version of the bill, H.R. 11500. The majority in the committee stressed its virtues as environmental policy, the minority its drawbacks as energy policy. After a tough, six-day fight on the floor it passed with a 291–81 vote and went to conference. Both bills were widely seen as tough, but many differences separated the two complex, contentious pieces of legislation. After meeting more than twenty times, the conferees finally filed a conference report in early December.

By this time, it had become clear that President Ford was considering a veto of the bill. Moreover, the 93rd Congress was in its waning days (it adjourned December 20). Any delay in transmitting the bill to the president might open the door to a pocket veto; given the bill's tortuous passage through the 93rd Congress, this might actually kill it. The bill's supporters in the House decided upon a bold stratagem: they would seek to suspend the rules and send the bill directly to the floor without passing through the Rules Committee. If this move succeeded, it would save time. It would also demonstrate that the bill probably had enough support to override a veto, for the suspension of the rules would require a two-thirds majority. On December 9 the sponsors tried this maneuver, and failed, by a vote of 212–150. They had no other choice but to follow the normal procedure, and brought the bill to the floor on December 13. The conference report was adopted on a voice vote, bill manager Morris Udall explaining candidly that he wished to avoid demonstrating yet again that "we didn't have a two-thirds vote." The delays had now put Ford in a position to use the pocket veto if he wished.[26] The most persuasive argument the bill's defenders could muster was that the next, more liberal Congress might write an even more extreme bill. This argument failed to move the president. At the end of the month he pocket-vetoed the bill, saying it would curtail coal production at a critical time.

Part of this story departs from the scripts of the veto threat and SVB models. According to the veto threat model, once the Nixon administration signaled its willingness to accept the Senate bill, the president should not have vetoed the bill. But Watergate intervened and Nixon was removed from the picture. By the time Ford finally threatened to veto the bill, there was no time to rework the laboriously crafted con-

[26] The Senate also adopted the report by voice vote and sent it to the president December 16. Congress adjourned four days later.

ference report nor sufficient support to avoid the pocket veto via a special rule.

Obviously, the bargaining would take a different course in the 94th Congress. For one thing, the influx of so many Democrats made the legislation's sponsors confident that they had enough votes to override a veto, at least if the bill was positioned correctly. Accordingly, they reintroduced virtually the same bill that had been vetoed, as S. 7 in the Senate and H.R. 25 in the House. The administration introduced its own bill and noted changes it would require to support S. 7. The Senate Interior Committee adopted several of these but rejected others; another change was added on the floor. The bill then passed the Senate 84–13 in March.

Udall was open about his strategy for the House bill. He fully expected Ford to veto the bill; the real issue was success or failure in the override attempt. The bill's opponents agreed. Representative Sam Steiger, who led the Republicans fighting the 1974 bill, conceded immediate defeat. "Sustaining the veto – that's the only way we can go now." The House Interior Committee, looking ahead to the override, made several major changes to the bill, all aimed at alleviating the criticisms the administration had leveled against the first bill. Some of these changes came straight from the administration's own bill. Once the bill reached the floor, some members pressed to strengthen its environmental regulation, but over the course of several stormy days Udall resisted all these efforts, reminding members of the enormous difficulty in reaching an agreement with the Senate the previous year. The House finally approved the bill by the overwhelming margin of 333–86 in mid-March.

Because of the care taken to coordinate both versions of the legislation, the Conference Committee reconciled the bills fairly easily. The Senate adopted the conference report by a voice vote, the House by a vote of 293–115 on May 7. The dramatic difference in the House vote reflected no major change in the bill but an enormous lobbying effort by the administration, coal industry, and utility companies. As unemployment rose throughout 1975, opponents of the bill labeled it a job killer. The argument proved effective in the era of stagflation.

To no one's surprise, Ford vetoed the bill, on May 20. The House voted to defer its override attempt until after Memorial Day. Both sides escalated their lobbying efforts. The president himself stepped in to cajole old friends. Perhaps the high point of the confrontation occurred when an extraordinary joint session of the House and Senate Interior Committees confronted a panel of administration spokesmen, including energy czar Frank Zarb, in a crowded hearing room. Under glaring television lights, the committee members and administration leaders engaged in a freewheeling, sometimes brutal debate over the bill's merits. On June 10 the House finally voted on the override attempt. The vote was 278–143. The veto was sustained, by a margin of three votes.

The second strip-mining veto displays the distinctive pattern of the override model. Members carefully calibrated the bill with an eye to the override; the president then vetoed an unattractive bill hoping for success in the override.

Ford vetoed three other landmark bills. His veto of the Freedom of Information Act amendments follows the script of the override model and provides a particularly nice example of the threat model in action. The veto of the common-site picketing bill involved a last-minute switch by the president from support to opposition, in the face of Ronald Reagan's primary challenge. I discuss the apparently anomalous veto bargaining involving oil import fees in the penultimate section.

REAGAN

As a president Ronald Reagan had many assets: his ability to project warmth and conviction over television and radio, a wealth of practical political experience, a clear conception of his presidency, and, for the most part, skilled subordinates. But few assets were as valuable as a Republican Senate.

As I discussed in Chapter 5, a split party Congress transforms veto politics. With a unified, hostile Congress, the veto directly extracts policy concessions. With a split party Congress, the president's veto power works primarily to alter the bicameral bargaining on Capitol Hill. It strengthens the bargaining position of the chamber controlled by his copartisans, particularly if the president is far from the hostile chamber but not too distant from his supporters in the friendly one. When *CQ Almanac* wrote in 1986, "Throughout his presidency, Ronald Reagan's success in Congress had come in large part because of his ability and willingness to strike a deal at the right moment, even on issues that involved his fundamental principles," it captured the essence of a president's veto strategy with a split party Congress (1986:360). He should appear a man of principle, ready to use his veto. Otherwise, the veto will do little to strengthen the friendly chamber in its negotiations with the hostile one. But a nonrecalcitrant president must be able to compromise when his copartisans have wrung every concession possible from their counterparts. Otherwise he risks bargaining breakdowns and overrides. Reagan proved very deft at this form of veto bargaining.

In 1987, however, the Democrats captured the Senate. The nation's postwar experiment with a split party Congress was over. The administration now faced a hostile Congress, and in this configuration the veto became for Reagan what it had been for Truman in 1946–47, Eisenhower in 1959–60, Ford in 1975–76, and later would become for George Bush.

The Split Congress Vetoes

Reagan vetoed three landmark bills in the split party Congress. Of these vetoes, by far the most interesting is that of the Anti-Apartheid Act, for it illustrates the limits as well as the potency of veto power in a split party Congress.

The Anti-Apartheid Act.   Reagan seems consistently to have viewed South Africa as a sideshow in the larger struggle with communism. His administration's favored policy toward South Africa, "constructive engagement" with the Botha government coupled with hostility to the leftist African National Congress, attempted to minimize the chance of Communists coming to power. In contrast, members of Congress evaluated events in South Africa from the perspective of their constituents, who increasingly saw the South African government as immoral and racist. Over time, conflict between the administration and Capitol Hill – including most Republicans – was inevitable (*CQ Almanac* 1986:359–73).

In 1985, both houses passed a relatively mild bill imposing sanctions on South Africa. Reagan agreed to impose some of the sanctions by executive order and Majority Leader Robert Dole and Senate Foreign Relations Committee Chair Richard Lugar then killed the conference bill in the Senate, via a filibuster. This resolution provided only a temporary respite for the administration, however. In 1986, in the face of a brutal crackdown in South Africa, the House took up H.R. 4868. As amended on the floor, the bill suspended virtually all trade with South Africa and forced all U.S. businesses to depart that country within six months. In this form the bill had no chance of passage in the Senate but the fact that it passed the House at all – similar amendments had been overwhelmingly rejected in 1985 – signaled a change in sentiment in the face of the events in South Africa.

The real question, then, was the sentiment in the Republican Senate. Would it opt for a slight increase in sanctions, which the president either could accept or head off with mild executive action? If so, would the threat of a presidential veto strengthen the Senate's hand sufficiently to restrain the House? Alternatively, would the Senate press for more severe sanctions, ones the Republican president might veto?

To put some backbone in the Senate Foreign Relations Committee,

Reagan took to the airwaves. In a nationwide television speech, he called on Congress to "to resist this emotional clamor for punitive sanctions." The speech flopped, confirming senators' perception of a president badly out of step with the country. Support in the Senate for bolstering the sanctions was bipartisan and so strong that Chairman Lugar resolved to proceed with a "moderate" bill. The president's speech did serve, however, as a clear veto threat, for Reagan appeared bellicose and intransigent. Under the circumstances, Lugar stated, any bill would need at least 2–1 support in the Senate. "If we are serious about legislation, we will look for what will have the most support," he declared to committee members. The bill they crafted had the support on the committee of all but the most conservative Republicans, such as Jesse Helms. Floor amendments wrought changes in the committee's bill, but whenever one sanction was tightened, another was relaxed. The final bill passed 84–14.

Lugar still had to prevail with the House. To do so he produced a powerful argument, and took an ingenious action. He pointed out that the end of the session was near. If bargaining between the Senate and House over the final bill became protracted and produced nothing until the close of the session, Reagan would surely pocket-veto the bill. Congressmen would then have nothing to take the voters in the upcoming election of November 4. The best way to expedite the bargaining and avoid a pocket veto was total capitulation by the House to the Senate's moderate bill. Moreover, only a bill closely resembling the Senate's could hope to beat a regular veto. To cap his argument, Lugar appointed Jesse Helms as one of the two senators for the conference committee, thereby assuring a deadlocked conference if the House tried to tighten anything in the bill. Very reluctantly, liberals and the leaders of the Black Caucus agreed to accept the Senate's bill, thus eliminating the need for a conference. The Senate's bill flew through the House with a 308–77 vote.

The president now had ten days before he needed to act. He used every one of them, lobbying Senators and carefully counting noses. Finally, on the last day he could, he vetoed the bill. An override in the House was, of course, a foregone conclusion. The best the administration could hope for was a very narrow victory in the Senate. To bolster support there, White House aides circulated among Foreign Relations Committee members a draft executive order issuing more sanctions. This move followed hints in the president's veto message that he would unilaterally impose some sanctions if the Senate sustained his veto. A later letter to congressional leaders made the hint a promise. Subsequently, administration lobbyists secured pledges from six senators to support the administration if the vote were sufficiently close. Despite the administration's efforts, Lugar's bill received the support of seventy-eight senators. Some twenty-one voted to sustain the veto, a shortfall of twelve votes. Even had the six fence-sitters supported the president, he still would have been six votes shy of the necessary margin. *Congressional Quarterly* scored the override as the "most serious defeat Reagan had suffered on a foreign issue" up to that time, and a "stunning blow" for the Reagan administration.

The enactment of the Anti-Apartheid Act illustrates the limits of veto power in a split party Congress. The circumstances are worth underscoring: the president was badly out of step with the country, irreconcilably at odds with members of the other party, and quite far from all but the most extreme fringe of his copartisans in the one chamber his party controlled. In such circumstances, despite split party control of Congress, the override model kicked in. Exactly as the model of split party Congresses in Chapter 5 indicates, the more extreme chamber was effectively cut out of the bargaining. Lugar's hard-ball tactics with the House leadership show how this works in practice. The president's obvious veto threat in his television speech drove the Senate to the override region. The president then gambled heavily on a long-shot override attempt, and lost.

Other Split Congress Vetoes.   The two remaining vetoes of landmark vetoes in this period are less interesting. The first, the veto of an anti-crime bill in the 97th Congress, was a straightforward case of sequential veto bargaining. In the last hours of the session, Congress passed a hastily thrown together package of anticrime measures. Among the bill's provisions was the creation of a cabinet-level "drug czar," a symbolic move that provoked strong objections from stakeholders in the existing bureaucracies. Reagan pocket-vetoed the bill but announced his willingness to support a bill without the czar. The 98th Congress promptly repassed the bill, dropping the offending provision. The president signed the bill into law.

The remaining split Congress veto pitted Reagan against almost the entire 99th Congress. The bill was a clean-water measure that dispensed massive amounts of pork all over the country, in the form of sewage treatment plants. Objecting to the massive expenditures, Reagan pocket-vetoed the bill. Although the veto would clearly have been overridden, even a successful override would have been moot in the short run since the program had an adequate cushion of existing money. The next Congress – the unified, hostile 100th Congress – followed the script of the override model and Congress repassed the bill virtually unmodified. The president vetoed it again, and Congress promptly overrode the veto.

Veto Bargaining

The 100th Congress

Veto bargaining between Reagan and the 100th Congress assumed its most interesting form in the maneuvering surrounding a massive, omnibus trade bill.

The Trade Veto. The new Democratic Congress made a fast start with high-priority trade legislation. In 1987, both chambers passed a huge omnibus trade bill, H.R. 3, by overwhelming margins. The legislation was extraordinarily complex: nine Senate and fourteen House committees had been involved in the drafting. Each chamber's version of the bill was more than a thousand pages long. The conference committee included 44 senators and a staggering 155 House members, who worked in seventeen subgroups. Not surprisingly the conference committee, which began work in September 1987, began to flag. Little was accomplished during the heated budget negotiations between Congress and president that followed the Black October stock market crash. But when the new session opened, the leadership put the bill high on its agenda.

Going into conference, H.R. 3 contained one piece of certain veto bait: the so-called Gephardt amendment, which required the president to retaliate against Japan unless it reduced its huge trade surplus with the United States or ended "unfair" trade practices. Two other provisions drew veto threats: severe sanctions directed at Toshiba for exporting restricted technology to the Soviet Union, and mandatory notification of plant closings. Additionally, the administration opposed other sections of the bill, including a provision requiring disclosure of foreign ownership of U.S. companies or real estate.

The key architects of the bill, Senator Lloyd Bentsen and Representative Dan Rostenkowski, worked with administration trade officials to weaken some of the bill's more objectionable portions. They expunged the Gephardt amendment, among many other changes. Remaining, however, were the provisions about plant-closing notification, Toshiba sanctions, and foreign investment disclosure. By April 1988 the conference report was finally ready, but it came festooned with veto threats.

The wily Speaker of the House, Jim Wright, decided to make no more concessions to the president. The House passed the bill 312–107, suggesting the Speaker had plenty of votes to override a veto. In the Senate, however, a last-minute push by the administration and a dispute over provisions limiting the export of Alaskan oil stiffened Republican opposition. The bill passed 63–36, short of the critical 2–1 margin. Although the final bill was now complete and due for presentation to the

240

president, Speaker Wright, in an unusually imaginative manipulation of legislative procedure, attempted to erase the Alaskan oil provision from the bill via a drafting procedure intended for correcting minor typographical errors. Minority Leader Robert Dole scotched the maneuver in the Senate and the final bill, including the Alaskan oil provision, went to President Reagan.

The president waited almost two weeks to veto the bill. When he did, he cited the plant-closing provision as particularly obnoxious. He passed over other items that had drawn veto threats, such as the Toshiba sanctions, and emphasized his opposition to the Alaskan oil provisions, among other minor items. Within hours the House voted to override the veto, 308–113, a wide margin. The Senate put off action until after the Memorial Day recess. When it returned, it sustained the veto by a vote of 61–37, a margin of five votes.[27]

The first round of veto bargaining graphically illustrates the power of veto threats. Reagan's threats persuaded Congress to drop the Gephardt amendment and otherwise calibrate the bill for an override. The unexpected failure in the Senate – confirmed by Speaker Wright's desperate attempt to rewrite a finalized bill – illustrates the uncertainty inherent in many override attempts.

The override model predicts that Congress would simply repass the trade bill unchanged, hoping for a better outcome in the Senate. This is what happened – almost. The ingenious Wright saw further opportunities for legislative legerdemain.

Within hours of the failed override, Wright repackaged the omnibus bill. First, he removed the plant-closing section of the bill, which enjoyed large bipartisan popularity, and placed it in a separate bill. In essence, Wright challenged Reagan to veto provisions supported by many of his copartisans and popular with the voters, a veto sure to be overridden. Then Wright took the remainder of the omnibus bill, deleted the Alaskan oil provisions (perhaps to make up for the absence of the popular plant-closing provision), and placed it in a new bill. The new bill was thus calibrated to attract about the same number of votes as the old one and stood an excellent chance of beating a veto.

The plant-closing bill passed the Senate 72–23; a week later it passed the House 286–136. Reagan reluctantly signed the bill. In early August the Senate repassed the omnibus bill, this time by the vote of 85–11. Dropping the Alaskan oil provisions had made the bill veto-proof. The

[27] One of the five was Majority Leader Robert Byrd who, seeing the override attempt going down to defeat, had voted with the minority. He did this to preserve his right to request another override vote, should he be able to convert senators even after the failed override. This subtle parliamentary maneuver had no impact in the trade veto but played a critical role in the Highway Reauthorization override.

House followed suit with another enormously lopsided vote. Again Reagan reluctantly signed the bill.

In sum, Reagan's veto threats removed many items, and the veto itself killed the Alaskan provisions. Given the huge Democratic opposition and the support within his own party for the bills, he had done well – but if the Senate had been controlled by Republicans he would certainly have done far better.

Other Notable Vetoes of the 100th Congress. The remaining two vetoes of landmark legislation in the 100th Congress also show the override model at work. In the civil rights restoration act, Congress passed a tough bill calibrated for the override attempt. Reagan's veto was overturned by a margin of eight votes in the Senate. The veto of a gigantic highway and mass-transit bill followed a similar script, though the veto failed by a single vote.

ANOMALIES: THE MISSING VETOES

The vetoes in Table 8.1 reveal three cases of "missing vetoes." Two of these – Reagan and the plant-closing bill and Bush and the civil rights bill – apparently contradict the override model. The third – Ford and oil import fees – seems to violate the SVB model. I examine each in turn.

Violations of the Override Model

In these two cases, Reagan and the plant-closing bill and Bush and the civil rights bill, the president vetoed a bill and the veto was narrowly sustained. As the override model predicts, Congress repassed the bills virtually unchanged. The override model then predicts another veto, since the president has a chance to kill the bill if the override fails and bargaining breaks down. But in these two cases, the president did not reveto the round 2 bills despite an absence of concessions. Instead, he signed them. Why?

The Plant-Closing Bill. As I discussed earlier, the plant-closing bill was one of the two successor bills to the omnibus trade bill vetoed by President Reagan. The stand-alone plant-closing bill simply repeated the provisions from the omnibus bill and thus contained no concessions on plant-closing. But the circumstances were very special: the extremely popular plant-closing provisions had been stripped out of an omnibus bill. Shorn of the other provisions in the omnibus bill (which went into the other successor bill), the plant-closing bill was veto-proof, as indi-

242

cated by its extremely lopsided margins of passage. The override model predicts a veto of an unmodified, repassed bill because the override has a chance to succeed. No such chance existed for the plant-closing bill.

Bush and the Civil Rights Bill. In 1989, the Republican-dominated Supreme Court announced opinions in six cases involving job discrimination. In each case the Court narrowed the reach of the law or available remedies. Since the decisions involved statutory interpretation, Congress could reverse them simply by passing new law, which the heavily Democratic 101st Congress determined to do. The Senate Labor and Human Relations Committee drafted S. 2104, to reverse the rulings. The bill drew an immediate veto threat from the Bush administration but the Senate passed the bill 65–34. The administration branded the bill a "quota bill," a label that stuck.

In the House, both the Education and Labor Committee and the Judiciary Committee worked on a version of the bill, H.R. 4000. The House approved the bill 272–154. Thus, in both the House and the Senate, the bill appeared unlikely to beat a veto. In conference, the conferees scaled back the bill. The bill's sponsor, Ted Kennedy, predicted the bill would be veto-proof in the Senate, though others were less certain. Despite the concessions, the administration continued to issue veto threats. The Senate adopted the conference report 62–34, and the House did so 273–154. Clearly, if the bill was going to beat the veto, it would do so very narrowly. Five days later, to no one's surprise, Bush vetoed the bill. The Senate failed to override by a single vote, 66–34, and the measure died in the 101st Congress.

When the 102nd Congress opened, the bill's sponsors tried again. In the House the successor bill was H.R. 1, an appellation signaling the bill's significance to the Democratic leadership. Initially, the bill's sponsors in the House tried to dodge the "quota bill" label by targeting its provisions more broadly for women. But by the time the bill had navigated the House, the Senate, and the Conference Committee, it strongly resembled the bill passed the previous year. The bill included at best minor concessions.

Up to this point, the legislative history of the civil rights veto contains no surprises: it is exactly what the override model predicts. But now comes a surprise. The Senate adopted the conference report by a vote of 93–5, much greater than the 62–43 vote for the predecessor. The vote in the House followed suit, 381–38, up from 273–154. And the president signed the bill.

What happened? The answer takes but two words: Clarence Thomas. Between the two bills came the bruising struggle in the Senate over Clarence Thomas's appointment to the Supreme Court. During the fight, television beamed into living rooms across the country pictures of Republicans apparently attacking the legacy of the civil rights movement. Many Republican senators were understandably reluctant to back yet another assault on the civil rights bill. As Minority Leader Bob Dole explained, "From our Republican standpoint, it's better to be in a position of supporting a bill rather than going against Danforth [the bill's sponsor in the Senate – and the floor manager for the Thomas nomination] trying to override a veto." A veto would have been almost certainly futile, accomplishing nothing except further embarrassment for the Republicans, including the president. In short, the distribution of preferences on the civil right bill – perhaps even the president's – had shifted dramatically between the two rounds of bargaining. With the new distribution, support for essentially the same bill was much greater and the president's veto calculation different.

A Violation of the SVB Model

Suppose Congress passes a bill and the president vetoes it, and the margin to sustain is overwhelming. Or, the vote on passage is so close Congress does not even try to override. Then the SVB model predicts that the successor bill, if there is one, should include concessions. If it does not, the president should certainly not sign the bill. The veto bargaining over oil import fees seems to violate the model twice: first, the successor bill contained no concessions; and second, the president signed it.

The Oil Import Fee Veto. In January 1975 President Ford announced a dramatic action to conserve energy during the oil crisis. He would impose a fee on imported oil, raising it three dollars, in three one-dollar increments beginning on February 1. Congress moved to block the price rise. The action in the subsequent veto differs dramatically from that studied in the rest of this book, for President Ford began the process with a unilateral policy initiative. The case thus involved *administrative* policy making rather than *statutory* policy making, in Ferejohn and Shipan's phrase.[28] The sequence of play in administrative policy making, and thus the basic nature of the game, is quite different from that in statutory policy making. But let us see how the case played out.

The House Ways and Means Committee reported H.R. 1767 in Feb-

---

[28] Ferejohn and Shipan 1990 very carefully examines vetoes and administrative policy making. For more details, additionally see Ferejohn and and Eskridge 1992, and Eskridge 1994.

ruary. This bill nullified the price rise and suspended the president's authority to raise import fees for ninety days, thus reversing his administrative action. The floor approved the bill 309–114. The Senate Finance Committee quickly reported the bill without amendments and the Senate approved it 66–28. This vote boded ill for the administration, for counts of the remaining senators indicated a probable override in the event of a veto (*CQ Almanac* 1975:193). But the nose counts involved the comparisons between *the bill* – that is, no increase in fee – and the *status quo absent the bill*, namely an apparent three-dollar increase in fees. In early March, Ford vetoed the bill. But he simultaneously announced a compromise. If Congress sustained the veto he would voluntarily suspend the remaining two-dollar increase in the fee for sixty days, pending an overall agreement on energy policy. Thus, he used his ability to take administrative action to redefine the choice facing the wavering congressmen. No longer did they face a choice between a zero increase and a *three*-dollar increase. Instead, their choice was between a zero increase and a *one*-dollar increase. This compromise so altered the calculations that the Democratic leadership in both chambers indefinitely deferred plans for an override vote, which the White House confidently predicted it would win (*CQ Almanac* 1975:195).

But an even more dramatic move was in store. As the two sides moved into the second round of the veto bargaining, the Circuit Court of the District of Columbia intervened. The court ruled that Ford had exceeded his authority in imposing the import fee. The administration appealed the decision to the Supreme Court but effectively the Circuit Court had switched the reversion point in the bargaining back to a zero increase. Moreover, it destroyed Ford's ability to maneuver through administrative action. The remaining bargaining would now be statutory, and take place from a status quo of a zero increase. Not surprisingly, the successor bill then passed by Congress allowed no increases in oil import fees. Moreover, given the court's action, a veto would be futile. The president signed the bill.[29]

In sum, close inspection finds no counterexamples to the models among the three cases of missing vetoes. Instead, the models provide a basis for understanding what happened in three very special cases, the first involving a unique maneuver that rendered a successor bill vetoproof, the second involving a large change in the actors' preferences between the two bills, and the third involving administrative action and judicial intervention to change the status quo.

---

[29] The agreement on oil import fees was part of the deal surrounding S. 622 (PL 94–163), the Energy Policy and Conservation Act.

CONCLUSION

The models highlight a handful of factors in veto politics: the ideological distance between president and Congress, whether Congress is unified or split party, the location of the veto override players, uncertainty about the president's preferences, the location of status quo policies, and the press of urgent problems and the inherent uncertainty of the legislative process. According to the models, these factors shape the veto strategy of the president and the legislative strategy of Congress. However, as complicated as the models may seem, they remain simplified abstractions. In contrast, the case studies reveal tangled events and complex policies. As real cases inevitably are, they are finely textured and much denser with detail than any simple model ever could be (or should be). Savoring details and celebrating complexity require no models. Understanding the order beneath the details does. By examining some of the most important vetoes of the postwar period, I have tried to show that the models provide an interpretive framework for making sense of the details. The real politics of real vetoes are rich and complex, but simple models make them understandable.

9

Conclusion

VETO BARGAINING AND THE FIRST CLINTON ADMINISTRATION

To observers in 1992, the election of Bill Clinton seemed to mark an end to the era of divided government. After twelve long years a Democrat was back in the White House. The House of Representatives remained the rock-solid bastion of the Democratic Party, as it had since 1955 and apparently always would. The Democrats held the chamber by a 258 to 176 advantage, with one Independent. The Democrats also held the sometimes volatile Senate with the solid margin of 57–43, unchanged from the 102nd Congress.

The ideological distribution of senators in the 103rd Congress is shown in the top panel of Figure 9.1.[1] Strikingly clear is the polarization of the Senate. On the left was a large block of very liberal Democrats, on the right a substantial group of conservative Republicans, and on the far right an isolated group of extreme conservatives. The middle was thinly populated. Given this configuration, the Democratic leadership in the Senate favored a "start left" rather than a "start center" strategy.[2] In other words, whenever possible, legislative initiatives were shaped to appeal to liberal Democrats and then include concessions to pick up a few moderates, rather than appeal to a larger bipartisan supermajority. Given the nearly empty center, the policy costs of gaining the extra Republican votes were often prohibitively steep, at least for a very liberal Democratic caucus.

The 103rd Congress moved briskly to pass an impressive array of legislation, ultimately totaling nine important and ten landmark enact-

---

[1] The figure is based on the same data and methods used for Figure 8.1.

[2] Haynes Johnson and David Broder (1996:301–32) describe debates in the White House and among the Democratic leadership over the two strategies for the Clinton health care plan. A "start left" strategy was chosen for the health care plan.

247

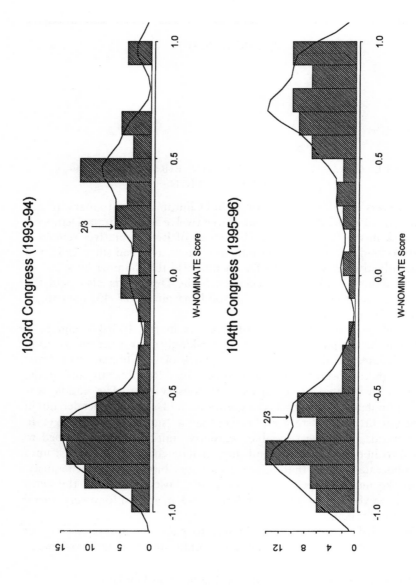

Figure 9.1. The Makeup of the Senate: The 103rd versus 104th Congress

ments, a very respectable record (Cameron et al. 1996; Mayhew 1995). Many of these initiatives, such as a tax increase for upper-income voters, absolutely infuriated the Republicans. What might be called the populist right was even more enraged by changes in social policy. The new president, who had run as a moderate Democrat, now backed gays in the military, supported affirmative action, and advocated gun controls. The reaction on the right was sharp. Vicious, ultraconservative radio commentators daily excoriated the "draft-dodging" president and his "femi-nazi" wife. The subsequent collapse of the administration's center-piece, a wildly ambitious plan for national health insurance, left the Clinton presidency stumbling.

The midterm election of 1994 brought the incumbent party a jaw-dropping reversal of fortune. For the first time in forty years, since Eisenhower lost his Republican Congress in 1954, the public stripped control of the legislature from the party of a sitting president. House seats, supposedly safer than those in Brezhnev's Supreme Soviet, tumbled like ninepins – but only if held by a Democrat. The GOP gained fifty-three seats in the House and eight seats in the Senate. Not a single incumbent Republican was defeated. The House Democrats most likely to lose were moderates who had faithfully supported the Democratic leadership's agenda (Brady, Cogan, and Rivers 1995; Ferejohn 1996). The repudiation of the president's party was unmistakable. At the same time, the incoming Republicans were militant, mobilized, and united behind leaders of proven parliamentary skill.

The bottom panel of Figure 9.1 shows the resulting configuration in the Senate, the critical terrain over the next two years since the House was so overwhelmingly conservative.[3] If the 103rd Senate had been polarized, the 104th was set for a civil war. The large block of very liberal Senators on the left was smaller in size. But the peak of the block had actually moved further left. The block of conservative Republicans was of course much larger, but its peak was much further right. The center was even thinner than before. The polarization was more extreme than even the 80th Congress of 1947–48 (compare Figure 9.1 with Figure 8.1).

What could the president do in the face of an electoral catastrophe? The 1946 Rowe Memorandum had sketched a strategy for a president who faced a comparable disaster (recall the discussion in Chapter 8). The president should begin by appearing conciliatory – after all, his party had just suffered a sharp and unmistakable rebuke from the voters. But then, as the militant opposition took disturbingly extreme positions and the electorate began to have second thoughts, the president should

---

[3] The data are based on roll call votes through December 1995.

shift from conciliation to conflict. He would have to pick his shots carefully, but a veto strategy could set the overconfident opposition on its ear.

Clinton indeed followed the broad outlines of the Rowe strategy. In the weeks after the election, the president was subdued and conciliatory. In contrast, the Republicans were triumphant. They saw no need to compromise the principles that had brought them victory and were happy to display their passions, no matter how extreme, before the mass media. As late as June 1995, the president declared at a Montana town meeting, "I don't want to have a pile of vetoes. So here I am – all dressed up and ready to cooperate. . . . I want to cooperate with Congress but it takes two to tango" (*CQ Weekly Report*, June 3, 1995:1559). Within a week, he issued his first veto. By late summer a year later, he had threatened more than three dozen bills and actually used the veto pen sixteen times (see Table 9.1). He blocked key portions of the Republican agenda and used veto bargaining to reshape others. Moreover, he did all this while recasting his image and boosting his popularity. Not since Eisenhower in 1959 had a president used the veto so effectively to reshape his presidency. I detail the highlights of this remarkable performance here.

But 1995–96 was hardly a replay of 1959–60 or even 1947–48. A striking difference was the way Clinton used vetoes to alter his policy reputation. In 1947–48, Truman's veto strategy moved him to the *left*; in 1959–60, Eisenhower's moved him to the *right*. In other words, their vetoes reshaped their reputations in the "natural" direction given their partisan identification, which was also the direction most useful in extracting policy concessions during veto bargaining. This process is easily understood in light of Chapter 4's model of sequential veto bargaining. But Clinton's vetoes repositioned him to the *right* – away from the "natural" reputation of a Democrat and away from the position that would extract maximum concessions. How could this be? In fact, doesn't this move contradict the model, in a particularly simple and devastating way? The answer is no. In fact the model explains how Clinton's "transformation" worked.

Truman and Clinton: Moving Left versus Moving Right

During the 79th Congress of 1945–46, liberals cast a cold eye on Truman. They found "the little man in the White House" unappealing as a personality and unreliable as a politician. But with the arrival of the Republican 80th Congress in 1947, Truman seemed to move left with a lurch: using the veto and the bully pulpit, he battled the reactionaries on every front.

Figure 9.2 takes a closer look at Truman's move left. The left-hand panel shows in stylized form Truman and the 79th Congress (1945–46). In the figure, the status quo policy sq represents a legacy from the New Deal and is shown as quite liberal. The ideal point for the 79th Congress, labeled C, indicates a somewhat less liberal legislature. The range of possible presidential types is show by the interval bordered by $\underline{t}$ and $\overline{t}$. That is, Truman may have been a centrist, corresponding to the type shown as $\overline{t}$. Or he may have been a liberal, indicated by $\underline{t}$. Or he may have been something in between. No one could be sure, since in the preference configuration of the 79th Congress both the moderate Truman and the liberal Truman almost always would behave the same way, signing the bills presented to him by Congress as it modified the legacy of the New Deal.

The right-hand panel shows the same Truman in 1947, but now with a Republican Congress. As the conservative Congress tried to set its impress on the nation, the moderate Truman and the liberal Truman separated themselves. Truman's blizzard of vetoes soon revealed he was no moderate: the types between τ and $\overline{t}$ would not have acted as Truman did. For example, a moderate probably would have accepted the Republican's third income tax bill but Truman vetoed it. Of course, discovering just how liberal the president was on each issue required case-by-case testing. In most cases, he revealed himself to be extremely liberal. In short, there was uncertainty about Truman's convictions, uncertainty that could not be resolved in 1945–46, given the configuration of Congress and president. Liberals could view him with justifiable suspicion (i.e., see his type as $\overline{t}$). In the configuration of 1947–48 the uncertainty was resolved, and Truman seemed to "move left" (a type closer to $\underline{t}$). But Truman did not really change. Rather, *his strategic situation changed*. In that configuration he could take actions that recast his reputation, and he did so in a way that would extract maximum concessions from Congress.

Figure 9.3 analyzes Clinton's move to the right. As Clinton began his presidency, Congress moved to address the conservative legacy of the Reagan and Bush administrations. As it did so, there was genuine uncertainty about the president's convictions. As shown in stylized form in the left-hand panel of Figure 9.3, Clinton might be a moderate $\overline{t}_1$. Or, as many suspected, he might be an extreme liberal ($\underline{t}$). There was no doubt about the Democratic 103rd Congress, though: the Democratic caucus was quite liberal and much of the legislation produced by the 103rd Congress could be portrayed as liberal. (In the figure, C again denotes Congress's ideal point.) Given the complexion of the congressional leadership and its legislative agenda, moderate-Clinton and liberal-Clinton would *both* be accommodators. Those inclined to see a liberal could

Table 9.1. *President Clinton's first-term vetoes*

Initial bill	History	Successor	History
Authorizations			
H.R. 1158: FY95 rescissions + disaster relief package	Veto threat, few concessions; 61–38 in S, 235–189 in H, vetoed 6/7/95; no override attempt	H.R. 1944	Concessions; passes H276–151, S 90–7; president signs
S 21: Bosnia arms embargo	Veto threat, concessions: 69–29, 298–198 vetoed 8/11/95; no override attempt	None	
H.R. 1058: Investor lawsuit bill	No threat; passes 65–30, 320–102; vetoed 12/19/95; overridden 319–100, 68–30	—	
H.R. 1530: FY96 defense authorization	Threat on missile defenses, size; S concession but replaced in conference; 267–149, 51–43; vetoed 12/28/95 citing missile defense, minor provisions; override fails in H 240–156	S 1124	Dropped missile defenses, most minor provisions; 287–129, 56–34; president signs
H.R. 4: Welfare reform	A successor to H.R. 2491 containing only welfare provisions; few or no concessions from successor; threat; passed 52–47, 245–178; vetoed 1/9/96; no override attempt	H.R. 3734	Threat aimed at Medicaid provisions; capitulation; many concessions from previous bill; 78–21, 328–101; president signs
H.R. 1833: Late-term abortions	Threat; passes 54–44, 286–129; vetoed 4/10/96; overridden in H 9/19 285–137; fails in S 57–41 9/27/96; died	None in 104th Congress	

Bill	Action		
H.R. 1561: FY96–97 foreign aid and State Department authorization	Attempt to kill 3 agencies draws threat; concessions in conference; passes 226–172, 52–44; vetoed 4/12/96 citing remaining Taiwan and Vietnam provisions; override fails 234–188	None in 104th Congress	
H.R. 956: Product liability lawsuits	Threat; cloture after filibuster; no concessions; passed 59–40, 259–158; vetoed 5/2/96; override fails 258–163	None in 104th Congress	
H.R. 743: Labor-management teams	Threat due to undermining employee protections; no concessions; 221–202, 53–46, president vetoes 7/30/96; no override attempt	None in 104th Congress	
H.R. 2902: Silvio O. Conte Wildlife Refuge	Administration opposed restrictions on eminent domain; no concessions	None in 104th Congress	
Appropriations			
H.R. 1854: FY96 legislative branch appropriations	Threat; 305–101 and 94–4; vetoed 10/3/95; no override attempt	H.R. 2492	No concessions, president signs (joint deal on executive branch funding)
H.J. Res. 115: Continuing resolution	Threat; passed 224–172, voice in S; vetoed 11/13/95; government shuts down; no override attempt	H.J. Res. 122	421–4, voice (first of many continuing resolutions)
H.R. 2586: Debt limit extension	Threat on default provisions and riders; passes 49–47, 219–185; vetoed 11/13/95; no override attempt	H.R. 3136	Congress almost totally capitulates. 328–91, voice, signed 3/29/96
H.R. 2491: Budget balancing reconciliation bill	Threat at Medicaid, Medicare reductions, welfare provisions, others; concessions in S and some on Medicaid in conference; passed 237–189, 52–47; vetoed 12/6/95; no override attempt		Parts included in appropriations bills, plus H.R. 4 (welfare)

Table 9.1. *(cont.)*

Initial bill	History	Successor	History
H.R. 1977: FY96 interior appropriations	Threat directed at S provisions on mining patent and Tongass Forest, cuts; concessions on patents in conference after 2 rejections in H; passed 244–181, 58–40; vetoed 12/23/95	H.R. 2880 (CR), H.R. 3019 (omnibus)	Funded briefly in CR H.R. 2880, which contained concessions on environment, 371–42, 82–8; H.R. 3019 drew threat over environmental provisions, S made concessions; passed 88–11, 399–25; signed
H.R. 2099: FY96 VA-HUD appropriation	Threat over cuts, especially Ameri-Corp; H moves to more moderate S position in conference; passed 227–190, 54–44; vetoed 12/18/95	H.R. 2880, H.R. 3019	Funded briefly in continuing resolution at conference levels, with minor concessions
H.R. 2076: FY96 commerce, justice, state, judiciary appropriation	Threat on police hiring cuts; no concessions; passed 50–48, 256–166; vetoed 12/19/95; override fails 240–159	H.R. 2880, H.R. 3019	Noncontroversial portions stripped out and passed in two separate bills, signed; remainder funded briefly under continuing resolution H.R. 2880, then in omnibus H.R. 3019

Note: H = House; S = Senate.
Source: CQ *Almanac* 1995, 1996; CQ *Weekly Reports*, various issues 1995–96.

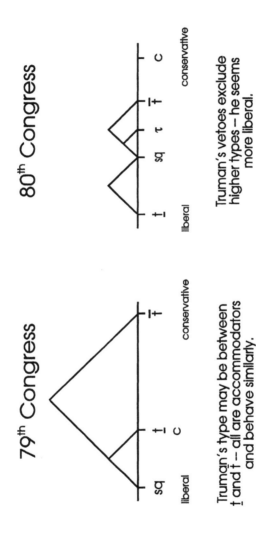

Figure 9.2. Truman and the 79th and 80th Congresses: Using Vetoes to Move Left

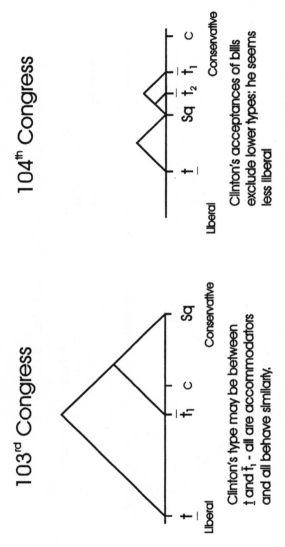

Figure 9.3. Clinton and the 103rd and 104th Congresses: Using Vetoes to Move Right

interpret Clinton's failure to distance himself from Congress's liberal enactments as confirmation of their belief. The clinching moment was the president's gamble on a highly regulatory health care plan. His support for the plan seemed to confirm voters' suspicions: the president probably was a big-government liberal.

The right-hand panel of Figure 9.3 shows Clinton in 1995, as the Republican Congress moved to alter liberal policies, including those enacted over the previous two years. In the figure, the ideal points for each presidential type correspond to those in the left-hand panel, though the indifference points labeling the types differ from the left-hand panel because the respective status quo policies differ. Many suspected the president of being a liberal (a type in the left end of the type space) but much uncertainty remained. None of the types would be an accommodator in this configuration so all would use a veto strategy against Congress. But if the president were really an extreme liberal he would force Congress to move to the override point (somewhere in the liberal range of the policy space), as predicted by the override model. Enactments would come through overrides, if they came at all. On the other hand, if Clinton were actually a moderate, then Congress and the administration might be able to work out agreements via sequential veto bargaining. Congress would have to compromise but ultimately the president would sign a sufficiently moderate bill. This is in fact what happened, over and over (I discuss the history shortly). The president announced his support for budget rescissions, while forcing Congress to rework them. He (ultimately) endorsed a rapid path to a balanced budget, but pried concessions from Congress. He declined to veto a bill banning gay marriages. In contrast, Truman had remorselessly vetoed the red-baiting McCarran Internal Security Act of 1950, a somewhat comparable bill in the tenor of its times.

In terms of the model, Clinton's actions excluded the types in the lower end of the type space, the extreme liberals (i.e., the types between $\underline{t}$ and $\bar{t}_2$).[4] He forced many to reevaluate their impression of him. To these voters and commentators, he seemed to have moved to the center. But he had probably always been there, on most issues. He had not changed; his strategic situation had. Moreover, the genuine uncertainty about his exact preferences on many issues – an ambiguity that clearly frustrated his Republican opponents – was extremely useful in extracting concessions from Congress. The president had promised to "end welfare as we know it." Would he really veto a bill that did just that? He would, twice, before signing a third bill. He threatened to veto a military appro-

---

[4] The indifference point, τ, for the override player would be located to the left of $\bar{t}_2$ in the diagram.

priations bill. Would he really do it? Not if the bill included money for his troops in Bosnia – but he would use the veto to strip strategic missile defenses from the defense authorization bill. And so on. The uncertainty about his preferences allowed him to use the veto to shape his reputation issue-by-issue, in the process extracting concessions.

Veto Bargaining in the First Clinton Administration

As the preceding discussion suggested, the broad contours of veto bargaining in the 104th Congress were determined by two factors. First, the congressional Democrats who were defeated in 1994 were not the most extreme liberals. In fact, extreme liberals did fairly well in the 1994 election. Moderate Democrats held the seats that were most vulnerable to a Republican surge, and it was they whom conservative Republicans replaced. As a consequence, the Democratic rump remaining in the 104th Congress was even *more* liberal than it had been in the 103rd Congress (Brady et al. 1995:19–20). Consequently, the already depleted center almost ceased to exist. The result for the location of the veto override player is shown in the bottom panel of Figure 9.1. The point marked ⅔ shows the approximate location of the veto override player in the Senate – a liberal Democrat. Consequently, if the Republicans were forced to craft a veto-proof bill, they could count on making steep policy concessions.

Second, the president was no Truman. Clinton sometimes took liberal positions, especially on social issues and most notably with his health care plan. But as a governor he had been a leader of the "New Democrats" – a moderate – and he had run as one in 1992. On many issues he would be less liberal than the override player in the Senate.

Once the president played (or, in many cases, threatened to play) the veto card, these two factors meant the Republicans would almost always find it more attractive to craft a signable bill than an unbeatable one. The veto bargaining in the 104th Congress therefore followed the script of the sequential veto bargaining model rather than the override model.

The Clinton administration reveals a piquant irony of the American system of separated powers. Defeat allowed the president to act more effectively than had victory. And the enactments hammered out through adversarial veto bargaining were more popular with voters than were the enactments passed by a Democratic majority in 1993–94, and almost certainly more popular than those an unfettered Republican majority would have enacted in 1995–96. In the end, neither party received a clear-cut victory. Only the voters did.

Conclusion

The Clinton presidency confirms rather then contradicts the historical experience on divided government, summarized in the regression model shown in Figure 1.1. Despite occasional interruptions, we live in an age of divided government. As I argued in Chapter 1, the current era may well be the greatest period of divided government in our national history. Yet, electoral eras can end overnight; that is the lesson of 1896. Perhaps we too live on the edge of an electoral precipice. However, in the immortal words of Nathan Detroit, that is not the way to bet. The forces that brought us to this era remain somewhat mysterious but there is no reason to believe they will not persist, at least in the near to medium run (Fiorina 1996).

What the Clinton experience does show is that divided government at the end of the century is quite different from that of, say, Eisenhower's middle congresses. In the mid-1950s a strong center bridged the congressional parties. Within the broad middle ground a centrist president could govern coalition-style, as a "hidden-hand" president (Greenstein 1982). Veto bargaining had its place, but absent an activist wing of the opposition – like the one that emerged with the 1958 election – its role was relatively circumscribed. In contrast, the center of today's congressional party system is nearly empty. Many of the seats held in the 1950s by Southern Democrats, reactionaries on race and labor but often moderate on other issues, are now held by very conservative Republicans. The Democrats are thus more unified, and more liberal, than they have been in fifty years. Among the Republicans, men and women of the center – the Rockefellers, Percys, Goodells, Chase Smiths, and Warrens – are an increasingly dim memory (Rohde 1991:137–63; Rae 1989). It is a long step from Everett Dirksen to Newt Gingrich. In the environment at the turn of the century, divided government means veto bargaining.

It is a sure bet, therefore, that veto bargaining will shape many of the most consequential legislative enactments of the near future, at least so long as divided government persists. But will those enactments be particularly important? It is a common form of ahistoricism to see current problems as uniquely important just because one happens to be close to them. Nonetheless, the legislative battles of the coming years may be consequential for an unexpected reason: the demise of global communism and the concurrent collapse of the Soviet empire.

The postwar era was built on the bedrock of anticommunism. Truman and the 80th Congress forged a bipartisan foreign policy explicitly based on containing communism. That policy persisted for almost fifty years. The domestic policies that appeared in the late 1940s, blossomed in the 1950s, and grew through the 1960s partially reflected the same forces. For example, American housing policy created a nation of home owners, a new yeomanry in the battle against communism. Many circumstances led to the policy but the desirability of that end was certainly one. A motivation for early civil rights policy, beginning with the desegregation of the military, was the desire to remove the international embarrassment of Jim Crow. Affirmative action policy then tried to create a well-educated black middle-class firmly attached to American institutions. Again, many forces were at play but the danger of an isolated and alienated portion of the population was more striking when the battle with global communism was more salient. Federal support for education was explicitly linked to anticommunism; so too was science policy. The gigantic tax subsidy for private health insurance, along with Medicare, provided the middle class the benefits of socialized medicine, without the socialism. The examples proliferate.

Each of these programs had politics that extended far beyond anticommunism. They created constituencies that persist after the end of communism. Nonetheless, they were predicated on a world in which American democracy competed with global communism. That world is now gone. With it went the coalitions and rationales that supported not only American foreign policy but important parts of the domestic political economy as well. What will ultimately emerge remains unclear. Most obviously, American foreign policy will be re-created from top to bottom to reflect the new configuration of power and the challenges of a new economic order. This process is likely to take a decade or more. But the domestic state will also be reshaped. No part of the structure created in the postwar years – health, welfare, civil rights, and housing policy; science, education, and technology policy; environmental and resource development policy; trade and tax policy – will remain exactly what it was. If divided government persists, much of the new political economy will be forged in the heat of veto bargaining.

And it may not be a bad thing, at least from the perspective of the average voter. Not only are the congressional parties polarized with respect to each other, they are arguably quite far from much of the electorate. Veto bargaining tends to move policy toward a center occupied by voters but disproportionately abandoned by the parties. So long as the presidency remains in the hands of the Democrats and Congress in those of the Republicans, the moderating effect of veto bargaining will infuriate partisans of the right just as earlier, when the Republicans controlled the White House and the Democrats Capitol Hill, it infuriated partisans of the left. Voters may find the discord inherent in interbranch bargaining unseemly and distasteful. The results, however, are apt to prove surprisingly palatable.

Conclusion

For two and a half decades after the Second World War, the intellectual framework for the study of American government was provided by the masterful synthesis fashioned by V. O. Key, Robert Dahl, David Truman, the contributors to the Michigan school of voting studies, and other leaders in political science's behavioral moment. The behavioral synthesis joined an account of voting behavior (the Michigan school's empirical studies), an account of policy making (the theories of pluralism and presidential government), and an account of institutional change (the notion of critical elections). Together, these components captured in elegant shorthand most of American politics, at least since the emergence of the university-based discipline of political science in the 1880s.

Beginning in the mid-to-late 1960s, the behavioral synthesis began to unravel. What went wrong? Two factors stand out. The first factor is implied by the description comparativist Robert Bates offers of his own field: "The field of development lacks a core body of deductive theory; it proceeds inductively instead. . . . In a field without theory, precedents assume the status of laws" (1988:499). When new events occurred, the "laws" of American politics melted away. These events included the movement politics of the 1960s and 1970s, the mysterious disappearance of realigning elections, the rise of split-ticket voting, the resurgence of congressional parties, and the reappearance of divided government. The second factor was new ideas, most rooted in rational choice analysis. For example, Mancur Olson's logic of collective action attacked the foundations of pluralism while Morris Fiorina's reconceptualization of party identification removed the linchpin of the Michigan model. The two-pronged assault from unexpected events and new concepts left the behaviorists' tidy system in disarray.

By the mid-1970s the behavioral synthesis was increasingly tattered, yet nothing had emerged to replace it. Without the cohesion of a unifying vision, the academic study of American politics splintered into semi-autonomous subfields – Congress, presidency, voting behavior, public opinion, law and courts, and so on. In each subfield professionalized scholarship flourished but the subfields rarely spoke to one another. Lost was a concern for issues that spanned the subfields, including the operation of the separation-of-powers system.

During the past decade or so, a successor to the behavioral synthesis has appeared, the research program I called in Chapter 1 rational choice institutionalism. This research program harks back to earlier institutionalisms, including those of Madison and Hamilton, Ford and Wilson, and

Edward S. Corwin. But it is distinctively different in its paradigm, its method, and its vision.

A New Institutionalism

The distinctive paradigm of analytical institutionalism is most evident in the branch devoted to studying constitutions. In a recent essay Roger Myerson lays out the pieces:

> The structure of a democratic political system consists of the offices that politicians may seek, the constitutional powers associated with these offices, and the procedures by which candidates are elected to these offices. These structures together form a complex incentive system for politicians, determining what kinds of political decisions and strategies will be rewarded. Thus, the constitutional *structure* of a democracy may influence the *conduct* of its politicians and the *performance* of its government. (1995:77; emphasis added)

The aim of the structure-conduct-performance paradigm is threefold. The first aim is to trace how governmental structures create incentives for governmental officials and voters. Examples of such structures are first-past-the-post legislative elections, the no-confidence vote in parliamentary systems, and the separation of powers. The second aim is to analyze how those incentives shape the conduct of political actors. Thus, for example, one would show why first-past-the-post elections lead to two-party systems with convergent parties, how the no-confidence vote creates disciplined parties within a legislature, and how the separation of powers fosters interbranch bargaining.[5] The third aim is to uncover the consequences for the performance of the system. For instance, one would evaluate how convergence parties affect the welfare of the electorate (Myerson 1995:78–79).

The method for implementing the structure-conduct-performance paradigm represents a break with earlier traditions as well. The first step in implementing the paradigm is to use noncooperative game theory – the purest form of rational choice analysis – to construct deductive models in which the links between structure, conduct, and performance are explicit. Moreover, as Myerson notes, the aim is to create an *abundance* of models:

> We need to develop a literature in which many such [game-theoretic] models are analyzed, because any one tractable model can only consider a few simple aspects of constitutional structure and political behavior. By examining many such models, and by relating the theoretical analysis to empirical findings from com-

---

[5] These examples draw upon Myerson and Weber 1993, Feddersen 1992, Diermeier and Feddersen 1996, and Cox 1997. References to other examples may be found in Myerson 1995.

parative politics, we can gradually build a better understanding of the significance of different political institutions.

The second step is to use systematic empirical evidence to evaluate the resulting models, calibrate them, and investigate their properties.

The underlying vision is perhaps the most radical element in the program. Though this vision is rarely articulated, the use of the structure-conduct-performance paradigm is revealing. The paradigm originates not in political science but the branch of economics known as industrial organization, the subfield that studies the performance of industries. For many years, industrial organization was one of the least theoretical and most empirical parts of economics. Research was relentlessly inductive, moving from case studies of industries and firms to cross-industry statistical analysis. By the mid-1970s, most economists regarded the field as a failure. Forty years of unabated inductivism had uncovered only a handful of reliable, systematic patterns. The theoretical notions that had guided the research looked increasingly ad hoc. Research was at a standstill. Then, in the 1980s, a revolution occurred. The new solution concepts developed in game theory (described in Chapter 4) transformed the field; indeed, many entered economics through the study of firms' strategy and tactics. Models proliferated, allowing the analysis of hundreds of industry configurations and forms of strategic competition. This orgy of model building subsided in the late 1980s and empiricism picked up again, but now guided by the models. Spinoffs from the revolution include a revamped approach to strategy in business schools, and the new "economics of organization," which has made its presence felt not only in economics but in political science.[6]

What would the study of American politics look like if it drew more heavily on industrial organization as a model? First, the intellectual contours of the field would be shaped much more by models of fundamental strategic situations than is true at present. Models of bargaining, signaling, screening, tournaments, commitments, and so on would be deployed across the subfields as the occasion warranted. As a consequence, the field would be much more comparative across the subfields. Congress, courts, presidency, bureaucracy, and electoral systems would be seen less as sui generis than as illustrative of particular strategic issues. The special features and histories of individual institutions would continue to receive close scrutiny. But they would serve more as laboratories for elaborating and empirically investigating causal mechanisms and somewhat less as freestanding objects for organizing the field. Second, concerns that span the subfields would receive more attention than at

[6] To see the former, consult Milgrom and Roberts 1992; on the latter, see Holmstrom and Tirole 1989, and Moe 1984.

present. The separation of powers, for example, would not be quite the orphan that it is today. The macroperformance of the system would surely receive more attention. Third, the links between theory and data would be closer than has typically been the case. Natural history has its place, as does completely abstract model building. But central to an industrial-organization-style political science is combining well-elaborated causal mechanisms with systematic, on-point evidence. Finally, an industrial-organization-style American politics would fit more comfortably with and have more to contribute to comparative politics than it seems to at present.

A Laboratory for Institutionalism

Veto bargaining offers a natural laboratory for experimenting with these ideas, and that has been one of the goals of this book. Thus, I began with a fundamental structure in American politics, the separation-of-powers system. The structure implies interbranch bargaining. Accordingly, I used noncooperative game theory to construct several models of interbranch bargaining. The models allowed me to explore the incentives facing presidents and Congress during bargaining and to deduce their likely conduct. I then used systematic empirical evidence to evaluate the models.

How successful was this experiment in analytical institutionalism? In Chapter 3, I reviewed criteria that are typically used to evaluate scientific theories. How do the models stack up against those criteria? The models explain the natural history of the veto and solve empirical puzzles, including ones they were not designed to solve. They make predictions outside the initial data, which turn out to be correct, for example, concerning deadline effects. They turn apparent counterexamples (like Clinton's shift to the center, or the missing vetoes) into solved problems. They provide a framework for interpreting and understanding history, including specific cases of veto bargaining. No rival model or models display their reach and power in explaining veto bargaining. The models are certainly not the final word on veto bargaining or the presidential veto – far from it. But measured against stringent criteria, far more stringent than often employed in social science, they perform pretty well.

The payoff from this experiment in rational choice institutionalism is not simply insights into the conduct of the president and Congress. The payoff includes lessons about the performance of the separation-of-powers system. For example, the presidential veto does not automatically turn intervals of divided government into periods of policy gridlock, because vetoes are hardly "bullets" for important legislation. Instead, vetoes are bargaining tools that shape agreements. And, when the parties are polarized and government is divided, veto bargaining moderates policy to the advantage of nonpolarized voters.

This study just scratches the surface of veto bargaining, which is ubiquitous in the separation-of-powers system. For example, the Supreme Court has a veto over legislation. Lower courts can veto the actions of administrative agencies. Congress has worked hard to devise its own veto over administrative actions, despite interference from the Supreme Court. In addition, the floors of the House and the Senate have a veto over the work of conference committees; the Senate has veto power over presidential treaties; the Senate may veto high-level presidential appointments, including Supreme Court nominees; and so on. Nor is this reliance on veto mechanisms restricted to the federal government. Similar mechanisms abound throughout state and local governments. The methods on display in this book can be adapted to study the full range of veto mechanisms. The result will be a better understanding of American government.

Lessons for Studying the Presidency

Very few scholars of the presidency are enthusiasts of rational choice theory. Instead, most scholars adhere either to historical institutionalism or to quantitative behavioralism.[7] The antipathy for rational choice theory among both groups is easy to understand. For practitioners of historical institutionalism, the rational choice approach has seemed too abstract and too removed from real politics. For them, rational choice theory has meant empty propositions about the uninteresting. For diehard, number-crunching behavioralists, rational choice theory has seemed too contemptuous of empirical evidence. For them, it has meant untestable propositions about the unobservable.

Rational choice theory is far better suited to the study of the presidency than either group suspects. Rational choice is not magic; regardless of the method, bad social science is always easier to produce than good. Used appropriately and thoughtfully, however, rational choice theory can direct systematic empirical analysis into new and profitable avenues, and supply theoretical foundations for work that had functioned hitherto as descriptions. It renders intelligible real politics made by real presidents.

Skeptics are entitled to the following rejoinder. In Chapter 3 (they might argue) I posited an applicability scale for rational choice theory. Situations at the high end of the scale are well suited to rational choice

---

[7] Illustrative of the first approach is Pious 1979; illustrative of the second is Edwards 1989 or King and Ragsdale 1988. Rational choice studies of the presidency include Miller 1993, Moe 1985, and Sullivan 1988.

analysis. Those at the low end are poorly suited for that type of inquiry. Over the next five chapters I applied rational choice theory to veto bargaining, a type of politics that clearly resides at the high end of the scale (I suggested as much myself). Granted, this exercise was useful since failure there would have implied failure everywhere. But success at the high end of the scale (if Chapters 4–8 be counted a success) tells us nothing about the prospects for success lower on the scale. *And that's where most presidential politics lies.*

This is a cogent argument, but one I reject. Much more of presidential politics resides at the high end of the applicability scale than skeptics believe. However, the best way to prove this point is through demonstration, not argumentation. Nonetheless, in an effort to encourage others to produce those demonstrations, I offer a brief counterargument to the skeptics.

The Applicability Scale Revisited.   Richard Pious has advanced the useful concept of presidential "prerogative power" (1979: chap. 2). One can distinguish three levels of prerogative power, depending on an activity's proximity to constitutional foundations. The first is explicitly grounded in Articles I and II of the Constitution and includes, beside the veto, nominations and treaty making. The second level involves actions that take place in the interstices of the Constitution. They are governed by what earlier generations of political scientists called our "unwritten constitution." Many of these activities, despite the silence of the written Constitution, have become routine, are repetitious, and are rarely contested as activities however much their content may be. Examples include managing the bureaucracy, formulating and pressing a legislative program, constructing the presidential budget, "going public" to pressure Congress, intervening in selected labor disputes, conducting personal diplomacy, and pursuing presidential objectives in the courts, for instance, via test cases or the solicitor general's amicus briefs (Neustadt 1982). Activities at the third level border on Caesarism. Examples include Lincoln's suspension of habeas corpus, Truman's seizure of the steel mills, Nixon's bombing of Cambodia, Reagan's pursuit of covert activities in Nicaragua (the Iran-Contra scandal), and above all Andrew Johnson's battle with Congress over reconstructing the defeated South. At this level, presidential prerogative government may contravene statutes or even the Constitution itself. It pushes the separation of powers to the breaking point and sometimes precipitates a constitutional crisis.

The first level constitutes the core of the institutional presidency, for it is hard-wired into the office by the Constitution. For the reasons I discussed in Chapter 3, activities at this level reside at the "high" end

266

of the applicability scale. For them, the structure-conduct-performance paradigm offers a natural framework in which rational choice theory can be used productively. Interesting work on appointments, treaties, and executive agreements is under way. The coming years will surely see more research of this kind.

The second level includes much of modern presidential politics. A few works explore the applicability of rational choice theory to this middle range but for the most part this is virgin territory (Calvert et al. 1989; Snyder and Weingast 1994). The key to applying rational choice theory here is the recognition that "structures" include more than constitutionally entrenched entities or procedures. They also include structural features that are malleable over the long haul but fixed in the short run. Examples include bureaus, congressional committees, congressional procedures like the 1974 Budget Act or the Senate's Rule XXII (governing filibusters), the procedural conventions established under the aegis of the Administrative Procedures Act, the organization and standard operating procedures of the federal judiciary, and procedures internal to the Supreme Court such as the rules governing which cases it hears. All these are extraconstitutional and hence changeable, at least in the long run. But for models targeted at midrange politics, they can be taken as fixed "structures" *in the short run*. Given this, midrange prerogative government can be modeled using the same techniques I employed in this book, provided one is sensitive to the historical contingency of the structures. Since many of these interesting activities are frequently repeated even in a "short run," systematic empirical evidence can be used to evaluate the models.

Ultimately, this approach to midrange politics will be completely satisfying only if short-run "structures" can themselves be explained via rational choice theory. For example, the rules of the game established by the Administrative Procedures Act can be taken as fixed in the short run. But taking the long view, the rules themselves – including the shaping influence of presidents – need to be explained using the structure-conduct-performance paradigm. Attempts to explain shifting institutional forms and procedures can be seen as a distinctly rational choice contribution to the newly emerging subfield of American Political Development, and a contending alternative to approaches other than rational choice, such as that offered in Steven Skowronek's provocative *The Politics Presidents Make*. Terry Moe's deft analysis of the development of the organizational presidency provides a model for how this research might proceed (1985; 1993).

Politics at the third level of prerogative government combines all the problems at the lower levels with new ones. Consider, for example, Andrew Johnson's confrontation with Congress over Reconstruction, which led to the severest crisis in the history of the presidency. Part of this confrontation involved veto bargaining over the Reconstruction Act and other bills. This part of the story can be understood with the models in this book. Part of the confrontation involved a struggle over policies administered by the army and by the Freedman's bureau. This part of the story resembles similar struggles over bureaucratic policy analyzed in existing level 2 models, such as Snyder and Weingast's study of presidential influence at the National Labor Relations Board (NLRB). Parts of the confrontation, however, involved an assault on the separation-of-powers system itself. Examples include Johnson's effort to cow Congress with military force by attempting (unsuccessfully) to create an Army of the Atlantic headquartered in the District of Columbia, and his ultimate dismissal of Secretary of War Edwin Stanton in flagrant violation of the Tenure of Office Act. What determines the outcome in a full-fledged constitutional crisis between the branches? The answer, like the power of constitutionalism itself, lies outside the Constitution and in the sentiments of the people (Weingast 1997). How much rational choice has to say about such matters is an open question but one well worth exploring.

Rational Choice and the Presidency. In sum I make no claim that rational choice theory, even in the form of rational choice institutionalism, is the best way to study all aspects of the presidency. The "personal presidency" – charisma, personal magnetism, special skill in picking subordinates, and so on – is important but probably lies beyond the bounds of rational choice analysis. Parts of the institutional presidency may prove elusive as well. I do assert, however, that presidential studies have been unduly bichromatic, limited to the hues of descriptive institutionalism and quantitative behavioralism. There is a richer palette that scholars can draw upon, and the result will be a more vivid and interesting portrait of the presidency.

The Significance of the Separation-of-Powers System

I opened this book by quoting from Gordon Wood's magisterial study of early American political thought. In Wood's account (1969), the Founders put the separation of powers at the center of the American political system. In so doing, they bequeathed an enigma to generations of political scientists. What is the true significance of the separation-of-powers system?

One response to the enigma is to see the separation-of-powers system as a botched parliamentary system. But it is hardly that. Persisting in

268

this error leads to canards about gridlock and pipe dreams about disciplined political parties. It means missing the actual strengths and real weaknesses of the American system.

Another way to understand the enigma is to view the separation-of-powers system as a "presidential" system. But this approach also mischaracterizes the American system. To view a system of genuinely tandem institutions as somehow "presidential" is to misplace the interbranch bargaining that is central to the American system. Of course, presidents are important, often critically so; but when and how they are important depends on a complex and variable balance of power between the branches.

The American system is neither a botched parliamentary system nor a presidential system. It is something quite different from either. It is a system predicated on internal checks and balances, a system in which interbranch bargaining is not a minor component but oftimes a major one. The long-standing fear about the American system is that gridlock inevitably follows whenever policy differences between the branches are severe. The evidence mustered in this book demonstrates that even in adversarial circumstances and even in the type of bargaining most likely to lead to stalemate, the separation-of-powers system is regularly able to forge agreements. It does so *through* interbranch bargaining rather than *despite* it. When examined through the lenses of careful theory and systematic evidence, the performance of the separation-of-powers system is surprising. We have yet to grasp its true significance.

References

Aldrich, John. 1995. *Why Parties: The Origin and Transformation of Party Politics in America.* Chicago: University of Chicago Press.

Alesina, Alberto, and Howard Rosenthal. 1995. *Partisan Politics, Divided Government, and the Economy.* Cambridge: Cambridge University Press.

Ambrose, Stephen E. 1984. *Eisenhower.* Vol. 2: The President. New York: Simon and Schuster.

American Political Science Association. 1950. *Toward a More Responsible Two-Party System.* Washington, D.C.: APSA.

Arnold, R. Douglas. 1979. *Congress and the Bureaucracy: A Theory of Influence.* New Haven: Yale University Press.

Arrow, Kenneth J., and Seppo Honkapohja, eds. 1985. *Frontiers of Economics.* New York: Basil Blackwell.

Ashenfelter, Orley, and Richard Layard, eds. 1986. *Handbook of Labor Economics.* Amsterdam: North-Holland.

Aumann, Robert J. 1985. "What Is Game Theory Trying to Accomplish?" Pp. 28–87 in *Frontiers of Economics,* edited by Kenneth J. Arrow and Seppo Honkapohja. New York: Basil Blackwell.

Austen-Smith, David. 1992. "Strategic Models of Talk in Politics." *International Political Science Review* 13:45–58.

Bachrach, Peter, and Morton Baratz. 1962. "The Two Faces of Power." *American Political Science Review* 56:947–52.

Banks, Jeffrey. 1991. *Signaling Models in Political Science.* Chur: Harwood Academic Press.

Baron, David. 1996. "A Dynamic Theory of Collective Goods Programs." *American Political Science Review* 90:316–30.

Bartholomew, D. J. 1977. "The Analysis of Data Arising from Stochastic Processes." Pp. 145–74 in *The Analysis of Survey Data,* vol. 2: Model Fitting, edited by Colm O'Muircheartaigh and Clive Payne. London: John Wiley and Sons.

Bates, Robert. 1988. "Lessons from History, or the Perfidy of the English Exceptionalism and the Significance of Historical France." *World Politics* 40: 499–516.

271

References

Bates, Robert, Avner Greif, Margaret Levi, Jean-Laurent Rosenthal, and Barry Weingast. 1998. *Analytical Narratives*. Princeton: Princeton University Press.

Beck, Nathaniel, and Simon Jackman. 1998. "Beyond Linearity by Default: Generalized Additive Models." *American Journal of Political Science* 42 (2):596–627.

Becker, Richard A., John M. Chambers, and Allan R. Wilks. 1988. *The New S Language: A Programming Environment for Data Analysis and Graphics*. Pacific Grove, Calif.: Wadsworth and Brooks/Cole Advanced Books and Software.

Belkin, Aaron, and Philip E. Tetlock, eds. 1996. *Counterfactual Thought Experiments in World Politics*. Princeton: Princeton University Press.

Berman, Larry. 1990. *Looking Back on the Reagan Presidency*. Baltimore: Johns Hopkins University Press.

Bessette, Joseph M., and Jeffrey Tulis, eds. 1981a. *The Presidency in the Constitutional Order*. Baton Rouge: Louisiana State University Press.

1981b. "The Constitution, Politics, and the Presidency." Pp. 3–30 in *The Presidency in the Constitutional Order*, edited by Joseph M. Bessette and Jeffrey Tulis. Baton Rouge: Louisiana State University Press.

Bond, Jon R., and Richard Fleisher. 1990. *The President in the Legislative Arena*. Chicago: University of Chicago Press.

Brady, David. 1988. *Critical Elections and Congressional Policy Making*. Stanford, Calif.: Stanford University Press.

Brady, David, John Cogan, and Douglas Rivers. 1995. "How the Republicans Captured the House: An Assessment of the 1994 Midterm Elections." Essays in Public Policy, no. 57. Hoover Institution, Stanford University.

Brams, Steven J., Paul J. Affuso, and D. Marc Kilgour. 1989. "Presidential Power: A Game-Theoretic Analysis." Pp. 55–74 in *The Presidency in American Politics*, edited by Paul Brace, Christine Harrington, and Gary King. New York: New York University Press.

Brandenburger, Adam. 1992. "Knowledge and Equilibrium in Games." *Journal of Economic Perspectives* 6:83–102.

Branyan, Robert L., and Lawrence H. Larsen. 1971. *The Eisenhower Administration, 1953–1961*. New York: Random House.

Bronowski, Jacob. 1977. "Humanism and the Growth of Knowledge." Pp. 74–104 in *A Sense of the Future: Essays in Natural Philosophy*. Cambridge, Mass.: MIT Press.

Bryce, James. 1888. *The American Commonwealth*. Vol. 1: *The National Government*. London: Macmillan.

Bueno de Mesquita, Bruce. 1996. "Counterfactuals and International Affairs: Some Insights from Game Theory." Pp. 211–29 in *Counterfactual Thought Experiments in World Politics*, edited by Aaron Belkin and Philip E. Tetlock. Princeton: Princeton University Press.

Burns, James McGregor. 1984. *Roosevelt, the Lion and the Fox*. New York: Harcourt, Brace, Jovanovich.

Cain, Bruce, John Ferejohn, and Morris Fiorina. 1987. *The Personal Vote: Constituency Service and Electoral Independence*. Cambridge, Mass.: Harvard University Press.

References

Calvert, Randall L., Mathew D. McCubbins, and Barry R. Weingast. 1989. "A Theory of Political Control and Agency Discretion." *American Journal of Political Science* 33:588–611.

Calvert, Randall L., Mark J. Moran, and Barry R. Weingast. 1987. "Congressional Influence over Policy Making: The Case of FTC." Pp. 493–522 in *Congress: Structure and Policy*, edited by Mathew D. McCubbins and Terry Sullivan. Cambridge: Cambridge University Press.

Camerer, Colin. 1995. "Individual Decision Making." Pp. 587–704 in *Handbook of Experimental Economics*, edited by John H. Kagel and Alvin E. Roth. Princeton: Princeton University Press.

Cameron, Charles M., and Susan Elmes. 1995. "A Theory of Sequential Veto Bargaining." Working Paper. Departments of Political Science and Economics, Columbia University.

Cameron, Charles M., William Howell, Scott Adler, and Charles Riemann. 1996. "Measuring the Institutional Performance of Congress in the Post-War Era: Surges and Slumps in the Production of Legislation, 1945–1994." Hoover Institution, Stanford University, April.

1997. "Divided Government and the Legislative Productivity of Congress." Paper presented at the annual meeting of the American Political Science Association, Washington, D.C., September.

Cameron, Charles M., Yuen Kwok, and Charles Riemann. 1995. "Veto Power: Presidential Vetoes and Congressional Policy Concessions, 1945–1992." Department of Political Science, Columbia University. Unpublished manuscript.

Cameron, Charles M., John Lapinski, and Charles Riemann. 1996. "Veto Threats: Testing Formal Theories of Political Rhetoric." Department of Political Science, Columbia University. Unpublished manuscript.

Carr, Edward Hallett. 1961. *What Is History?* New York: Vintage Books.

Chong, Dennis. 1995. "Rational Choice Theory's Mysterious Rivals." Pp. 37–59 in *The Rational Choice Controversy*, edited by Jeffrey Friedman. New Haven: Yale University Press.

Chubb, John E., and Paul E. Peterson, eds. 1985. *The New Direction in American Politics*. Washington, D.C.: Brookings Institution.

eds. 1989. *Can the Government Govern?* Washington, D.C.: Brookings Institution.

Cleveland, William S. 1993. *Visualizing Data*. Summit, N.J.: Hobart Press.

Cleveland, William S., Eric Grosse, and William M. Shyu. 1993. "Local Regression Models." Pp. 309–76 in *Statistical Models in S*, edited by John Chambers and Trevor Hastie. New York: Chapman and Hall.

Coleman, James. 1973. *The Mathematics of Collective Action*. London: Heinemann Educational Books.

Congressional Quarterly. 1985. *Members of Congress since 1789*. 3d ed. Washington, D.C.: Congressional Quarterly.

Congressional Quarterly (CQ) Almanac. Various issues.

Congressional Quarterly (CQ) Weekly Report. Various issues.

Copeland, Gary. 1983. "When Congress and President Collide: Why Presidents Veto Legislation." *Journal of Politics* 45 (August): 696–710.

273

References

Corwin, Edward S. 1940. *The President: Office and Powers*. New York: New York University Press.

  1957. *The President, Office and Powers, 1787–1957: History and Analysis of Practice and Opinion*. 4th rev. ed. New York: New York University Press.

Cox, Gary W. 1997. *Making Votes Count: Strategic Coordination in the World's Electoral Systems*. Cambridge: Cambridge University Press.

Cox, Gary W., and Samuel Kernell, eds. 1991. *The Politics of Divided Government*. Boulder, Colo.: Westview Press.

Cox, Gary W., and Mathew D. McCubbins. 1993. *Legislative Leviathan: Party Government in the House*. Berkeley: University of California Press.

Crawford, Vincent. 1991. "Thomas Schelling and the Analysis of Strategic Behavior." Pp. 265–94 in *Strategy and Choice*, edited by Richard J. Zeckhauser. Cambridge, Mass.: MIT Press.

Dahl, Robert. 1956. *Preface to Democratic Theory*. Chicago: University of Chicago Press.

Derthick, Martha, and Paul J. Quirk. 1985. *The Politics of Deregulation*. Washington, D.C.: Brookings Institution.

Diermeier, Daniel, and Timothy Feddersen. 1996. "Cohesion in Legislatures." Paper prepared for the annual meeting of the Midwest Political Science Association, Chicago.

Donovan, Arthur, Larry Laudan, and Rachel Laudan, eds. 1988. *Scrutinizing Science: Empirical Studies of Scientific Change*. Dordrecht: Kluwer Academic Publishers.

Donovan, Robert J. 1982. *Tumultuous Years. The Presidency of Harry S Truman, 1949–1953*. New York: W. W. Norton.

Dougan, William R., and Michael C. Munger. 1989. "The Rationality of Ideology." *Journal of Law and Economics* 32:119–41.

Downs, Anthony. 1957. *An Economic Theory of Democracy*. New York: Harper and Row.

Edwards, George C. 1989. *At the Margins: Presidential Leadership of Congress*. New Haven: Yale University Press.

Edwards, George C., John Kessel, and Bert Rockman. 1993. *Researching the Presidency: Vital Questions, New Approaches*. Pittsburgh: University of Pittsburgh Press.

Elster, Jon. 1979. *Ulysses and the Sirens*. Cambridge: Cambridge University Press.

  1983. *Explaining Technical Change*. Cambridge: Cambridge University Press.

Enders, Walter. 1995. *Applied Econometric Time Series*. New York: John Wiley and Sons.

Enelow, James, and Melvin Hinich. 1984. *The Spatial Theory of Voting*. Cambridge: Cambridge University Press.

Erikson, Robert S., Michael B. MacKuen, and James A. Stimson. 1995. "Dynamic Representation." *American Political Science Review* 89:543–65.

Eskridge, William N., Jr. 1991. "Reneging on History? Playing the Court/Congress/President Civil Rights Game." *California Law Review* 79:613–84.

  1994. *Dynamic Statutory Interpretation*. 1994. Cambridge, Mass.: Harvard University Press.

References

Everitt, Brian S. 1994. *A Handbook of Statistical Analyses Using S-Plus*. New York: Chapman & Hall.

Farrell, Joseph, and Robert Gibbons. 1989. "Cheap Talk Can Matter in Bargaining." *Journal of Economic Theory* 48:221–37.

Feddersen, Timothy. 1992. "A Voting Model Implying Duverger's Law and Positive Turnout." *American Journal of Political Science* 36 (4):938–62.

Ferejohn, John. 1974. *Pork Barrel Politics: Rivers and Harbors Legislation, 1947–1968*. Stanford, Calif.: Stanford University Press.

——— 1996. "Clinton and His Congresses: Electoral Realignment or Congressional Revolution?" New York University School of Law. Unpublished manuscript.

Ferejohn, John, and William Eskridge Jr. 1992. "The Article I, Section 7 Game." *Georgetown Law Journal* 80 (3):523–64.

Ferejohn, John, and Debra Satz. 1995. "Unification, Universalism, and Rational Choice Theory." *Critical Review* 9 (1–2):71–84.

Ferejohn, John, and Charles Shipan. 1990. "Congressional Influence on the Bureaucracy." *Journal of Law, Economics, and Organization* 6 (Special Issue): 1–20.

Feyerabend, Paul. 1978. *Against Method*. London: Verso.

Finley, Moses. 1985. *Ancient History: Evidence and Models*. New York: Penguin Books.

Fiorina, Morris. 1996. *Divided Government*. 2d ed. Boston: Allyn and Bacon.

Fish, Stanley. 1989. *Doing What Comes Naturally: Change, Rhetoric and the Practice of Theory in Literary and Legal Studies*. Durham, N.C.: Duke University Press.

Fisher, Roger, and William Ury. 1981. *Getting to Yes*. Boston: Houghton Mifflin.

Fogel, Robert. 1989. *Without Consent or Contract*. New York: Norton.

Ford, Gerald R. 1980. "The President and Congress." Pp. 21–39 in *The Virginia Papers on the Presidency*, vol. 2, edited by Kenneth W. Thompson. White Burkett Miller Center Forums, 1979, part II. Washington, D.C.: University Press of America.

Ford, Henry Jones. 1898. *The Rise and Growth of American Politics*. New York: Macmillan.

——— 1919. *The Cleveland Era: A Chronicle of the New Order in Politics*. New Haven: Yale University Press.

Fudenberg, Drew, and Jean Tirole. 1983. "Sequential Bargaining with Incomplete Information." *Review of Economic Studies* 50:221–47.

——— 1991a. "Perfect Bayesian Equilibrium and Sequential Equilibrium." *Journal of Economic Theory* 53:236–60.

——— 1991b. *Game Theory*. Cambridge, Mass.: MIT Press.

Gaventa, John. 1980. *Power and Powerlessness: Quiescence and Rebellion in an Appalachian Valley*. Urbana: University of Illinois Press.

Gibbons, Robert. 1992. *Game Theory for Applied Economics*. Princeton: Princeton University Press.

Gosnell, Harold F. 1980. *Truman's Crises*. Westport, Conn.: Greenwood Press.

Green, Donald P., and Ian Shapiro. 1994. *The Pathologies of Rational Choice*. New Haven: Yale University Press.

References

Greene, John Robert. 1992. *The Limits of Power*. Bloomington: Indiana University Press.

1995. *The Presidency of Gerald R. Ford*. Lawrence: University Press of Kansas.

Greenstein, Fred I. 1982. *The Hidden Hand Presidency*. New York: Basic Books.

Groseclose, Tim, and Nolan McCarty. 1996. "Presidential Vetoes: Bargaining, Blame Game, and Gridlock." Department of Political Science, Ohio State University. Unpublished manuscript.

Hamby, Alonzo L. 1973. *Beyond the New Deal: Harry S. Truman and American Liberalism*. New York: Columbia University Press.

ed. 1974. *Harry S. Truman and the Fair Deal*. Lexington, Mass.: D. C. Heath.

Hamilton, Alexander, James Madison, and John Jay. 1787. *The Federalist*. Reprint, New York: Modern Library Edition, 1937.

Hansen, John Mark. 1991. *Gaining Access: Congress and the Farm Lobby, 1919–1981*. Chicago: University of Chicago.

Hastie, Trevor J. 1993. "Generalized Additive Models." Pp. 249–308 in *Statistical Models in S*, edited by John M. Chambers and Trevor J. Hastie. New York: Chapman and Hall.

Heclo, Hugh. 1977. *Studying the Presidency: A Report to the Ford Foundation*. New York: Ford Foundation.

Heckman, James J., and James M. Snyder Jr. 1997. "Linear Probability Models of the Demand for Attributes with an Empirical Application to Estimating the Preferences of Legislators." *RAND Journal of Economics* 28 (0):S142–S189.

Hinich, Melvin J., and Michael C. Munger. 1994. *Ideology and the Theory of Political Choice*. Ann Arbor: University of Michigan Press.

Hoff, Samuel B. 1993. "Presidential Success in the Veto Process: The Legislative Record of Gerald R. Ford." Pp. 293–308 in *Gerald R. Ford and the Politics of Post-Watergate America*, vol. 1, edited by Bernard J. Firestone and A. Ugrinsky. Westport, Conn.: Greenwood Press.

Holmstrom, Bengt, and Jean Tirole. 1989. "The Theory of the Firm." Pp. 61–133 in *Handbook of Industrial Organization*, vol. 1, edited by Richard Schmalensee and Robert D. Willig. Amsterdam: North-Holland.

Hull, David L. 1988. *Science as a Process: An Evolutionary Account of the Social and Conceptual Development of Science*. Chicago: University of Chicago Press.

Huntington, Samuel. 1965. "Congressional Responses to the Twentieth Century." Pp. 5–31 in *The Congress and America's Future*, edited by David Truman. Englewood Cliffs, N.J.: Prentice-Hall.

Imbens, Guido W. 1992. "An Efficient Method of Moments Estimator for Discrete Choice Models with Choice-Based Sampling." *Econometrica* 45 (8): 1977–88.

Ingberman, Daniel, and Dennis Yao. 1991. "Presidential Commitment and the Veto." *American Journal of Political Science* 35 (2):357–89.

Jackson, Carlton. 1967. *Presidential Vetoes, 1792–1945*. Athens: University of Georgia Press.

276

References

Johnson, Haynes, and David S. Broder. 1996. *The System: The American Way of Politics at the Breaking Point*. Boston: Little, Brown.

Jones, Charles O. 1994. *The Presidency in a Separated System*. Washington, D.C.: Brookings Institution.

Kagel, John, and Alvin Roth, eds. 1995. *Handbook of Experimental Economics*. Princeton: Princeton University Press.

Keith, Nathaniel Schnieder. 1973. *Politics And the Housing Crisis since 1930*. New York: Universe Books.

Kelly, Sean. 1993. "Divided We Govern? A Reassessment." *Polity* 25:475–84.

Kennan, John. 1986. "The Economics of Strikes." Pp. 1091–137 in *Handbook of Labor Economics*, edited by Orley Ashenfelter and Richard Layard. Amsterdam: North-Holland.

Kennan, John, and Wilson, Robert. 1989. "Strategic Bargaining Models and Interpretation of Strike Data." *Journal of Applied Economics* 4:87–130.

——— 1990. "Strikes, Bargaining and Arbitration: New Developments. Can Strategic Bargaining Models Explain Collective Bargaining Data?" *AEA Papers and Proceedings* 80 (2):405–9.

——— 1993. "Bargaining with Private Information." *Journal of Economic Literature* 31 (March): 45–104.

Kernell, Samuel. 1991. "Facing an Opposition Congress." Pp. 87–112 in *The Politics of Divided Government*, edited by Gary Cox and Samuel Kernell. Boulder, Colo.: Westview Press.

Key, V. O., Jr. 1955. "A Theory of Critical Elections." *Journal of Politics* 17:3–18.

——— 1964. *Politics, Parties, and Pressure Groups*. 4th ed. New York: Thomas Y. Crowell.

Kiewiet, D. Roderick, and Mathew D. McCubbins. 1988. "Presidential Influence on Congressional Appropriations Decisions." *American Journal of Political Science* 32:713–36.

King, Gary. 1993. "The Methodology of Presidential Research." Pp. 387–412 in *Researching the Presidency: Vital Questions, New Approaches*, edited by George C. Edwards III, John H. Kessel, and Bert A. Rockman. Pittsburgh: University of Pittsburgh Press.

King, Gary, and Lyn Ragsdale. 1988. *The Elusive Executive: Discovering Statistical Patterns in the Presidency*. Washington, D.C.: CQ Press.

Kingdon, John W. 1984. *Agendas, Alternatives, and Public Policies*. Boston: Little, Brown.

Kiser, Edgar, and Margaret Levi. 1996. "Using Counterfactuals in Historical Analysis." Pp. 187–207 in *Counterfactual Thought Experiments in World Politics*, edited by Aaron Belkin and Philip E. Tetlock. Princeton: Princeton University Press.

Koford, Kenneth. 1989. "Dimensions in Congressional Voting." *American Political Science Review* 83:949–1062.

Krehbiel, Keith. 1991. *Information and Legislative Organization*. Ann Arbor: University of Michigan Press.

——— 1996. "Institutional and Partisan Sources of Gridlock: A Theory of Divided and Unified Government." *Journal of Theoretical Politics* 8 (1):7–39.

References

1998. *Pivotal Politics: A Theory of US Lawmaking*. Chicago: University of Chicago Press.

Kreps, David M. 1990a. *A Course in Microeconomic Theory*. Princeton: Princeton University Press.

1990b. "Corporate Culture and Economic Theory." Pp. 90–143 in *Perspectives on Positive Political Economy*, edited by James E. Alt and Kenneth A. Shepsle. Cambridge: Cambridge University Press.

Kreps, David M., and R. Wilson. 1982. "Reputation and Imperfect Information." *Journal of Economic Theory* 27:253–79.

1987. "Sequential Equilibria." *Econometrica* 50:863–99.

Kuhn, Thomas. 1962. *The Structure of Scientific Revolutions*. Chicago: University of Chicago Press.

Lafont, Jean-Jacques, and Jean Tirole. 1993. *A Theory of Incentives in Procurement and Regulation*. Cambridge, Mass.: MIT Press.

Laudan, Larry. 1977. *Progress and Its Problems: Toward a Theory of Scientific Growth*. Berkeley: University of California Press.

Lawless, J. F. 1982. *Statistical Models and Methods for Lifetime Data*. New York: John Wiley and Sons.

Lee, Alton R. 1966. *Truman and Taft-Hartley: A Question of Mandate*. Lexington: University of Kentucky Press.

LeMay, Michael C. 1987. *From Open Door to Dutch Door: An Analysis of U.S. Immigration Policy since 1820*. New York: Praeger.

Leuchtenburg, William E. 1973. *Beyond the New Deal: Harry S. Truman and American Liberalism*. New York: Columbia University Press.

Liao, Tim Futing. 1994. *Interpreting Probability Models: Logit, Probit, and Other Generalized Linear Models*. Thousand Oaks, Calif.: Sage.

Light, Paul.1982. *The President's Agenda*. Baltimore: Johns Hopkins University Press.

Linz, Juan. 1994. "Presidential or Parliamentary Democracy: Does It Make a Difference?" Pp. 3–87 in *The Failure of Presidential Democracy: Comparative Perspectives*, vol. 1, edited by Juan Linz and Arturo Valenzuela. Baltimore: Johns Hopkins University Press.

Lukes, Steven. 1974. *Power: A Radical View*. New York: Macmillan.

Manski, Charles F., and Steven R. Lerman. 1977. "The Estimation of Choice Probabilities from Choice Based Samples." *Econometrica* 45 (8):1977–88.

Manski, Charles F., and Daniel McFadden. 1981. "Alternative Estimators and Sample Designs for Discrete Choice Analysis." In *Structural Analysis of Discrete Data with Economic Applications*, edited by Charles F. Manski and Daniel McFadden. Cambridge: MIT Press.

Mason, Edward Campbell. 1891. *The Veto Power: Its Origin, Development and Function in the Government of the United States (1789–1889)*. Harvard Historical Monographs, no. 1. Boston: Ginn.

Matthews, Steven. 1989. "Veto Threats: Rhetoric in a Bargaining Game." *Quarterly Journal of Economics* 103:347–69.

Mayhew, David. 1974. *Congress: The Electoral Connection*. New Haven: Yale University Press.

References

1991. *Divided We Govern: Party Control, Lawmaking, and Investigations, 1946–1990.* New Haven: Yale University Press.

1995. "Clinton, the 103rd Congress, and Unified Party Control: What Are the Lessons?" Paper presented at a conference honoring Stanley Kelley Jr., Princeton University, October 27–28.

McCarty, Nolan. 1997. "Presidential Reputation and the Veto." *Economics and Politics* 9 (1):1–26.

McCubbins, Mathew, Roger Noll, and Barry Weingast. 1987. "Administrative Procedures as Instruments of Political Control." *Journal of Law, Economics, and Organization* 3:243–77.

McCullagh, P., and J. A. Nelder. 1989. *Generalized Linear Models.* 2d ed. New York: Chapman and Hall.

Milgrom, Paul R., and John Roberts. 1982. "Predation, Reputation, and Entry Deterrence." *Journal of Economic Theory* 27:280–312.

1992. *Economics, Organization, and Management.* Englewood Cliffs, N.J.: Prentice-Hall.

Miller, Gary J. 1993. "Formal Theory and the Presidency." Pp. 289–336 in *Researching the Presidency: Vital Questions, New Approaches*, edited by George C. Edwards, John Kessel, and Bert Rockman. Pittsburgh: University of Pittsburgh Press.

Milner, Helen V., and Peter B. Rosendorff. 1997. "Democratic Politics and International Trade Negotiations: Elections and Divided Government as Constraints on Trade Liberalization." *Journal of Conflict Resolution* 41:117–46.

Moe, Terry. 1984. "The New Economics of Organization." *American Journal of Political Science* 28:739–77.

1985. "The Politicized Presidency." Pp. 235–72 in *The New Direction in American Politics*, edited by John E. Chubb and Paul E. Peterson. Washington, D.C.: Brookings Institution.

1989. "The Politics of Bureaucratic Structure." Pp. 267–329 in *Can the Government Govern?*, edited by John E. Chubb and Paul E. Peterson. Washington, D.C.: Brookings Institution.

1993. "Presidents, Institutions, and Theory." Pp. 337–86 in *Researching the Presidency: Vital Questions, New Approaches* edited by George C. Edwards III, John H. Kessel, and Bert A. Rockman. Pittsburgh: University of Pittsburgh Press.

Moe, Terry, and Scott A. Wilson. 1994. "Presidents and the Politics of Structure." *Law and Contemporary Problems* 57:1–44.

Mouw, Calvin J., and Michael B. MacKuen. 1992. "The Strategic Agenda in Legislative Politics." *American Political Science Review* 86 (1):87–105.

Myerson, Roger B. 1978. "Refinements of the Nash Equilibrium Concept." *International Journal of the Game Theory* 7:73–80.

1991. *Game Theory: Analysis of Conflict.* Cambridge, Mass.: Harvard University Press.

1995. "Analysis of Democratic Institutions: Structure, Conduct, Performance." *Journal of Economic Perspectives* 9 (1):77–89.

Myerson, Roger B., and Robert Weber. 1993. "A Theory of Voting Equilibria." *American Political Science Review* 87 (1):102–14.

References

Nagal, Jack. 1975. *The Descriptive Analysis of Power*. New Haven: Yale University Press.

Nathan, Richard. 1990. "The Presidency after Reagan: Don't Change It – Make It Work." Pp. 195–206 in *Looking Back on the Reagen Presidency*, edited by Larry Berman. Baltimore: Johns Hopkins University Press.

Neustadt, Richard E. 1960. *Presidential Power*. New York: Macmillan.

———. 1973. "Congress and the Fair Deal: A Legislative Balance Sheet." Pp. 15–41 in *Harry S. Truman and the Fair Deal*, edited by Alonzo Hamby. Lexington, Mass.: D. C. Heath.

———. 1980. *Presidential Power*. New York: John Wiley and Sons.

———. 1982. "Presidential Leadership: The Clerk against the Preacher." Pp. 1–36 in *Problems and Prospects of Presidential Leadership in the Nineteen-eighties*, vol. 1, edited by James Sterling Young. Lanham, Md.: University Press of America.

North, Douglas. 1981. *Structure and Change in Economic History*. New York: Norton.

Olson, Mancur. 1965. *The Logic of Collective Action*. Cambridge, Mass.: Harvard University Press.

Ordeshook, Peter C. 1986. *Game Theory and Political Theory: An Introduction*. Cambridge: Cambridge University Press.

Ornstein, Norman J., Thomas Mann, and Michael J. Malbin. 1997. *Vital Statistics on Congress*. Washington, D.C.: Congressional Quarterly.

Osborne, Martin J., and Ariel Rubinstein. 1994. *A Course in Game Theory*. Cambridge, Mass.: MIT Press.

Pach, Chester J., and Richardson E. 1991. *The Presidency of Dwight D. Eisenhower*. Rev. ed. Lawrence: University Press of Kansas.

Page, Benjamin, and Robert Y. Shapiro. 1992. *The Rational Public: Fifty Years of Trends in American Public Preferences*. Chicago: University of Chicago Press.

Palmer, Matthew S. R. 1995. "Toward an Economics of Comparative Political Organization: Examining Ministerial Responsibility." *Journal of Law, Economics and Organization* 11(1):164–88.

Peterson, Mark A. 1990. *Legislating Together: The White House and Capitol Hill from Eisenhower to Reagan*. Cambridge, Mass.: Harvard University Press.

Pettit, Philip. 1991. "Decision Theory and Folk Philosophy." Pp. 147–175 in *Foundations of Decision Theory: Issues and Advances*, edited by Michael Bacharch and Susan Hurley. Oxford: Basil Blackwell.

Pious, Richard. 1979. *The American Presidency*. New York: Basic Books.

Poole, Keith T., and Howard Rosenthal. 1991. "On Dimensionalizing Roll Call Votes in the U.S. Congress." *American Political Science Review* 85:955–1060.

———. 1997. *Congress: A Political-Economic History of Roll Call Voting*. New York: Oxford University Press.

Poole, Keith T., and Howard Rosenthal. 1985. "A Spatial Model for Legislative Roll Call Analysis." *American Journal of Political Science* 29:357–84.

Popkin, Samual L., John Gorman, Jeffrey Smith, and Charles Phillips. 1976.

References

"Comment: Toward an Investment Theory of Voting Behavior: What Have You Done for Me Lately?" *American Political Science Review* 70:779–805.

Rae, Nicol. 1989. *The Decline and Fall of the Liberal Republicans from 1952 to the Present*. New York: Oxford University Press.

Raiffa, Howard. 1982. *The Art and Science of Negotiation*. Cambridge, Mass.: Harvard University Press.

Reichley, James A. 1981. *Conservatives in an Age of Change: The Nixon and Ford Administrations*. Washington, D.C.: Brookings Institution.

Richardson, Elmo D. 1979. *The Presidency of Dwight D. Eisenhower*. Lawrence: University Press of Kansas.

Rohde, David. 1989. "Something's Happening Here; What It Is Ain't Exactly Clear." Pp. 137–64 in *Home Style and Washington Work: Studies of Congressional Politics*, edited by Morris P. Fiorina and David Rohde. Ann Arbor: University of Michigan Press.

——— 1991. *Parties and Leaders in the Postreform House*. Chicago: University of Chicago Press.

Rohde, David, and Dennis Simon. 1985. "Presidential Vetoes and Congressional Response: A Study of Institutional Conflict." *American Journal of Political Science* 29:397–427.

Romer, Thomas, and Howard Rosenthal. 1978. "Political Resource Allocation, Controlled Agendas, and the Status Quo." *Public Choice* 33:27–44.

Ross, Dorothy. 1991. *The Origins of American Social Science*. Cambridge: Cambridge University Press.

Ross, Sheldon. 1993. *Introduction to Probability Models*. 5th ed. San Diego: Academic Press.

Roth, Alvin E. 1995. "Bargaining Experiments." Pp. 253–348 in *The Handbook of Experimental Economics*, edited by John Kagel and Alvin Roth. Princeton: Princeton University Press.

Rowe, James H., Jr. 1946. " 'Cooperation' or Conflict? The President's Relationships with an Opposition Congress." In Appendix A, "Oral History Interview with James H. Rowe Jr.," Harry S. Truman Library, Independence, Missouri, December 1979.

Rubenstein, Ariel. 1998. *Modeling Bounded Rationality*. Cambridge, Mass.: MIT Press.

Safire William. 1975. *Before the Fall: An Inside View of the Pre-Watergate White House*. Garden City, N.Y.: Doubleday.

Sah, Raaj K., and Joseph E. Stiglitz. 1986. "The Architecture of Economics Systems: Hierarchies and Polyarchies." *American Economic Review* 76:716–27.

Satz, Debra, and John Ferejohn. 1994. "Rational Choice and Social Theory." *Journal of Philosophy* 91:71–87.

Schap, David. 1986. "Executive Veto and Informational Strategy: A Structure-Induced Equilibrium Analysis." *American Journal of Political Science* 30:754–70.

Schattschneider, E. E. 1942. *Party Government*. New York: Holt, Reinhart and Winston.

References

Schelling, Thomas. 1960. *The Strategy of Conflict*. Cambridge, Mass.: Harvard University Press.

Schmalensee, Richard, and Robert Willig, eds. 1989. *Handbook of Industrial Organization*. Vol. 1. Amsterdam: North Holland.

Senate Library. 1992. *Presidential Vetoes, 1789–1988*. S. Pub. 102–12. Washington, D.C.: U.S. Government Printing Office.

Shepsle, Kenneth. A. 1986. "Institutional Equilibrium and Equilibrium Institutions." Pp. 51–81 in *Political Science: The Science of Politics*, edited by Herbert F. Weisberg. New York: Agathon Press.

Shepsle, Kenneth A., and Mark S. Bonchek. 1997. *Analyzing Politics: Rationality, Behavior, and Institutions*. New York: W. W. Norton.

Shepsle, Kenneth A., and Barry R. Weingast. 1981. "Structure-Induced Equilibrium and Legislative Choice." *Public Choice* 37:503–19.

——— 1984. "Political Solutions to Market Problems." *American Political Science Review* 78:417–34.

Shugart, Matthew Soberg, and John M. Carey. 1992. *Presidents and Assemblies: Constitutional Design and Electoral Dynamics*. Cambridge: Cambridge University Press.

Skowronek, Stephen. 1997. *The Politics Presidents Make: Leadership from John Adams to Bill Clinton*. Cambridge, Mass.: Belknap Press of Harvard University Press.

Smith, Eric R. A. N. 1989. *The Unchanging American Voter*. Berkeley: University of California Press.

Snyder, James M., Jr. 1992a. "The Dimensions of Voter Preferences: Voting on California Ballot Propositions, 1974–1990." Working Paper. Department of Economics, University of Chicago.

——— 1992b. "Committee Power, Structure-Induced Equilibria, and Roll Call Votes." *American Journal of Political Science* 36:1–30.

Snyder, Susan, and Barry Weingast. 1994. "The American System of Shared Powers: The President, Congress, and the NLRB." Hoover Institution, Stanford University. Unpublished manuscript.

Sobel, Joel, and Ichiro Takahashi. 1983. "A Multistage Model of Bargaining." *Review of Economic Studies* 51:411–26.

Spitzer, Robert J. 1988. *The Presidential Veto: Touchstone of the American Presidency*. Albany: State University of New York Press.

Stewart, Charles, III, and Barry R. Weingast. 1992. "Stacking the Senate, Changing the Nation: Republican Rotton Boroughs, Statehood Politics and American Political Development." *Studies in American Political Development* 6: 223–72.

Sullivan, Terry. 1988. "Headcounts, Expectations, and Presidential Coalitions in Congress." *American Journal of Political Science* 32:567–89.

Sundquist, James L. 1968. *Politics and Policy: The Eisenhower, Kennedy, and Johnson Years*. Washington, D.C.: Brookings Institution.

——— 1973. *Dynamics of the Party System*. Washington, D.C.: Brookings Institution.

——— 1988. "Needed: A Political Theory for the New Era of Coalition Government in the United States." *Political Science Quarterly* 103:613–35.

References

Sutton, John. 1986. "Non-Cooperative Bargaining Theory: An Introduction." *Review of Economic Studies* 53:709–24.

1991. *Sunk Costs and Market Structure: Price Competition, Advertising, and the Evolution of Cooperation.* Cambridge, Mass.: MIT Press.

Taft, William Howard. 1916. *The President and His Powers.* New York: Columbia University Press. Originally published as *Our Chief Magistrate and His Powers.*

Taylor, Howard M., and Samuel Karlin. 1984. *An Introduction to Stochastic Modeling.* Orlando, Fla.: Academic Press.

Taylor, Michael. 1987. *The Possibility of Cooperation.* Cambridge: Cambridge University Press.

1989. "Structure, Culture and Action in the Explanation of Social Change." *Politics and Society* 17:115–62.

Tulis, Jeffrey. 1987. *The Rhetorical Presidency.* Princeton: Princeton University Press.

Tuma, Nancy Brandon, and Michael T. Hannan. 1984. *Social Dynamics: Models and Methods.* Orlando, Fla.: Academic Press.

Venables, W. N., and B. D. Ripley. 1994. *Modern Applied Statistics with S-Plus.* Statistics and Computing. New York: Springer-Verlag.

Watson, Richard A. 1993. *Presidential Vetoes and Public Policy.* Lawrence: University Press of Kansas.

Weingast, Barry R. 1996. "Off-the-Path Behavior: A Game-Theoretic Approach to Counterfactuals and Its Implications for Political and Historical Analysis." Pp. 230–43 in *Counterfactual Thought Experiments in World Politics,* edited by Aaron Belkin and Philip E. Tetlock. Princeton: Princeton University Press.

1997. "The Political Foundations of Democracy and the Rule of Law." *American Political Science Review* 91 (2):245–63.

White, Harrison C. 1970. *Chains of Opportunity.* Cambridge, Mass.: Harvard University Press.

Wilson, Woodrow. 1908. *Constitutional Government in the United States.* New York: Columbia University Press.

Witte, John F. 1985. *The Politics and Development of the Federal Income Tax.* Madison: University of Wisconsin Press.

Wood, Gordon S. 1969. *The Creation of the American Republic, 1776–1787.* Chapel Hill: University of North Carolina Press.

Wooley, John. 1991. "Institutions, Election Cycles, and the Presidential Vetoes." *American Journal of Political Science* 35:279–302.

Woolgar, Steve. 1988. *Science, the Very Idea.* New York: Tavistock Publications.

Young, Peyton, ed. 1991. *Negotiation Analysis.* Ann Arbor: University of Michigan Press.

1998. *Individual Strategy and Social Structure: An Evolutionary Theory of Institutions.* Princeton: Princeton University Press.

Zaller, John. 1992. *The Nature and Origins of Mass Opinion.* Cambridge: Cambridge University Press.

Index

Index

Index

287

Index

Index

Index

291

Index